PRAISE

"Ninja Selling is the most phenomenal sales system I've encountered. It not only changes how you sell, it changes *your* life."
—Dawn Deeter, PhD, Distinguished Chair of Relational Selling and Marketing; Director of Kansas State University National Strategic Selling Institute

"Regardless of your industry, Ninja Selling is the gold standard of solutions-based selling. I have found no other book on sales that covers everything from mindset to actions in as comprehensive of a manner."
—Nolan Matthias, cofounder of Mortgage 360, author of *Golf Balls Don't Float—72 Life and Business Lessons* and *The Mortgaged Millionaire*

"Thanks for putting the humanity back in selling. The Ninja program reminds me of emergency directions on an airplane: Put your own oxygen mask on, so that you can better help others. That's what Ninja is to me—oxygen."
—Jennings Doyle, Windermere Real Estate, Seattle, Washington

"*Ninja Selling*® is like a seat belt. It's always there; you know you should use it, and it's dangerous not to!"
—Laura Reynolds, Ruhl&Ruhl Realtors, Davenport, Iowa

"This is the best sales training I have ever had. I have been through the Cisco Professional certification, the Polycom Certified Sales Expert, Microsoft Solution Selling, and more. Ninja is by far the best breakdown of the sales process I have ever seen."
—Jim Merrion, Coldwell Banker, Boulder, Colorado

NINJA 気 SELLING

Subtle Skills. Big Results.

NINJA 気 SELLING

Subtle Skills. Big Results.

LARRY KENDALL

*The goal of Ninja Selling is to help you increase
your income per hour so you can have a life.*

GREENLEAF
BOOK GROUP PRESS

This publication is designed to provide accurate and authoritative information in regard to the subject matter covered. It is sold with the understanding that the publisher and author are not engaged in rendering professional services. If expert assistance is required, the services of a competent professional should be sought.

Published by Greenleaf Book Group Press
Austin, Texas
www.gbgpress.com

Copyright ©2017-2023 Larry Kendall

All rights reserved.

No part of this book may be reproduced, stored in a retrieval system, or transmitted by any means, electronic, mechanical, photocopying, recording, or otherwise, without written permission from the copyright holder.

Distributed by Greenleaf Book Group

For ordering information or special discounts for bulk purchases, please contact Greenleaf Book Group at PO Box 91869, Austin, TX 78709, 512.891.6100.

Design and composition by Greenleaf Book Group
Cover design by Greenleaf Book Group
Cover image: ©Shutterstock/Olga Lyubkina
Interior image: ©Shutterstock/Sergio Hayashi
Interior graphics: Anne Vetter

Cataloging-in-Publication data is available.

Print ISBN: 978-1-62634-284-2

eBook ISBN: 978-1-62634-285-9

Part of the Tree Neutral® program, which offsets the number of trees consumed in the production and printing of this book by taking proactive steps, such as planting trees in direct proportion to the number of trees used: www.treeneutral.com

TreeNeutral

Printed in the United States of America on acid-free paper

18 19 20 21 22 23   14 13 12 11 10 9 8 7

First Edition – Updated 2023

This book is dedicated to Jimmy D. (The Original Ninja) and all my partners at The Group, Inc. Real Estate. Their inspiration and practice of these principles made this book possible.

And to our Ninja Instructors, who are committed to changing lives and the sales industry.

CONTENTS

Foreword   xiii
Preface: The Ninja Way   xv
Acknowledgments   xxiii
Introduction   1

PRINCIPLE 1: PERSONAL MASTERY

Chapter 1: The Ninja Mind-Set   13
Chapter 2: Good Vibrations   15
Chapter 3: Controlling Your Emotional Energy   18
Chapter 4: Rituals   21
Chapter 5: The Ninja Morning Routine   24
Chapter 6: What You Focus on Expands   27
Chapter 7: Learning to Run Your Brain   32
Chapter 8: My Results Formula   37
Chapter 9: Creating Your Future   41
Chapter 10: Eight Key Steps to Proper Programming   44
Chapter 11: The Power of Affirmations   47
Chapter 12: The Power of Focus   50

PRINCIPLE 2: STOP SELLING! START SOLVING!

Chapter 13: The Pursuer-Distancer Dance   57
Chapter 14: Creating Value   59
Chapter 15: Asking the Right Questions   62

Chapter 16: The FORD Questions   66
Chapter 17: The Power of FORD   70
Chapter 18: What Will People Pay For?   73
Chapter 19: Creating Your Value Proposition   79
Chapter 20: Building Your Brand   83
Chapter 21: A Proactive Trusted Advisor   88

PRINCIPLE 3: NINJA BUSINESS STRATEGY
Chapter 22: Working Smart   97
Chapter 23: The Power of FLOW   102
Chapter 24: You Are Either Visible or Invisible   106
Chapter 25: The Power of 8 in 8   114
Chapter 26: How Do You Generate Business?   120
Chapter 27: The Ninja Nine—Your Five Daily Habits   124
Chapter 28: The Ninja Nine—Your Four Weekly Habits   132
Chapter 29: What Holds You Back?   145
Chapter 30: Building Your Database   148
Chapter 31: Formatting and Using Your Database   157
Chapter 32: The Power of PIE Time   165

PRINCIPLE 4: CONNECT AND COMMUNICATE
Chapter 33: The Platinum Rule and Personalities   172
Chapter 34: Decision Strategies   179
Chapter 35: The Power of Pretend   181
Chapter 36: Giving Permission   185
Chapter 37: Ninja Consultation   187
Chapter 38: Ninja Consultation Step 1: Connection   196
Chapter 39: Ninja Consultation Step 2: Information   201
Chapter 40: Ninja Consultation Step 3: Solution   206

Chapter 41: Ninja Consultation Step 4: Proposal   211

Chapter 42: Helping Customers Make Good Decisions   219

Conclusion: The Ninja Path   222

APPENDICES

Appendix A: The Ten-Step Buyer Process   226

Appendix B: The Art and Science of Showing Property   251

Appendix C: Soft Closing Questions   255

Appendix D: Seller Decisions   261

Appendix E: The Sixteen-Step Seller Process   266

Appendix F: Pricing on the Bridge   293

Appendix G: Dynamic Pricing   295

Appendix H: Your Next Transaction Is Embedded in This One   298

Afterword: The Ninja Prayer   300

Index   302

About the Author   317

FOREWORD

It kept happening. It seemed like wherever and whenever I spoke before a group, some top-producing area Realtor® would approach me afterward and say, "Have you heard of Larry Kendall?" Naturally, it didn't take long before I started wondering, *Just who is this Larry Kendall everyone's talking about?* And it didn't take long to find out.

Larry was a very successful Realtor who grew an award-winning real estate firm called The Group and then began teaching other Realtors how to become much more successful utilizing something he called the Ninja Selling® System.

Ninjas were an ancient sect of warriors who were so startlingly effective, some concluded they must have supernatural powers. In reality, they weren't magical; they were just *really good* at what they did. Whatever the mission, no matter how impossible, no matter what the odds or obstacles, they got it done. And made it look effortless.

This also turned out to be a pretty accurate description of Larry. And, for that matter, of the people coming out of his system, who were fanned out across the country, all achieving astonishing levels of success.

That, however, was not the best part. The best part—and the reason that I have since become such a total fan of Larry's and of what he does—was that they were achieving all this success not through high-pressure tactics, manipulative techniques, or brutally long hours, but simply by putting their focus on one thing: bringing exceptional value to their clients.

They were, as I came to learn, the very embodiment of what I like to call go-givers. The Ninja Selling System's stated goal is to help you increase your income per hour, so you can have a full life. It is also a system that can help your business become a lot more fun and a lot less stressful as well as a lot more profitable. Yet Ninja Selling is about so much more than that. It is a way of conducting business that allows you to be absolutely laser-focused on bringing value to others. I loved discovering that, and after meeting Larry and getting to know him, it also made complete sense. Of course. How could he not do (and teach) business that way? That's who he is.

And now, all these years later, I have the privilege of introducing Larry to you through the pages that follow. As you go through these pages, you'll learn the mind-set behind the stellar successes, the principles that make Ninja Selling work, and the specific strategies that Larry and his people use. You'll be inspired by the stories and real-life examples Larry offers from his portfolio of Ninja Selling superstars. The processes they follow are so clearly laid out that you'll find yourself murmuring as you read, "That's easy—I can do that." And the beauty of it is: You can. When you combine a winning philosophy and a winning system/strategy, your success is virtually guaranteed.

Ninja Selling will work for any personality type, not just the extrovert or "people person." Larry's system is not about the salesperson. It's about the client. What *Ninja Selling* will teach you is how to communicate exceptional value to your clientele. And like beauty itself, that value is a quality that *always* exists in the eyes of the beholder.

While this book is geared directly to today's Realtor, its success principles apply equally well across the board. As a matter of fact, more and more professionals—bankers, accountants, insurance professionals, and a multitude of others in a host of different fields—are now enthusiastically embracing the Ninja Selling System because of the soaring professional heights it takes them to. In other words, regardless of what line of work you are in, you will benefit enormously from reading *Ninja Selling*.

Enjoy this fantastic book! And, as Larry often says:

"*Be awesome—and help somebody.*"
—Bob Burg, coauthor of **The Go-Giver**

P.S. If you are a sales leader, division manager, or company CEO, I suggest you have every salesperson on your team read, devour, and apply the information in this book. I can promise you the results will be . . . *nincredible.*

PREFACE

THE NINJA WAY

What if you could be a very successful salesperson without ever putting yourself in the position of being rejected by your customer? Does fear of rejection hold you back? Welcome to Ninja Selling®, a user-friendly selling system where your customers will never feel pressure from you or be put in the awkward position of rejecting you. Ninja Selling is a very different approach to sales.

Many sales books and training programs have been developed by top salespeople who share the techniques that worked for them. Many of these people have what we call *big power personalities*, and their techniques work because of their power personalities. However, according to the DISC Personality Assessment, less than 20 percent of the US population has this power type of personality. What about a selling system that works for the rest of us? Those of us who are introverts? Or people who may be uncomfortable with combative selling or power tactics?

A good selling system works for all personality types and relies on four characteristics:

1. It is a documented and proven process that is written down. You can hand it to someone. You hold in your hands the Ninja Selling System.

2. It gives you predictable results. If you work the system, the system works for you. A favorite Ninja mantra is TSW—The System Works! (Sometimes referred to as This Stuff Works!)

3. It gives you predictable results regardless of your personality or gender. The Ninja Selling System focuses on teachable skills that are effective for everyone.

4. It gives you predictable results regardless of the market you are in. Ninja Selling works for all types of selling, regardless of product, service, or market.

Ninja Selling was originally designed for real estate sales, but we have found it applies to any area of sales or life improvement. Bankers, accountants, insurance agents, engineers, fundraisers, and even surgeons who want to improve their bedside manners have taken Ninja classes.

ON-PURPOSE SELLING

Because the Ninja Selling system gives you predictable results, you can now be an *on-purpose* salesperson versus an *on-accident* salesperson who has no system. On-accident salespeople are hunters and gatherers, roaming the market until they accidentally run into a customer who says yes. How much more productive would it be to have a purpose in everything you do, and know that it works. Would this increase your income per hour?

NATE'S STORY

A good example of an on-purpose salesperson is a young man named Nate Buie. Nate has a very unique personality—outgoing, funny, smart, loveable, irreverent, and caring. He is also hardworking and fluent in Spanish. Nate joined our company at the age of twenty-three. His previous experience consisted of being a pizza driver. He felt it gave him an advantage because he knew all the streets. Within three years, Nate was doing 163 transactions a year. (The national average is six.) Nate worked the system, and the system worked for Nate.

THE FOUR PRINCIPLES

Ninja Selling is built around four principles. This book is organized into four sections based on these principles.

- **Principle 1: Personal Mastery.** Your success in sales and in life is largely a function of your ability to control your thoughts and your energy. Ninja Selling teaches you how to run your brain and program yourself for success. It starts with learning how to focus your energy, so you are able to bring out your best and the best in others.

- **Principle 2: Stop Selling! Start Solving!** People love to buy, but they hate to be sold. Customers are attracted to value. The Ninja system teaches you to stop selling and start learning to create value.

- **Principle 3: Ninja Business Strategy.** Ninja teaches you a business strategy that will generate a continuous flow of customers coming to you. It focuses your attention first on people who know you, like you, and trust you. You spend your time, money, and energy building relationships before chasing strangers.

- **Principle 4: Connect and Communicate.** Ninja is built around the science of the customer—what customers value and how they make decisions to get it. We will teach you a step-by-step process for both buyers and sellers that helps them make good decisions.

NINJAS VERSUS SAMURAIS

In ancient Japan, the emperor's palace guard was composed of samurai. They were the best fighters in the land and lived in the palace to protect the emperor. They enjoyed the best clothes, food, accommodations, and weapons. However, over time their egos grew, and they became self-centered and lazy—sometimes even refusing to go on missions for their ruler.

Naturally, the emperor became very concerned about the protection of his empire as well as his own safety. He decided he needed a plan B—a backup force that he could count on. Yet he didn't want to alienate the samurai, lest they get upset and overthrow him.

The emperor hit upon the idea of training his gardeners in the martial arts and using them as his backup army. They would need to accomplish their missions at night, so no one would see them, and then be back at work in the garden the next day. These invisible warriors became known as ninjas—quiet, unassuming, talented people who got results without the ego.

Unfortunately, many top salespeople take on the characteristics of samurai—lots of flash and ego. Most customers are turned off by this typical image of a salesperson.

Ninjas are more focused on their customers than themselves. They don't seem to be salespeople. They sell without selling. Their mission is to deliver world-class results from down-to-earth people. As a result, Ninjas are more likeable and user-friendly than samurai salespeople.

- **Real Estate Licensee.** According to the Association of Real Estate License Law Officials (ARELLO), there are an estimated three million active real estate licensees in the United States as of November 2022.

- **Realtors.** According to the National Association of Realtors®, there are 1,598,117 Realtors in the United States as of November 2022. A Realtor® is a real estate licensee who is serious enough about selling real estate that he or she joins the national, state, and local real estate associations. Realtors subscribe to the rules of these organizations and to their code of ethics. Throughout this book, we will use the word *Realtor* to refer to this group—as differentiated from real estate licensees.

- **Ninja.** A Realtor who follows the Ninja Selling System and achieves big results without the ego.

INCREASE YOUR INCOME PER HOUR

Can a career in real estate sales become addictive? Can you wake up in the morning and realize that you have been working every day and yet are not making any money?

How does Ninja Selling help you increase your income per hour so you can have a life? By helping you focus on what we call the *vital few*.

There are a lot of ways to sell real estate. But what is the best way? The most efficient way? The way that will generate the highest income per hour? Have you ever heard of Pareto's principle? It is sometimes called the 80/20 rule.

Vilfredo Pareto was an Italian economist who discovered that 20 percent of the world's population enjoys 80 percent of the world's wealth. He later confirmed the 80/20 principle is at work in most areas of life—20 percent of the land produces 80 percent of the food, 20 percent of the plants produce 80 percent of the oxygen, and so on. Pareto also proved that 80 percent of our results come from just 20 percent (or less) of our activities. He called these activities the *vital few*. Two excellent books on this subject are *The 80/20 Principle* and *Living the 80/20 Way* by Richard Koch.

What are the vital few activities that will give you the greatest results in your real estate career? *Ninja Selling* documents forty years of research on the vital few activities that will increase your income per hour.

GINA'S STORY

Gina Theriault is a Colorado mom. She and her husband, Brad, have five kids in their blended family. While Gina is a seventeen-year veteran of real estate sales, June marked eleven months without a closing, the longest dry spell of her career.

"It was scary," she says. "We'd maxed our credit cards and were using up the line of credit on our home. I knew something had to change. I signed up for the Ninja Selling training, even though I really could not justify the cost."

In the five months after the Ninja training, from June to November, Gina earned $155,000—changing her business, her family, and her life. The most remarkable part of her story is that Gina's youngest son, Lochlan, is a special-needs child requiring extra care. As a result, Gina is only able to sell real estate from 8:00 a.m. to 2:00 p.m. five days a week, while Lochlan is in school. Gina has to make every minute count. She had to focus on the vital few. The Ninja Selling System helped her dramatically increase her income per hour so she could have a life.

The goal of this book is to give you a step-by-step process that will help you do the same. What if tomorrow morning you woke up without fear—fear of rejection, fear of not having enough, fear of where the next deal will come from? What if you woke up with a feeling of peace, clarity, purpose, focus, and abundance; with the confidence that you have a system that will produce predictable results for you so you can be on purpose in your life; with a feeling of connectedness to your friends, family, and clients? What if you had the realization that you are here to create not to compete? What if you had the belief, skills, and confidence to have, do, be, and give whatever you want? And, you could do it your way by being yourself, being genuine. Would your life be different? Would your life have changed?

Welcome to the Ninja Way.

ACKNOWLEDGMENTS

Thank you, Pat—my wife of fifty-four years—for your love, persistence, and support, without which this book would not be a reality. Thank you also to my kids, Kristin and Matt, for your support in helping our family live the Ninja lifestyle: Think big, live simple, make a difference. Thanks also to my friend and fellow instructor, Don Tennessen, for helping me create the Ninja Installation and to Lauren Roesener for your passion and commitment in building the Ninja Nation. I also want to thank my editor, Joan Tapper, for taking my words and making them sing.

INTRODUCTION

Did you know great salespeople are not necessarily born that way? They can be made. I'm living proof of that. Given my background, I was ill equipped for a career in sales. I grew up in Council Grove, Kansas, a small town of about 2,300 people. When I was in first grade, I contracted encephalitis, a disease of the brain and central nervous system. The disease left me with paralysis of one leg and slurred speech. I wasn't the last kid picked to play on a team; I was *never* picked! My greatest fear was being asked to read aloud in class and the other kids laughing at my slurred speech.

During this period, what kept me going and kept my spirits up was my mom. She was an encourager. She kept telling me, "You're going to be OK. You'll get better. Someday, you'll be able to walk and talk normally." I learned a lot from her about the power of encouragement.

And she was right! By the time I reached high school, I was playing sports and could talk without the slur.

But I remained an introvert. I made it through high school, college, and the army and found myself with a wife and ten-month-old daughter living in Fort Collins, Colorado, with no job. What do you do if you want to live someplace and you can't find a job? You go into sales. Anyone can find a job in commission sales. So I started a job as a real estate salesman—not a particularly good career choice for an introvert.

The first thing I needed was some sales training, so I immediately signed up for a huge sales rally being held in Denver, Colorado. It had all the big-name speakers and sales experts of the time. That day, I received a heavy dose of what I now call Depression-Era Selling—sales techniques that are heavily loaded with manipulation, intimidation, and tricks to outwit the customer. The underlying belief systems were built around scarcity and competition.

I was taught that selling is a numbers game, and you have to cold call a certain number of strangers a day until a certain number of them buy. They "buy or they die," I was told. "You have to get ten nos before you get your first yes."

One trainer, speaking on closing techniques, said that when the customer refuses to buy, he opens his briefcase and pulls out a toothbrush. When the customer asks, "What's that?" the salesman replies, "I'm not leaving until you sign the contract."

Another talked about the importance of mental preparation: "When I get out of my car and head up to their front door, I think to myself, *They've got my money in their pocket!*"

I left the sales rally sick to my stomach. What had I gotten myself into? *There has got to be a better way*, I thought, and I intended to find it.

WHEN THE STUDENT IS READY, THE TEACHER WILL APPEAR

I was ready and, as if by a miracle, an amazing group of teachers began to appear in my life. They have made all the difference for me, for our company (The Group, Inc. Real Estate), and for Ninja Selling.

The first was Lou Tice of the Pacific Institute, who taught me how to run my brain and start reprogramming my old self-concept into a new, more positive and powerful self.

Marshall Thurber taught me the very important lesson that the universe is set up around abundance not scarcity, and that the key to success is creation and cooperation, not competition. Marshall is a master teacher who has influenced millions of people.

Through Marshall, I met Tony Robbins and invited him to teach our partners at The Group, Inc. He was very young then, twenty-four, and later said we were the first corporation to hire him.

Through Marshall, I also met Thomas Crum, who introduced me to Aikido and conflict resolution at his Windstar Ranch in Aspen, Colorado. In addition, he taught me about energy and how to move it with my mind.

Dr. James Loehr, the amazing sports psychologist who works with world-famous Olympic and professional athletes (as well as "corporate athletes"), was living in Colorado at the time, and I was fortunate enough to take his classes and learn the keys to putting oneself into a peak performance state. I believe the principles he teaches apply, whether you are coaching top salespeople or top athletes and CEOs.

Robert Kiyosaki appeared in my life during this time, and we became good friends. Robert was doing a series of workshops called Money and You, Creating Wealth, and Powerful Presentations. Robert is probably best known for his *Rich Dad Poor Dad* books and recordings. However, I remember him most as a master teacher. Again, this relationship came about through Marshall Thurber.

Tom Peters's book (with Bob Waterman), *In Search of Excellence*, was number one on *The New York Times* Best Sellers list, and we were able to bring Peters to Fort Collins, Colorado. I was fortunate enough to spend a day with him (and an hour privately), asking him about our company, where we wanted to go and how to get there, and creating a new approach to selling.

All of these teachers had a profound influence on me, our company, and this book. There have been many more teachers since, but these were the earliest and the most influential. I want to thank them for their life-changing impact.

Interestingly, none of these teachers were in sales or sales training. Yet we applied what they taught to our sales approach and how we worked with our customers, and we saw dramatic, positive results. In 1991, The Group, Inc. Real Estate Associates was recognized by Real Trends as the most productive real estate company in America in terms of transactions per sales associate. We have had that ranking nearly every year since.

Ninja Selling is the system that got us there.

NINJA SELLING IS BORN

By 1994, we had documented and tested our sales systems in our *sales laboratory* at The Group, Inc. That fall, we taught our first Ninja Selling course at the Colorado Real Estate convention. With more than 440 people in attendance, it was the largest continuing education real estate class ever taught in the state.

We named the course Ninja Selling, because one of The Group's sales partners, Jim Dunlap (known as Jimmy D.), was nicknamed *The Ninja* by our office staff. Jimmy D. had great sales volumes and great customer satisfaction and referrals. He seemed to do it all effortlessly, quietly, and humbly—very ninja-like. He had the highest income per hour of anyone in our company and was able to have a life outside of real estate. We felt he was a great role model for many salespeople.

In 1998, I was invited by Howard Brinton to share the Ninja Selling story on his national Star Power program. Because of him, Ninja Selling had become nationally known and began attracting the attention of national real estate speakers and instructors.

Two years later, the Certified Residential Specialist (CRS) instructors of the National Association of Realtors called me and said they had listened to the Brinton interview. They asked, "If we come to Colorado, will you teach us Ninja Selling?" I enthusiastically agreed, although I was nervous about teaching the seventeen best instructors in our industry. Could I and Ninja Selling measure up to their standards?

They loved the Ninja Selling System and gave me a standing ovation at the end of the day. Walt Frey, a senior instructor for CRS, came up to me after the class and said, "Larry, what you have here could change our industry! I would like to work with you to teach Ninja Selling throughout the industry."

And so my life and Ninja Selling were forever altered. Walt and his team spread the Ninja gospel throughout the land. I can never thank him enough. In 2007, I began teaching Ninja Selling full time.

Today, we have more than 50,000 Ninja Selling graduates in the Ninja Nation.

In his book *To Sell Is Human*, Daniel Pink documents the history of selling. He describes how selling has changed over the years and what a modern, relevant sales approach looks like today. He's basically describing Ninja Selling. We have been practicing this sales system for more than thirty years and have been teaching workshops on it for more than two decades. We've proven it works. Now it is finally documented in this book. We hope *Ninja Selling* improves your business and your life!

A Note from the Original Ninja

I grew up in southwestern Colorado in a small town in the 1960s and '70s. My mom had three kids, three jobs, and no husband. I struggled in school, earning marginal results at best. We moved to Fort Collins, Colorado, in 1974, when I was fourteen, and my mother remarried. My high school counselor told me that my only viable job future was in agriculture—farming. He told me college would be a waste of money. A major insurance company also told me, based on its standardized testing, that I had no ability to sell anything. They wouldn't even grant me an interview.

Fast forward to 1985: I had been in the real estate business for about eight months and was doing well as a rookie. I had been invited to interview at The Group, Inc. for a sales broker position. The Group was a powerhouse in the Fort Collins real estate industry, and I knew only the best got to work there. The man I was meeting that day was Larry

Kendall. I had already heard a lot about him; he was described to me as a visionary, a sharp businessman, a cult-like leader, brilliantly intelligent, unapproachable, ahead of his time, tough, and much, much more.

As I entered his office, he stood to greet me. Surely, I thought, this man will size me up instantly and realize what I've been told before—that I am not capable of performing on the level that The Group requires. Instead, his hand firmly grasped mine, and he greeted me with confidence, humility, and genuine warmth. He made me feel welcome at once. And he gave me the ride of a lifetime.

My name is Jim Dunlap. Some people call me Jimmy D. Many in the real estate business call me the Original Ninja.[1] I have lived an amazing life. I have been blessed with a grand journey and adventures that I could never have imagined. Larry unlocked the best part within me. The style of business that is now called Ninja Selling was what I had to do in order to pursue my dreams, including professional road cycling and being the best I could be for my family and the people around me. I now have a degenerative disease, and I am no longer able to sell real estate, but I'm still able to encourage other Ninjas to be their best and to follow the Ninja Path.

Thousands of people have written and reached out to me in other ways to express their gratitude and to tell me that through my Ninja style of thinking and being in real estate, their lives have changed forever for the better. I deeply appreciate that, but this profound gratitude is owed to Larry. He worked diligently, incrementally, and consistently

---

1 You can contact Jimmy D. directly at Ride123@aol.com.

for twenty years to create and perfect the Ninja Selling program. I am just a fortunate guy who did what I did, with his guidance and support.

You can share in the words and wisdom that I have been fortunate to experience by reading this book. It offers you a way out of your present circumstance and your known limits and shines light on the path to your personal and professional mastery.

Yes, this book has the power to help you make more money in your career. More importantly, it will change your life. It will alter your ability to connect deeply and honestly with the people in your world and to be the best you can be. Fortunately for the world, Larry put his words and wisdom on paper. Perhaps, just as I was given the key to become the best I could be through Larry, you will find your key to unlock the best of you in this book.

Principle 1

PERSONAL MASTERY

> "For things to change for you, first you must change."
> **—Jim Rohn**

The Ninja Path starts with a commitment to mastery, to being the very best you can be. Let's start with a definition of mastery from Stewart Emery, and then we'll give you the Three Keys to Success to get you on the mastery path.

Stewart Emery's simple four-paragraph treatise on "Mastery" has had a profound impact on my life and the lives of my partners in The Group, Inc. We felt if we could get everyone on the same page—this page—we could achieve the miracles Stewart talks about.

Today, I encourage our Ninjas to read this page each day for thirty days when they graduate from our classes. Many can recite it from memory. Many more have written me about the positive impact it has had on their lives. I invite you to read and practice it.

MASTERY

Mastery in one's career and consciousness growth simply requires that we constantly produce results beyond and out of the ordinary. Mastery is a product of consistently going beyond our limits. For most people, it starts with technical excellence in a chosen field and a *commitment to that excellence*. If you are willing to commit yourself to excellence, to surround yourself with things that represent this, and miracles, your life will change. (When we speak of miracles, we speak of events or experiences in the real world, which are beyond the ordinary.)

It's remarkable how much mediocrity we live with, surrounding ourselves with daily reminders that the average is the acceptable. Our world suffers from terminal normality. Take a moment to assess all of the things around you that promote your being "average." These are the things that keep you powerless to go beyond a "limit" you arbitrarily set for yourself. The first step to mastery is the removal of everything in your environment that represents mediocrity, removing those things that are limiting. One way is to surround yourself with friends who ask more of you than you do. Didn't some of your best teachers, coaches, parents, etc.?

Another step on the path to mastery is the removal of resentment toward masters. Develop compassion for yourself so that you can be in the presence of masters and grow from the experience. Rather than comparing yourself and resenting people who have mastery, remain open and receptive; let the experience be like the planting of a seed

> within you that, with nourishment, will grow into your own individual mastery.
>
> You see, we are all ordinary. But a master, rather than condemning himself for his "ordinariness," will embrace it and use it as a foundation for building the extraordinary. Rather than using it as an excuse for inactivity, he will use it as a vehicle for correcting, which is essential in the process of attaining mastery. You must be able to correct yourself without invalidating or condemning yourself, to accept results and improve upon them. Correct, don't protect. Correction is essential to power and mastery.
>
> Stewart Emery

The Three Keys

There are three keys to mastery and success in your life and your business.

1. **Your Mind-Set.** How do you run your brain? What is your mental programming? Do you have the ability to focus, to control your thoughts and your energy? Ninja Principle 1 will help you develop the mental programs and focused energy to achieve your life and business goals.

2. **Your Skill Set.** The next step to mastery is technical excellence in your chosen field and a commitment to that excellence. Principles 2 and 4 will give you the specific processes to create value in the world and help your customers make good decisions. You will need to develop these skills with practice.

3. **Your Actions.** Principle 3 gives you the specific actions you can take to create a continuous flow of customers coming to you.

The Ninja System only works if you put it into action. Your discipline in putting your skills into action consistently will determine your results. As Jimmy D., the original Ninja, says, "Life happens at the level of movement, not words."

All three of these keys are critical, but the most important of the three is your mind-set. You may have the skills and be taking the right actions, but if you bring the wrong energy or attitude to the game, your mind-set will override the other two. Principle 1, personal mastery, is devoted to helping you create the Ninja mind-set.

Your mind-set is a function of your programming. This will become clear to you as we explore how your brain works. We will show you how to program your mind—and in some cases reprogram it. One of the most powerful programming methods is using positive affirmations stated in the first person.

> **"One of the most powerful methods to program your mind is to use positive affirmations stated in the first person."**

To help you, we are going to do something unusual in this section. At times, I am going to present the text of this book in first person—that is as "I." *I will put these sections in italics* so they will stand out for you. When you read the text in first person, you will personalize and internalize the message, and it will serve as an affirmation for you. It is much more powerful than if you read the words *you* or *we*.

Chapter 1

THE NINJA MIND-SET

A psychologist once told me, "At any given point in time, a human chooses to be either a player or a victim."

My cell phone rang, and a very excited voice said, "Hi Larry! This is Maria Vitale! I don't know if you remember me, but I was in your Ninja Installation class a couple of months ago. I'm so excited! I just walked out of my seventh closing for the month of December, and I have two more! I'll have nine closings in December! I owe it all to God and the Ninja Installation. I just wanted to call and personally thank you."

"Bravo, Maria!" I said. "I'm very proud of you." (Keep in mind the national average is six transactions a year and Maria is doing nine in one month!) "What was the one thing you learned in the Ninja Installation that helped you the most?"

"Oh, that's easy," Maria said. "It was the Ninja mind-set—specifically the morning routine you taught me."

"The morning routine?" I asked. (We will teach you this morning routine in Chapter 5.)

"Yes!" Maria exclaimed. "You see, Larry, you don't know my story. I'm a single mom with two little boys. I've been flat broke and living in my mom's basement for the last several months, trying to get started in real estate. Larry, when you lose your marriage and your home, you're flat broke, and you're living in your mother's basement with two kids under the age of three, what kind of a mind-set do you develop—player or victim?"

"Victim," I said.

"Exactly! I had a victim mind-set," declared Maria. "What I realized was that I was surrounded by potential buyers and sellers, but *nobody wants to work with a victim! People prefer to work with players.* The minute I changed my mind-set and energy to a player, people wanted to work with me, and I started writing contracts. Oh, and Larry, with this closing today, I put a deposit on a home. I bought a home for 181K. The boys and I are moving out of the basement. We are going to have our own place!"

When Maria stopped broadcasting on the victim channel and started broadcasting on the player channel, she changed her vibe, her relationships, her career, and her life.

Chapter 2

GOOD VIBRATIONS

Everything in the universe consists of energy that is vibrating at its own frequency, including you. For example, middle C on the piano vibrates at 261 hertz (cycles per second), which makes the tone middle C. Each musical note has a different frequency of vibration. Putting these vibrations together in patterns is what makes music.

I paid my way through college playing rock and roll. When we played shows, we had two perfectly tuned guitars sitting on either side of the stage. If we plucked a string on one of the guitars, guess what would happen to the other one? That same string would vibrate. There would be a transfer of energy (a sound wave) across the stage from one guitar to the other—from a sender to a receiver.

This is the same science at work behind radio and television transmissions—energy is sent at a frequency from a sender to a receiver. We call the different frequencies *channels*.

YOUR VIBE
As a human, I am both a sender and a receiver of energy. I broadcast energy at a frequency based on what I am thinking and feeling. Others receive this energy and call it my vibe.

Have you ever picked up someone's vibe? Do they pick up your vibe? How important is the vibe in sales? In trust? Can you pick up the vibe of someone who is angry? Depressed? Happy? In love? What is your vibe? What are you broadcasting? Victim or player? Nobody wants to be around a victim. Customers prefer to work with players.

You control your vibe with your thoughts and feelings. Your vibe can actually be measured with special instruments that show its colors (frequencies of energy) coming off your body. These frequencies and colors are a product of what you are thinking and feeling.

Control your thoughts, control your feelings (your emotional energy), and you will control your vibe. You decide the frequencies—that is, the channels—you broadcast and receive on. Ninjas know this and are constantly sending and receiving energy that empowers them and others.

Have you ever been around someone who makes you feel good just by being around them? You are picking up on their positive energy—their positive vibe. Similarly, have you ever been around somebody who is so toxic that you feel lighter, brighter, and more alive when he or she leaves your presence? That is all about energy. Everything in your environment—including people—either gives you energy or takes energy away.

Ninjas are masters of creating, sending, and receiving good vibrations. You can learn all the Ninja skills in this book, but they are unlikely to work for you if you're projecting fear, anger, and scarcity. This negative vibe will get picked up by customers, and they will avoid you.

✳ Like attracts like: People radiating positive energy will naturally move away from you if you are radiating negative energy, and people radiating negative energy will naturally be attracted to you, bringing their fear, anger, grief, and negativity into your life.

You will start feeling like a victim, not realizing what your thoughts, feelings, and actions are creating in your life. Before long, you are spiraling downward.

Fortunately, the laws of vibration work in both directions. I have seen people who are down and out change their thoughts, feelings, and vibrational frequency, and start spiraling up, ultimately achieving unbelievable success and happiness in their life. Maria did it.

Change your vibe. Change your world.

> *Ninjas are masters of creating, sending, and receiving good vibrations.*

Chapter 3

CONTROLLING YOUR EMOTIONAL ENERGY

Your emotional energy ranges from negative to positive (horizontal scale) and from low to high (vertical scale). As a result, you are in one of four energy quadrants when you are awake.

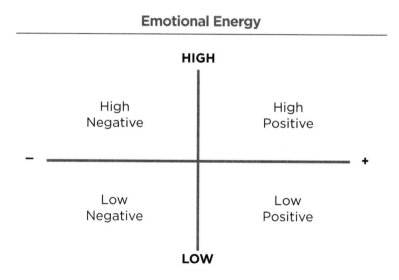

What are some of the emotions you might experience in each of these quadrants?

- **High Negative:** anger, fear, frustration, revenge, negative expectation

- **Low Negative:** sadness, guilt, depression, aloneness, negative expectation
- **High Positive:** happiness, inspiration, confidence, love, positive expectation
- **Low Positive:** contentment, relaxation, safety, love, positive expectation

I was first introduced to these energy quadrants by Dr. James Loehr, a sports psychologist who works with professional and Olympic athletes. According to Dr. Loehr's research, athletes perform at their best when they are in the high positive quadrant. In fact, he calls it the Performance Quadrant.

In sales, you are a corporate athlete. When it is time for you to perform—to meet with a customer—you need to have strategies you can use to move yourself into the high positive quadrant.

PLAYER AND VICTIM QUADRANTS

My observation is that players tend to live most of their lives in the high and low positive quadrants. They will have occasional episodes where they find themselves in the negative quadrants, because they are human and stuff happens. But they don't stay there very long. They learn from the experience, adjust, and move back to the positive quadrants. They have what we call *response-ability*—the ability to respond. Their experience on the dark side is only an episode.

Victims, on the other hand, tend to live most of their lives in the negative quadrants. When something happens in their life that causes anger or depression, they move to the negative quadrants and seem to get stuck there. They don't have response-ability and can't seem to find their way back to the positive side. Their negative energy and vibe start a feedback loop that affects their relationship with those around them.

Maria experienced this when she was in victim mode, and she realized that nobody wants to work with a victim.

Can you observe other humans and tell what energy quadrant they are in by their vibe? Most of us can, and so can our friends and customers. Again, people prefer to work with people who are in the positive energy quadrants.

To clarify, if you are in the high positive quadrant, you are not pumped up so high that you are hyper and scattered. To the contrary, you are cool, confident, positive, and focused. You have a nonanxious presence. You are very attentive and notice the slightest changes in your client or the environment. You pick up subtle and hidden nuances. You are very connected to your client and what is going on. You feel in control and confident in your skills and your ability to help your customer make good decisions. You are in a peak performance state.

How do you move yourself into this peak performance state?

- First, you need to have a proven process that delivers predictable results.
- Second, you need to develop your skills to deliver the process confidently.
- Third, you need to use a pregame ritual to help you focus and perform at your best.

Chapter 4

RITUALS

Rituals are something you do right before you perform. They are designed to help you get focused and prepared, so you will perform at your best—at your peak. Golfers have a preshot ritual they carry out each time they play. Free-throw shooters also have a preshot ritual. I have a pregame ritual I go through right before I start a workshop or just before I walk on stage to speak. Top salespeople have a pregame ritual they practice before they meet with their customers. All peak performers that I know have a pregame ritual.

Use a pregame ritual to move yourself into the high positive (performance) quadrant right before it is time to perform. Some people listen to a particular piece of music; others use visualization or affirmation. Some sit quietly and meditate or relax their breathing. Others focus on their clients—their needs and how to connect with them in the opening two minutes. (This is a mental rehearsal.)

When I walk past Tami Spaulding's office and hear a certain bit of music and see her shining her shoes, I know she is about to go on a listing appointment. She is going through her pregame ritual.

You cannot stay in the high positive quadrant all the time. It consumes too much energy. So when you are not performing, what quadrant do you want to be in? You got it—low positive. As a Ninja, you are always moving between the high and low positive quadrants. Notice that the feelings in these two quadrants are similar. The only real differences are the amount of energy and the focus required.

STRATEGIES TO COUNTERACT THE DARK SIDE

Rituals can also be used to help you get back on track when you are in trouble. What happens when you find yourself in the high negative or low negative quadrants—the dark side? You are human, and you'll end up in these quadrants sooner or later. And, if you get stuck there, you'll develop a victim mind-set. The key is to quickly recognize where you are and move out of there. How fast is your response-ability? Ninjas develop strategies to move out of those quadrants quickly, so the experience there is only an episode—hopefully, a very short one.

Here are some ways you can move out of negative quadrants:

- **Gratitude.** Focus on what you are grateful for. It will take your mind off the negative emotions of the moment.
- **Exercise.** Activity works out anger and frustration, and it's difficult to be depressed while exercising.
- **Music.** Positive, uplifting music can bring you back to the positive quadrants.
- **Nature.** Take a hike or go for a drive. Being in nature tends to heal you and puts life in perspective.
- **Learn.** Take a class or a lesson, read a book, or learn something new.
- **Escape.** Go to a movie or a ballgame, and mentally check out for a while.
- **Positive people.** Have lunch or spend time with someone who is emanating good vibrations.
- **Mentors and coaches.** When you find yourself on the dark side, turn to your mentors and coaches for help.

AVOID THE TRAPS

When many people find themselves in a negative quadrant, they immediately seek out others who are also in a negative quadrant. Misery loves company. This is a trap. Other traps are drugs, alcohol, food, and shopping (spending money you don't have). They make you feel better in the short run but tend to keep you in negative quadrants in the longer run.

The quality of your life will be a direct result of how much of your life you spend in the positive quadrants, on the bright side of life, and how little time you spend on the dark side. You have a choice in the matter. The decision is yours.

Chapter 5

THE NINJA MORNING ROUTINE

Routines are different from rituals. Routines are activities you do every day. For example, how many hours of sleep do you get per night? What is your exercise routine? What are your daily dietary habits? What time do you get to work? What are the activities you do each day to build relationships and generate business? Is your routine healthy and successful?

What you do every day is more important than what you do once in a while, because routines have a compounding effect over time. We can predict success in sales by simply observing a sales associate's daily routine.

Maria Vitale changed her life and career by choosing to be a player versus a victim. How did she do it? She credits the Ninja Morning Routine as one of the reasons.

The Ninja Morning Routine consists of four simple steps:

1. **Gratitude.** Give thanks for what you have, those around you, and who you are.
2. **Positive Reading.** Read something positive to start your day, even just a few pages.
3. **Affirmations/Visualizations.** Focus on a goal as if you have already achieved it.
4. **Write two personal notes.** Focus on others.

The first step is gratitude therapy. Gratitude, being in a state of thankfulness, is very powerful energy. Maria learned that, even when she was flat broke and living in her mother's basement with two small children, there were still things to be grateful for. Taking time to give thanks does a couple of very important things.

First, gratitude puts you in a state of positive humility, which is a very important part of the Ninja Selling philosophy. When the ego gets out of control, a person starts spiraling downward. Customers and friends don't enjoy being in the presence of an egomaniac and tend to move away. They gravitate toward humble, yet confident people who emanate good vibrations.

Second, giving thanks sets up a positive vibrational state. When you start feeling good and are emanating good vibrations, this, in turn, opens you up to receive new possibilities and opportunities flowing into your life. Dr. Michael Beckwith says it best: "You cannot bring anything new into your life until you are grateful for what you have now."

Here's a subtle but very important point: What you are feeling is more important than what you are thinking.

Thoughts get you headed in the right direction, but you have to really feel it in your body to get results. It's your feelings that determine your vibrational frequency and your sending/receiving channels. You decide this every day.

Get into the habit of programming yourself every day to be vibrating and sending/receiving energy frequencies of gratitude, love, abundance, and positive expectations.

BEGIN WITH GRATITUDE

I believe in the power of visualization or mental rehearsal. However, I have found it works best if you start with an attitude of gratitude. I often see people who have read books or taken classes on the power of visualization and then immediately visualize what it is that they want to have in their lives. If they are not careful, this can become a trap.

> "*Never take anything for granted. Every day is a gift.*"

Without the gratitude step, nothing new can come into their lives. Also, their mind can play funny games. People sometimes tell me that when they start visualizing what they want in their lives, they are reminded that they don't have it. In fact, there is a lot they don't have, and they suddenly start dwelling on all that they lack. They slip into scarcity. What started out as a positive exercise turns into a negative one and, consequently, produces negative vibrations.

When students tell me how a visualization experience turned negative for them, I ask if they started their visualization with gratitude. In every case, they say no. Always start with gratitude. Bring a person, object, or experience to mind. Feel the love and thanksgiving for that person, object, or experience. This opens you up to receive.

If you want to read more about the science of gratitude, read *Thanks! How the New Science of Gratitude Can Make You Happier* by Dr. Robert Emmons.

EVERY DAY IS A GIFT!

As you learn how energy works, and begin to receive success in your life, it is easy to slip into a mind-set that you are somehow master of the universe and can make anything happen. Well, you can make a lot happen by learning how the universe works, but you always need to remember you didn't create it, and you need to continuously have an attitude of gratitude.

Never take anything for granted. Every day is a gift.

We instill this philosophy at The Group, Inc. I always start our weekly sales meetings by asking, "What day is this?" Everyone replies in unison, "It's another day in paradise!" And that's our attitude of gratitude.

Now that you are in the positive energy quadrants, let's help you discover customers, transactions, and opportunities with your "onboard Google search engine."

Chapter 6

WHAT YOU FOCUS ON EXPANDS

At the base of your brain is a dense group of cells called the reticular formation. This part of your brain is about the size of your little finger, and every cell in your body is wired into it. It is called the Reticular Activating System (RAS). In computer terms, the RAS is your central processing unit. An illustration of the brain showing the location of the RAS is shown below.

Drawing of the Human Brain

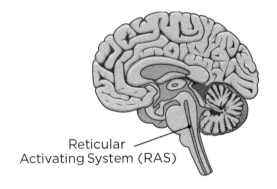

Reticular Activating System (RAS)

The RAS operates as your onboard Google search engine. Program in what you are looking for, and RAS will seek and find it. It operates on two pathways – love and fear. These two pathways are mutually exclusive. You can only be on one or the other. As a result, love is the absence of fear and fear is the absence of love.

Reticular Activating System

YOUR BRAIN'S FILTERING / FOCUSING DEVICE

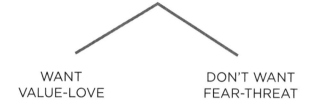

WANT
VALUE-LOVE

DON'T WANT
FEAR-THREAT

One pathway handles searches based on what you want, value, or love. The other handles searches based on what you fear or don't want. You do the programming—and determine the pathway—with your thoughts. Anything that doesn't fit the search is filtered out.

Whatever you focus on expands. In other words, you will see more of it. Your RAS will help you notice things you weren't seeing before and will improve or hurt your performance based on how you program it. The following is an example of how your RAS works:

Think of a car you really like or value. It may be the make and model you are driving right now. Imagine you and I are riding in your car. When a car like yours (or the car you want) goes by, do you notice it? Of course you do. Why? Because you value that car, and your RAS opens up and spots it. I have a different favorite car. When it goes by, I'm the one who notices it. You don't notice the cars that are important to me, and I don't notice the cars that are important to you. We only see the cars we value. We are two people in the same car going down the same road having two totally different experiences based on our different RAS programming. We see different things based on what we have programmed as valuable into our RAS.

Another example: You decide to buy new furniture for your living room. Suddenly, just when you are ready to make the purchase, you notice furniture sales popping up everywhere. Actually, stores run furniture ads and sales continuously. You only notice them now because it's important to you. Your RAS opened up and let this information into your awareness.

You will learn to use your RAS to spot the buyers, sellers, and transactions hidden in the crowd. *→ opportunities*

THE POWER OF YOUR RAS

Your RAS is a very powerful determiner of performance. Programing your RAS with your thoughts is especially easy to observe in sports. For instance, let's say you are a golfer, and as you approach the green, you notice a large sand trap creating an obstacle in your path. You repeat to yourself, "Stay out of that trap. Stay out of that trap." But where does the ball go? Into the trap! Why? Because that is where you programmed it to go. What you focus on expands! Think about it. Your onboard computer, your RAS, flashed "Trap! Trap! Trap!" Every cell in your body is focused on the trap. Of course the ball goes into it.

You programmed your RAS to go down the fear pathway. Experienced golfers know when they start down that path they are having dark thoughts. They immediately arrest those negative thoughts (what they don't want) and replace them with positive thoughts (what they want). These golfers shift over to the "want, value, love" pathway by focusing on the green, the hole, or wherever it is they want the ball to land.

The way your RAS works is a good news/bad news story. The good news: What you focus on expands. The bad news: What you focus on expands. As an example, have you ever wanted to get out of debt? I used to have that goal, and I would have episodes of getting out of debt. But then, after a while, I would be back in debt deeper than ever. One day, I remembered my own teaching: "What you focus on expands." If you focus on your debt, your debt will expand. So I shifted my focus to being free and clear. How will it feel to be free and clear? I enjoyed that feeling and focused on it, and within five years, we were indeed, free and clear.

Your RAS isn't judgmental. It doesn't discern right from wrong or positive from negative. It simply brings into your awareness whatever you choose to think about or focus on. So make sure you are focusing on what you want. Focus on the green, not the trap. Focus on making the free throw, instead of not missing the free throw. Focus on gratitude, wealth, and abundance, instead of fear and scarcity. Your RAS can quickly start a feedback loop that's either positive or negative.

When Mother Teresa was invited to an antiwar rally, she declined the invitation. "When you have a peace rally, I will attend," she said. She understood. Focus on what you want (peace) versus what you don't want (war). Another example of this shift in perspective is that we used to have a War on Cancer, and now we have a Race for the Cure.

THE QUALITY OF MY LIFE

The quality of my life will be determined, in large part, by the amount of time I spend on the positive pathway of my RAS. Being able to recognize I am going down the negative pathway, arresting those thoughts, changing them, and heading down the positive path is a very important skill for me to develop.

The player lives on the positive path. Victims tend to spend most of their lives focusing on what they don't want and, as a result, manifesting more of what they don't want in a negative feedback loop. Your Ninja Morning Routine and having positive, measurable goals will help you stay on the positive RAS pathway.

Unfortunately, most people have not taken the time to write down positive, measurable goals. As a result, they can't tell you what they want. Instead, they tell you what they don't want. One way to positively program your RAS is through a life list.

When he was fifteen, adventurer John Goddard made a list of the things he wanted to do in his life. Then he set about doing them. He and his list became famous. Some called him "the original Indiana Jones," and his 127-item list became the inspiration for the hit movie *The Bucket List*, starring Jack Nicholson and Morgan Freeman.

About fifteen years ago, we invited Dr. Goddard to come to our company and share his stories. We filled the Lincoln Center with 1,200 of our salespeople, clients, and families to hear him talk and see his photos. For me, the most powerful moment that night was when Dr. Goddard said, "The quality of your life is the quality of your list."

> *Focus on what you want. . . . What you focus on expands!*

Your list programs your RAS and magnetically draws you to those items. You begin to see opportunities that were hidden before. Make a list of what you want for yourself, your family, and for your career. Make a list of what brings you joy and everything you want to have, to do, to be, and to give in life. Your life list is your reasons for living list. It's your *why*. It's what motivates you to get up in the morning.

Start your life list now! Focus on what you want. Write it down, and put your RAS to work for you. What you focus on expands!

Chapter 7

LEARNING TO RUN YOUR BRAIN

A year after the following photo was taken, I contracted encephalitis—a disease of the brain. At that time, in the 1950s, two of the most feared diseases were polio and encephalitis. With encephalitis, the brain gets hot and swells, often causing unconsciousness. Many patients slip into a coma and die.

I was one of the lucky ones. I awoke from the coma, but the disease left me with a speech defect and paralysis of one leg. I was the kid in school who walked and talked funny and was often made fun of by the other kids. Needless to say, this created self-consciousness and insecurity that made me ill suited for a career in sales.

Nevertheless, I went into sales, and after five years, a breakthrough occurred when I met Lou Tice for the first time. Lou was a successful coach and psychologist who founded the Pacific Institute. He introduced me to the way our three brains work, and I started reprogramming the parts of my nonconscious brain that were holding me back.

I share this story because I actually used the science we cover in this chapter to change my life and career. I was the subject in this human laboratory. I know from personal experience that this stuff works!

YOUR THREE BRAINS

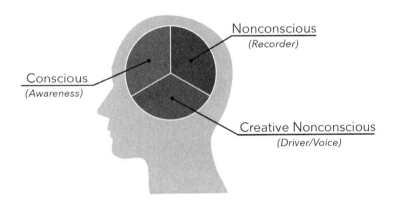

My conscious brain is what I am using to read this book. It is my awareness of what is going on around me right now—what I am seeing, hearing, smelling, feeling, tasting.

My nonconscious brain is like a recording device. It switched on and started recording while I was still in my mother's body. It records all experiences—everything I have ever seen, heard, and felt. It never forgets, and it never judges. My nonconscious assumes that everything it has recorded is the truth. These recordings become my program.

Examples of my program are my

- Self-image—how I see myself and believe others see me;
- Self-talk—what I say to myself;
- Self-esteem—how I feel about myself; and
- Beliefs—how I believe the world is, how it works, and my role in it.

Think of your conscious brain as your computer screen and your nonconscious brain as your hard drive and programmable software.

My creative nonconscious brain is the driver, or operating system, that runs my program. It forces me to behave consistently with my program. It acts as an autopilot, keeping me on track with my program.

THE LITTLE VOICE

Do you ever talk to yourself? Do you ever hear a little voice inside your head? That is often your creative nonconscious. Here's an experiment to show you how it works:

On a piece of paper, write down your income goal for this year. Once you have a number written down, double it, and write the doubled number down.

$ _____ Annual goal

$ _____ New goal (Annual goal × 2)

Did you hear a little voice? What did it say? Did it argue with you about the doubled number? Did it say, *No way! Not going to happen! You're kidding! You don't want to work that hard!* If the little voice argued with you, it's because the income goal is not in your program (your nonconscious). Imagine a computerized electronic voice saying, *Does not fit program! Does not fit program!* The goal is not on your hard drive. For you to achieve this goal, you will need to put it on there, on your program. We will show you how to do that.

What if the little voice said *Yes!* to the doubled goal? It *is* in your program. Just do it!

One of my business students at Colorado State University, Jake Shoptaugh, put it this way: "Setting goals is a function of the conscious mind. Reaching goals is a function of the nonconscious mind."

Jake made this profound statement in a paper he wrote after reading *The Answer* by John Assaraf and Murray Smith. The first hundred pages of this book offer a concise description, in simple language, of the way the brain works based on the research of award-winning scientists.

When I was growing up, we used the term *subconscious*. Scientists no longer use that word, because it implies that the subconscious is somehow less than the conscious. Today, scientists call this part of the brain the nonconscious, because they know it controls 96 to 98 percent of our behavior.

Want success? Learn to program your nonconscious. We will show you how.

YOUR NONCONSCIOUS CAN'T TAKE A JOKE!

Since your nonconscious mind is nonjudgmental, it records and believes anything that happens in the present moment, including your goals and affirmations that are stated in the present tense. It actually believes these things have happened, and they become part of your program. In his breakthrough 1963 book, *The Power of the Subconscious Mind*, Joseph Murphy, PhD, DD, states, "The subconscious can't take a joke."

Here's an example of how it works: Early in my real estate career, I weighed 205 pounds. My goal was to weigh 175 pounds. Occasionally, I'd get down to 175 pounds, only to return back to 205 pounds. I decided I needed to reprogram my nonconscious, so I started stating to myself, *"I enjoy weighing 175 pounds,"* when I actually weighed 205 pounds. At first, my little voice argued with me, but repeated enough times, my nonconscious began to believe I weighed 175 pounds. (It can't take a joke!) This became my new program, and my creative nonconscious drove me to behave according to that new program. I started modifying my diet and exercise and, over time, lost thirty pounds.

Your nonconscious is programmable. You control the programming, and we will show you how to do it.

Chapter 8

MY RESULTS FORMULA

My brain is my onboard hardware. My thoughts are the software. The electrical and chemical impulses called thoughts emanate energy in the form of waves and can be measured. Scientists estimate that I have more than fifty thousand thoughts each day. Where do my thoughts come from? Most of them come from my nonconscious program.

If I think about something enough, what happens? I begin to believe it. My fifty thousand thoughts a day start to accumulate and form my belief system. I begin to believe the world is a certain way, people are a certain way, and I am a certain way. This part of my belief system is my perceptual map—my worldview, the lens through which I see the world and my role in it.

I tend to act in accordance with my beliefs, my worldview, and my program. It is my actions that determine my results. My simple cause/effect formula looks like this:

My thoughts come from my nonconscious program and form my beliefs.

I take action based on my beliefs (programs).

My actions determine my results.

RESPONSIBILITY

Do you buy into this results formula? If you do, you must believe in the concept of *responsibility*: You are not just a passenger on this journey called *life*, you are also the captain.

The quality of my life is determined by the quality of my thinking. When I am thinking positive, loving thoughts—and feeling them—good things begin to happen because of the vibe I am broadcasting to others and the positive programming of my belief system.

I am responsible for the things I can control, which are my thoughts, beliefs, and actions. For these I take RESPONSIBILITY.

For the things I cannot control, I can control my response to them. In these situations, I take RESPONSE-ABILITY. I have the ability to respond. I can control my response.

Have you ever lost money in an investment? Have you ever had an accident, been injured, or had a serious illness? Most of us have had some or all of these experiences, yet we respond differently. Some are devastated, and their life spirals downward. They become victims. Victims don't seem to have the ability to respond to life's challenges. Others bounce back and become even stronger. They are the players.

The quality of my life is not so much determined by what happens to me as much as it is by how I respond to what happens. How I respond (my actions) is a function of my thoughts and beliefs.

JACK'S STORY

Jack Taylor had been a policeman for twenty-five years. He reached the rank of lieutenant in the Fort Collins Police Department and had served as a SWAT team leader and commander of the Larimer County Drug Task Force. After more than two decades of knocking down doors, chasing bad guys, and watching little kids crawling in meth labs, Jack decided he had seen enough. He wanted to spend the rest of his life doing something fun, positive, and rewarding. He decided on a career in real estate sales, joking that now he could take people in his car without having to put handcuffs on them. And, they could ride in the front seat.

But Jack had no sales experience. Since we didn't have an opening in any of our three Fort Collins offices, he went to our office in the neighboring town of Windsor. The weekend before he was to start work, Jack was driving his draft horses and wagon in a county fair rodeo. There was an accident. Jack was thrown off the eight-foot-high wagon seat and landed under the horses and wagon. The wagon rolled over him, breaking his neck.

The doctor stood over Jack in the hospital and said, "Jack, I have good news and bad news. The good news is you're alive, and you're not paralyzed. The bad news is you have a broken neck. We can do surgery now, or we can put you in a neck brace for six weeks and see if you heal." Jack chose the brace.

So there he was. Jack had given up his salaried position. He was to start his commission-selling job the next day. His office was in a strange town and market. He had a broken neck and could not work. Most people would give up under those circumstances. But Jack's a player. He has response-ability. Jack said, "I can still work the Ninja System. I can make my phone calls." And he did. He called all of his friends to let them know he was now in real estate sales.

> *"The quality of my life is not so much determined by what happens to me as much as it is by how I respond to what happens."*

Despite the cards he was dealt, Jack earned more than $300,000 his first twelve months in real estate sales and was named Rookie of the Year by the Board of Realtors.

I have a choice. I can choose to respond to the negative in a positive way, rather than letting it devastate me. I can choose to be a player. I can choose to take control of my thoughts and feelings. I can start this minute by programming myself for good vibrations.

Chapter 9

CREATING YOUR FUTURE

> *"You will be the same person in five years as you are today except for three things: The people you meet, the places you go, and the books you read."*
> —**Charles "Tremendous" Jones**

When Charlie "Tremendous" Jones told me this thirty years ago, it changed my thinking and my life. He is right. These three things program us, and I would add two more: your habits and your thoughts.

1. THE PEOPLE YOU MEET (FRIENDS AND MENTORS)

Have you ever heard that your income and your net worth will be the average of the five people you spend the most time with? Introduce me to your five best friends, let me spend some time with them, and I'll tell you an amazing amount about you. Birds of a feather flock together. Who are you flocking with? Players? Spectators? Victims? Choose your friends wisely.

Whenever a salesperson is in a slump, watch to see whom he or she is hanging out with. Are they going to lunch with other slumping salespeople or are they going to lunch with a player. Who are they sitting with at the sales meeting? If they are flocking with victims, I do a *pattern interrupt* and have them flock with the players. Their production usually increases immediately.

How do you pick a real estate company to join? Its brand? Its commission split? Its training program? Clearly, all of these are important.

But the most important consideration, in my opinion, is the people. Are they players? Are they the kind of people you want to be associated with, learn from, and flock with? Everything in your environment—including people—either gives you energy or takes energy away.

2. THE PLACES YOU GO

Travel expands your perceptual map, the lens through which you see the world. Your perspective changes with the number of countries and cultures you have visited. By seeing other parts of the world, travel will also make you feel even more grateful for what you have.

3. WHAT YOU READ (BOOKS AND MEDIA)

What books are you reading? Self-improvement books or romantic novels? What are you listening to? Recorded self-help books or talk radio? What are you watching? TED Talks and training videos or mindless videos and games?

Americans spend hours each day watching videos—TV, online, or mobile. Do you think most of this video is positive programming? How is a person to achieve mastery and greatness, fulfilling their life's dreams and passions, by spending hours each day watching videos? These people are not living their lives. They are spending their life watching others' lives.

4. YOUR HABITS

> *"People do not decide their futures. They decide their habits, and their habits decide their futures."*
> **—F.M. Alexander**

Your morning routine of gratitude, positive reading, affirmation, and writing personal notes are habits that will lead you to happiness and success. What is it that keeps so many salespeople from following these habits? Distractions and the inability to handle distractions. International business coach Robin Sharma calls it an addiction: "The enemy of Mastery is not mediocrity. It is distractions. The addiction to distractions ruins many potentially awesome lives."

Proper control of your thoughts and your focus will help you handle our modern world with its abundance of distractions.

5. YOUR THOUGHTS (VISUALIZATIONS AND AFFIRMATIONS)

> *"We become what we think about."*
> —James Allen

Your thoughts control your programming, your behavior, and your results.

Visualization: *My self-image is how I see myself. If I wish, I can reprogram my self-image—or parts of it—by simply and repeatedly visualizing myself as the person I want to become, as if I am that person now.*

Affirmation: *My self-talk is what I say to myself. What I say to myself becomes part of my program. I am saying what I want—not what I don't want. Even better, I say it as if I have it or am experiencing it right now.*

Chapter 10

EIGHT KEY STEPS TO PROPER PROGRAMMING

Have you ever tried visualizations or affirmations, and they didn't work for you? It may be because you weren't doing them properly.

The eight-step process listed below has been proven effective and is used by many successful people, from professional athletes to astronauts to salespeople. It is sometimes called *mental rehearsal* or *neural reconditioning*. To be effective, the process of programming or reprogramming your nonconscious needs to follow these eight steps:

1. **My Goal.** I make sure what I focus on is my goal, not someone else's goal for me. If it is not my goal, my nonconscious will fight it.

2. **Positive and Measurable.** My goal needs to be stated in the positive, that is, what I want—not what I don't want. Proper programming is *I enjoy being free and clear.* Improper programming would be *I want to get out of debt.* My RAS will focus on the debt, and what I focus on expands.

    My goal needs to be measurable. I need to be able to answer the question *How will I know when I've succeeded?* Vague goals such as happiness or success don't cut it. The nonconscious can't lock on to something so vague. Make the goal measurable and specific.

3. **First Person.** My goal needs to be stated in first person—*I*.

Some people have a tendency to use third person (their name), which is a mistake.

4. **Present Tense.** I state my goal in first person, present tense—as if it is happening right now. Remember: Your nonconscious can't take a joke. Your nonconscious only understands and relates to the present moment. As a result, all goals and affirmations need to be stated in the present tense. This is a big mistake many people make in goal setting.

   For example, the goal *I want to earn $250,000 this year* does not program. The nonconscious doesn't read future tense as an actual experience. In fact, it reads the statement as, *I am not earning $250,000 a year now.* Proper programming would be to state, *I enjoy earning $250,000 a year or more.* Here are some examples of proper and improper programming:

   Improper: *I want to lose thirty pounds.*
   Proper: *I enjoy weighing 175 pounds (ideal weight).*

   Improper: *I want to list more houses.*
   Proper: *I am grateful I list more than twenty-five houses a year.*

   Improper: *I want to get out of debt.*
   Proper: *I enjoy being free and clear.*

5. **Through My Eyes.** I see the goal or event through my own eyes. This gets back to first person versus a person who looks like you (third person). You need to see life through your own eyes, not as if you are watching a television show of your life.

6. **Sensory Specific.** I see, hear, feel, smell, and taste the experience. For example, if one of your goals is a trip to an Australian beach, see (through your eyes) what you would see walking on that beach. Hear the sounds of the ocean and the Australian accents of the people. Feel the sun on your face and the ocean breeze in your

hair. Feel the warm sand under your feet. Smell the salt breezes. You are there. Your nonconscious believes you are there.

7. **Daily for Thirty Days.** It takes time to program or reprogram the nonconscious. Your beliefs start to change after thirty days, if you have done this properly (as outlined above) and consistently (daily). In our Ninja Installation class, we have our Ninjas write their affirmations twenty-five times every morning. Increase your power by doing this exercise three times a day.

8. **Anchor.** Anchors remind us of the goal and put us in a particular state of mind about it. In the previous example, an anchor might be a poster of an Australian beach. Whenever you look at that poster, you are reminded of your goal and you go there in your mind—hearing the waves, feeling the sun and sand, and so on. Another anchor could be a dream board with pictures of the things that are on your life list.

Chapter 11
THE POWER OF AFFIRMATIONS

A properly written or stated affirmation is positive, specific, and expressed in the present tense.

Once you have prepared your affirmation, next you need to program it into your nonconscious. You do this by writing the affirmation over and over for thirty straight days. We recommend writing the affirmation twenty-five times a day. As you write it, remember to get into the *feeling* of having, doing, being, or giving it *now*. Strong feelings make the affirmation stronger.

To test your programming, write your affirmation once and then listen for your little voice, your creative nonconscious. What does it say? Does it say, *No way*? If it does, it is telling you the affirmation is not in the program. This is fairly typical of a new affirmation. It truly is not in your program. It will take some time—typically thirty days of continuously writing the affirmation—before the little voice starts to say, *Yes*. When this happens, the affirmation (goal) is in your program (nonconscious). Now, your creative nonconscious will begin to force you to behave in a manner that is consistent with it.

MARY LOU'S STORY

Mary Lou York is a Ninja in Austin, Texas. She attended the Ninja Training a number of years ago with Walt Frey as her instructor. Walt went over how to write affirmations and their power to reprogram the nonconscious, when you do them properly and repeatedly.

Mary Lou and a coworker were committed to writing their affirmations every day for thirty days, and they decided to hold each other accountable by sending each other their affirmations each day. It was a grind, and Mary Lou wanted to give up, but she kept going, because she promised her coworker she would do it.

One morning, about three weeks into the process, Mary Lou woke up not feeling very well and rolled over in bed to go back to sleep. Suddenly, a little voice said to her, *Mary Lou, get up! You earn $20,000 a month. You can't be lying in bed. Get up!*

And so Mary Lou got up and went to work. Later that day, a group of coworkers were heading out to lunch and invited Mary Lou to join them. Again, she heard the little voice say, *Mary Lou, you earn $20,000 a month. You can't be going to lunch with other agents—they won't be buying or selling with you.* And so Mary Lou started calling everyone in her referral base.

Mary Lou's nonconscious was being reprogrammed by her affirmations. Her creative nonconscious was forcing her to behave in accordance with her new program. The result: Mary Lou modified her behavior and earned $20,000 per month for the next six months! At that point she was hired to be the sales manager for her office and has been committed to sharing her "Ninja Experience" with her agents ever since!

MENTAL PUSH-UPS—JUST SEVEN MINUTES A DAY

We call affirmations *mental push-ups*. I'm sometimes asked, "Do I have to do these every day? Do I have to write my affirmations twenty-five times? Why can't I just write them once?" My response is, "How strong will you get if you only do one push-up every once in a while?"

> *A properly written or stated affirmation is positive, specific, and expressed in the present tense.*

If you write your twenty-five affirmations consistently every day, you will get stronger mentally. You will also program your nonconscious, and your creative nonconscious will cause you to behave consistently with your program. Writing my affirmations twenty-five times a day takes me about seven minutes. Does it work? I know it does because of my personal experience and the experiences of thousands of Ninjas.

Are you willing to invest seven minutes a day to find out?

Chapter 12

THE POWER OF FOCUS

*"Concentrate all your thoughts upon the work at hand.
The sun's rays do not burn white hot until brought into focus."*
—Alexander Graham Bell

As a kid, did you ever take a magnifying glass and focus the sun's rays on a tiny spot until it became so hot you could burn a hole in a piece of paper?

Focus!

Up to this point we have been constructing your belief system, your knowledge of how to run your brain (RAS), and how to control your emotional energy and vibe. This is your magnifying glass. This is your talent, your potential. We have been working on increasing the size of your magnifying glass. Now it is time to put your talent to work by learning to focus your magnifying glass.

YOUR NET FORWARD ENERGY RATIO

In their book *Enlightened Leadership*, Ed Oakley and Doug Krug identify a concept called the *Net Forward Energy Ratio* (NFER). They define this as the relationship between the positive mental energy pushing you toward your goal and the negative mental energy pulling you away from it. This force is calculated by the following equation:

**Net Forward Energy Ratio =
Productive Positive Mental Energy (can do) ÷
Nonproductive Negative Mental Energy (can't do)**

Nonproductive mental energy can also consist of distractions, partial attention, too many priorities, or lack of focus. Here's how your Net Forward Energy Ratio works:

Let's say the circle in the following illustration is you, and you have a goal you want to move toward. One voice, the 60 percent voice, says, *We can do it*. The other voice, the 40 percent voice, says, *No we can't*, or perhaps your 40 percent is distracted by other priorities.

The Power of Focus

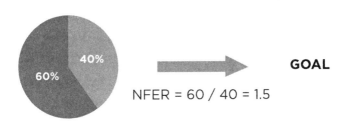

Your Net Forward Energy Ratio is 60/40 = 1.5. This is the same concept as the force it takes to get an airplane off the ground—you have 60 percent thrust and 40 percent drag. You have more thrust than drag, so you can get off the ground—barely. You will make progress toward the goal, but it will be slow, because you are only 60 percent focused.

By practicing the principles in this book, you will start to get more aligned and focused in your life. You will start to become more "on-purpose." As you continue your affirmations for thirty days, your little voice inside starts to say, Yes! Your Net Forward Energy Ratio starts to improve to 80/20 = 4.0. Notice that your results have more than doubled from 1.5 to 4.0, just by being a little more focused.

The Power of Focus

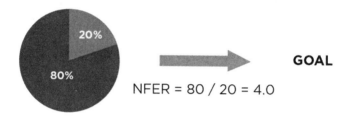

NFER = 80 / 20 = 4.0   **GOAL**

Keep working the system: daily gratitudes, performance quadrant, positive vibes, running your RAS in the positive channel, programming your nonconscious, focusing on your goals, limiting distractions. You will go to 90/10. Now your Net Forward Energy Ratio is 90/10 = 9.0. Your results doubled again! You went from 4.0 to 9.0 by just a little more focus. There is not much difference between 90/10 and 80/20, but look at the difference in the results. This is the exponential function at work.

The Power of Focus

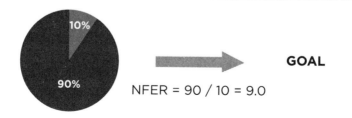

NFER = 90 / 10 = 9.0   **GOAL**

At this point, I have to warn you: This system runs just as fast in reverse. If you start to lose your focus, your results will drop in half very quickly. Jimmy D., the Original Ninja, became so successful as a salesman and a bicycle racer that the local cycling club asked him to be president. A small thing he thought, "Perhaps 10 percent of my time." His income dropped in half.

What would happen if you could put yourself into the focused state of consciousness we call *100 percent full-on*? Your little voice inside says, *Yes!* You are as focused as a laser. Your magnifying glass burns white hot. Your Net Forward Energy Ratio would be 100/0. What is 100/0? When I'm teaching workshops, I always get three answers to this question—100/0 = 0; 100/0 = 100; and the correct answer: 100/0 = ∞ (infinity).

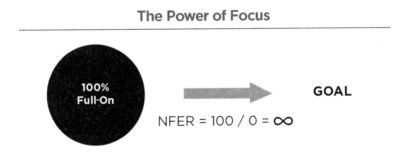

When someone gets in this state of focus, we don't know what might happen. We sometimes call it a miracle. Athletes call it being in the zone. And when athletes get in the zone, they often set world records. When salespeople get in the zone, they triple their incomes without working more hours. Maria Vitale (the broke single mom) closes nine transactions in thirty days and moves herself and her two boys out of her mother's basement. Nate Buie, the former pizza driver, earns more than $200,000 a year. It is an area often referred to as *miracles*.

According to Stewart Emery in "Mastery," miracles are events or experiences in the real world that are beyond the ordinary. Clearly, Maria's and Nate's results are beyond the ordinary.

Chad McWhinney, a close friend and very successful developer, believes in the Net Forward Energy Ratio formula so much that he changed his corporate logo to the infinity sign. He said to me, "Larry, if we can get everyone in our organization moving in the same direction with the same focus, we can accomplish miracles!" And they have.

Principle 2

STOP SELLING! START SOLVING!

People love to buy but they hate to be sold. So "Stop Selling!"

WHAT IS *SELLING*?

Webster's New World Dictionary describes selling in two different ways:

1. Selling, at its best is serving, and solving—often solving a need or want a customer didn't even know they had. The customer comes first. The word *sell* comes from an old English word, *sellan*, meaning to give. Giving service, counsel, and value is the highest form of selling and is the foundation of Ninja Selling. Is there any more noble purpose in life than to bring value to others? Our mission is to help you sell in this manner and to make it easy for both you and your clients.

2. Unfortunately, there is another form of selling. Selling at its worst is pitching and pushing—often resorting to high-pressure tactics and trickery. In fact, the slang description of selling in the dictionary is to *cheat, hoax, or dupe.* The salesperson is looking out for his own interests, not the customer's. Unfortunately, this form of selling is often depicted in movies and gives selling a bad image. It causes many to avoid a career in sales and others to avoid salespeople. It is to this form of selling that we say, "Stop Selling!" There is a better way—The Ninja Way.

When customers sense high-pressure tactics or manipulation, they either put up their defenses, causing the salesperson to push harder, or they run away, causing the salesperson to start chasing them. Would you like to attract customers rather than chase them? Principle 2 will teach you how to create value by asking the right questions and finding out what your customers want—and are willing to pay for. As a Ninja, you will be selling at its very best—solving, serving, and giving value. And, customers will beat a path to your door.

THE INTERNET HAS CHANGED SELLING IN A FEW PROFOUND WAYS

The days of high-pressure selling techniques are over. Perhaps you were taught combative selling; always be closing (ABC); you have to have ten nos to get your first yes; grind them down; they buy or they die. Customers no longer have to put up with these tactics. What's changed? The Internet has changed selling in two profound ways.

1. In the old days, the salesperson used superior product and market knowledge as a lever to manipulate or outwit the customer, who was at a distinct disadvantage. Today, however, most customers have done a great deal of research online, even before they enter the showroom, sales center, or open house. In some cases, they know more about the market and the product than the salesperson.

    A salesperson who launches into a pitch or engages in puffery is a turnoff to the customer. Customers want someone they can trust to help them make a good decision. Remember the importance of your vibe. Do customers get the vibe that you are there to help them or to sell them?

2. Since the advent of the Internet, pushy salespeople can be roasted by customers on social media. A salesperson's reputation can be made or broken by just one customer. On the positive side, when you do a great job for customers, and they feel you are their trusted advisor, they will tell their friends on social media. Today, the story your customers tell about you is more important than the story you tell about yourself.

Chapter 13

THE PURSUER-DISTANCER DANCE

In Ninja Selling, you can only help someone who is moving toward you. If they are moving away, they are distancing from you and not listening to you. How do you know if someone is distancing? You will feel in your body that you are pursuing. And the harder you pursue, the faster the person will distance themselves from you. This is what psychologists call the *pursuer-distancer dance*, and it occurs not only in sales but also in dating, family dynamics, and relationships.

Depression-era salespeople spend a lot of their time chasing prospects. Many are in pursuit mode most of the time and therefore gain a reputation for being pushy salespeople. As a result, both friends and customers tend to shy away when they see these salespeople coming.

THE FIRST STEP

The first step in Ninja Selling is to get people moving toward you—to *attract* them rather than pursue them. There are two critical aspects to this:

1. People tend to move toward someone they know, like, and trust—someone they feel good or comfortable with. The first step is to position yourself as a likable, trusted advisor, not as a salesperson.

2. People move toward value. If you have something they value, something they want, they will be attracted to you. *Your mission is to create value.*

Have you ever tried to catch a cat? We have a cat we named Freedom. When he gets out of the house, I cannot catch him. He'll pause just long enough for me to lunge for him, then he darts away. It's a game for him. The harder I pursue, the faster he distances. The only way I can catch him is to attract him with something he wants—something of value—such as food, love, or the warmth of the house. Whether it's your cat or your customer, they both are attracted by value.

> *The first step in Ninja Selling is to attract people rather than to pursue them.*

When it comes to customers, you create value by being likable and trustworthy, solving their problems, and making them feel good. You'll also need to be in what we call *flow* with them. Flow is the frequency of interactions with people—face-to-face, on the phone, through the mail, through email, through social media. The key is that these interactions need to create value; they should *not* be annoying mail, email, or phone calls from a pursuing salesperson.

Chapter 14

CREATING VALUE

What would you pay for a blank CD from the office supply store? Fifty cents? If we put something on the CD, such as the Ninja Selling System, that could improve your life and earn you hundreds of thousands of dollars, what would you pay for the CD? Certainly a lot more than fifty cents. We have created *value*.

THE LAW OF VALUE

In their wonderful book *The Go-Giver*, Bob Burg and John David Mann lay out five laws of success. One of these is the Law of Value: "Your true worth is determined by how much more you give in value than you receive in payment."

Simply put, if you are being hired by a seller to sell his or her house, and the owners are paying you a fee of $20,000, your mission is to demonstrate to them that you will earn or save them more than the $20,000 they are paying you.

You may be able to do this by selling the house for more money, selling it faster, reducing their stress, or lowering the risk that their house may not sell at all. This is what is known as creating value.

I find that many Realtors have a difficult time understanding the Law of Value. For some reason, they believe the seller should pay them a fee because the seller is their friend, because they sold them the house seven years ago, because this is the traditional fee schedule, or because it is company policy.

In the end, profit flows to those who create the most value. This book teaches you how to create value by solving a problem or bringing pleasure to the customer that is greater than what they pay you.

WHOLESALE AND RETAIL

Nate Buie is sitting with a seller in Greeley, Colorado, in a market where more than half of all home sales are foreclosures or short sales. He asks the seller, "Would you like to price your home at wholesale or at retail?"

The seller asks, "What do you mean?"

Nate responds, "There are really two markets right now. Because of the number of foreclosures, one market is based strictly on price—this is the wholesale market. At the same time, homes in 'cream-puff' condition are selling much higher—this is the retail market. You can sell your house in either market, but in between doesn't work."

"What are the numbers?" the seller asks.

Nate says, "The wholesale price will probably be about $150,000, and the retail price, if your property is fixed up, will be between $170,000 and $175,000."

"What will it cost me to go from wholesale to retail?" asks the seller.

"Based on investing in the places that will add the most value, I estimate $6,800," Nate replies.

"Let's do it!" states the seller.

The property sold in less than three weeks at $173,000—an increase of $23,000 above what it would have sold for in its previous condition. The seller invested $6,800 in repairs and paid Nate a fee of $10,380. Nate is a master Ninja and clearly demonstrated how he could create value for his seller.

WHAT DO PEOPLE VALUE?

People are willing to spend their time and money for two things:

1. Anything that solves their problem (eases their pain)

2. Anything that makes them feel good (brings them pleasure)

These are the two primary drivers that motivate people to take action. Think of ways you can solve their problem or make them feel good, and you will be creating value.

Here is an example of pain: An executive is being transferred from Chicago to Atlanta. She needs to sell her home in Chicago, find a home in Atlanta, and get her family moved to Atlanta. She's willing to pay real estate people large sums of money to help her solve this problem.

Here is an example of pleasure: A family has always had a dream of living in a certain neighborhood. It has great schools for the kids, a pool, and a clubhouse. It's closer to work, so the commute is less than half. As a result, they'll have more time with their family. They will pay real estate people large sums of money to help them realize this dream.

How do you know what your potential customers' problems are or what makes them feel good? How do you discover their pain and their pleasure? Ask them! Then start solving.

> *Ninja Selling is about asking the right questions to determine the customer's pain and pleasure and then offering a solution.*

What is one of the biggest complaints customers have about salespeople? They talk too much and don't listen. Ninjas talk less and listen more. Ninja Selling is about asking the right questions to determine the customer's pain and pleasure and then offering a solution if you have one. As you perfect your questioning and listening skills, you'll discover ways to offer solutions for needs (pain) and wants (pleasure) that customers didn't even know they had.

Chapter 15

ASKING THE RIGHT QUESTIONS

In a football game, one of the metrics is time of possession, or the amount of time each team has the ball. We use a similar metric in Ninja Selling, except the measurement is gauged by who is doing the talking. This person has possession of the conversation.

A rule of thumb for Ninja Selling is that the customer should be doing most of the talking—generally, about 75 percent of the time. When the customer is talking, several things are happening:

- The customer is more connected to the conversation, and, as the Ninja keeps asking questions, the customer *stays* connected to the conversation.

- The customer feels better about the conversation and the relationship, especially when asked about the familiar areas of life, such as family, occupation, recreation, and so on.

- The Ninja, through active listening skills, is learning more about the customer. We pick up the subtle and hidden personality traits, decision strategies, learning modality, and, most importantly, pain and pleasure.

THE TWO-MINUTE WARNING

Unfortunately, in most traditional sales presentations, the salesperson takes time of possession, often talking 90 percent or more of the time. Here's what happens in those instances:

- The customer becomes bored and mentally starts to drift off. Research shows that, unless the salesperson is a very compelling speaker, most customers will disconnect two minutes after the salesperson starts talking. We call this the *two-minute warning*. When the customer asks a question, your answer needs to be two minutes or less. If it will take more than two minutes, periodically check in with your customer by asking questions such as: "Are you with me so far?" or "What questions do you have so far?"

- As the salesperson continues to ramble, the customer starts to think the salesperson likes to hear himself talk. The customer is no longer the focus. The conversation is now salesperson centric versus customer centric, and the salesperson comes off as self-centered and pushy.

- When the salesperson is talking, he or she learns nothing about the customer. It's impossible to identify pain and pleasure (motivation), decision strategies (how the customer will make a decision), learning modalities (how the customer organizes information), or personality traits and body language (how to build rapport with the customer). The salesperson is simply "tellin' and sellin'."

THE SOCRATIC METHOD

Ninjas are masters of asking the right questions and are great listeners. We use the Socratic method. Who was Socrates? He was a Greek philosopher and teacher. What was his method of teaching? He asked great questions and was a great listener. Why?

- Asking questions keeps the student engaged and connected (as it does your customers).
- The answers lie within the student (as they do within your customers).

Socrates used his method of questioning to draw out the student and help the student become clear. The same philosophy of questioning applies in Ninja Selling. Your goal is to draw out your customers, help them become clear about their pain and pleasure, and help find a solution for it.

When you are really good at asking the right questions and helping your customers become clear, they will "close" you about 50 percent of the time. They will suddenly have an "aha!" and will tell you precisely what they want to buy and how they want to buy it. This is one of the most powerful and unique aspects of Ninja Selling. Questions become counseling. Ninjas don't make presentations; we have consultations.

> "Ninjas are masters of asking the right questions and are great listeners."

WHAT QUESTIONS DO I ASK?

Mike Malvey is a great friend and a partner at The Group, Inc. When he joined us, Mike expressed concern to me about finding a work/life balance. When he was with his family, he felt he should be at work. When he was at work, he felt he should be with his family.

Mike mentioned that his kids played sports, and he was spending a fair amount of time at their games and feeling guilty about it. I asked him to tell me what he did at these games.

"Well, the parents bring chairs," he said, "and we line them up on the sidelines and watch the game."

I responded: "Mike, I suggest that you leave your chair in the car. Instead of sitting down, I recommend you work the sidelines, getting to know the parents."

"What am I supposed to say?" Mike asked.

"I don't want you to *say* anything. I want you to *ask* questions and listen," I said.

"OK, then what questions shall I ask?" Mike said curiously and with a bit of sarcasm.

"Mike, the one question you *do not* want to ask is this: 'Do you know anyone who wants to buy or sell a house?' You will come off as a pursuing salesperson who is always looking for a deal, and the other parents will shy away from you. Instead, I recommend you ask the questions about their family, occupation, recreation, and dreams (FORD) and listen for changes that are causing pain or pleasure and that will drive their real estate decisions."

Chapter 16

THE FORD QUESTIONS

What are four of the most important parts of your life? How about your family? Your career? What do you do for fun? What are your hopes and dreams? We call these four core areas of your life your FORD (family, occupation, recreation, and dreams). Ninjas are masters of asking FORD questions.

F = Family/Friends

- Where are you originally from?
- How's the family?
- What is your son doing?
- When does your daughter graduate?
- Oh, you went skiing with the Carrolls? How are they doing?

O = Occupation

- What do you do during the day?
- How's business?
- What business are you in?
- How is everything at work?

R = Recreation

- What are you doing for fun?
- Did you go to the game last weekend?
- What trips do you have planned?

- Are you spending much time at your second home?
- How's your golf?
- How many ski days did you get this season?

D = Dreams

You will seldom ask someone directly, "What are your dreams?" Instead, *Dreams* is a category of questions dealing with the future:

- What are your plans for the holidays?
- Do you have any trips planned this summer?
- Your daughter is graduating this spring—what are her plans?

Are these easy questions to ask? Do people enjoy answering them? They love to talk about their family, their career, what they are doing for fun, and their goals. As they are sharing this information with you, they have time of possession, and they feel you care about them. Your relationship is being built.

YOUR NEXT QUESTION IS EMBEDDED IN THEIR LAST ANSWER.

Sometimes students ask me, "What do I say after I ask them where they're from or about their kids? Where do I go from there? I'm one and done."

Your next question is embedded in their answer. I learned this from a good friend and master Ninja Selling instructor, Peter Parnegg. Here's how it sounds:

"So, Justin, where are you from originally? Are you a native of Colorado?"

"No. I grew up in Lincoln, Nebraska, and went to the University of Nebraska."

"Really? I have friends who went to school there. When were you there?"

We discuss mutual friends, what they majored in, football games, and so on:

"So, what brought you to Colorado?"

"I was transferred out here with ABC Corp."

"ABC Corp. is a great company. How long have you been with them? How's business?"

Do you see how your next question is embedded in their last answer? It's easy. You are on a roll. Your customer has time of possession and is loving it. You are a Ninja. (Note: Be sensitive to cultural differences when asking FORD questions. In a few cultures, it is considered too personal to ask questions about someone's family.)

BEING PRESENT—LISTENING SKILLS

Most people talk at a rate of 150 to 180 words per minute. However, we are capable of listening 400 percent faster than that. As a result, if you aren't careful, you'll get bored as you listen, your mind will start to wander, and you'll check out. Or perhaps you will focus on the next question you are going to ask and not really listen to their answer. You'll end up disconnecting. Wherever you are, be there.

When asking FORD questions, you want to be totally present and focused on your customer, picking up on their subtle and hidden nuances.

> "It does not take sharp eyes to see the sun and the moon,
> nor does it take sharp ears to hear the thunderclap.
> Wisdom is not obvious. You must see the subtle and
> notice the hidden to be victorious."
> —**Sun Tzu**

What takes the FORD process from chitchat to power is the skill of listening for change—specifically change that affects pain and pleasure. That kind of change in someone's life will ultimately affect real estate decisions. Here are some examples:

- **Pain.** Examples include job loss, divorce, illness, an adult child moving back in, the last child leaving the nest, elderly parent moving in, or a longer commute.
- **Pleasure.** Examples include job promotion, inheritance, new baby, new hobby (golf, boating, etc.), last child leaving the nest, graduation, marriage.
- **Both.** Some changes can be both pain and pleasure. For example, the last child leaving the nest or an elderly parent moving in can be interpreted in different ways. I once saw a father, tears running down his cheeks, hugging his daughter right before she drove off to college. Meanwhile, the mother was standing at the front door, pumping her fist and mouthing, "Yes! Yes!"

Ninjas are very skilled at picking up the subtle nuances associated with these changes and then, at the appropriate time, offering a solution.

Ninja Selling So Far

Let's pause for a moment to summarize the Ninja Way of Selling:

- Stop selling and start attracting
- How do I attract? By creating value
- How do I create value? By solving a problem (pain) or making them feel good (pleasure)
- How do I discover their pain and pleasure? By asking the FORD questions and listening for change,
- Then offer a solution to their pain and pleasure
- STOP SELLING AND START SOLVING!

Chapter 17

THE POWER OF FORD

Why are the questions about family and friends, occupation, recreation, and dreams so simple and yet so powerful? The FORD questions represent people's core values. Is there anything more important to someone than family and friends? Their career? What brings them joy? Their hopes and dreams? When you ask about these four areas, you are touching their life and making an immediate personal connection.

Ninjas realize that we don't just sell real estate. Real estate is simply a vehicle we use to help people get more life in their four FORD areas. A Ninja's true purpose is to help people get more out of life.

Focus on your clients first, especially on what is motivating them in their four core values. So many real estate salespeople begin with the properties—the floor plan, price, condition, and so on. The bricks and sticks are important, but not as important as the people.

USING FORD

Ninjas use the FORD questions in three ways.

1. **Rapport.** FORD questions are a great way to build rapport—especially when meeting someone for the first time. There is an instant connection.

2. **Prospecting.** As you have just learned, if you are skilled at listening for change, you will discover pain and pleasure that will probably lead to a need for your services. This is a much

more effective way to discover business than blatantly asking, "Who do you know that wants to buy or sell a house?" It is also more user-friendly, attracting friends and customers toward you instead of pushing them away.

3. **Negotiating.** There are five primary negotiating points in a real estate contract. These are as follows:

   a. Price

   b. Terms

   c. Dates—closing and possession

   d. Inclusions and exclusions

   e. Contingencies

Most Realtors, as well as buyers and sellers, tend to focus on only one negotiating point—price. However, the Ninja is a master negotiator who understands there are five factors to be considered during negotiation. If you have negotiated on all five points and are still stuck, here's a strategy: Set the contract aside for a moment and focus on FORD.

Often, buyers and sellers get so caught up in the game of negotiation they lose focus on their priorities and why they are doing this in the first place. FORD questions help them refocus on what's important in their lives.

Ninja Nate Buie was involved in a tough negotiation. Buyer and seller had gone back and forth on many items and were now down to crunch time, where the contract either would be signed at $300,000 or the parties would walk away.

Nate asked the buyer, "Remind me again why this is the house you want to buy."

The buyer replied, "Because of the big backyard. It reminds me of the yard I grew up in as a kid. My dad and I played catch in that yard almost every night. I dream of playing catch in a yard like that with my son."

At that point, Nate asked, "Jared, in the overall scheme of life and your dreams for your son, how important is this cracked heat exchanger?" This $1,500 item was less than .005 of the sales price, but the buyer and seller were hung up on it. Nate's question brought the buyer back to his core values and his reasons for buying. He realized he had become caught up in a game of winning, instead of concentrating on his future happiness with his son. He signed the contract in an instant.

> *Ninjas realize that we don't just sell real estate. A Ninja's true purpose is to help people get more out of life.*

Chapter 18

WHAT WILL PEOPLE PAY FOR?

People are willing to pay money for two things: to solve a problem (pain relief) and to feel good (pleasure).

When people perceive that you can do these two things for them, they are naturally attracted to you. Now the question is: "*How much will they pay for these two things?*" That depends on how much value they perceive you are bringing to the party.

A survey of the ways Americans make buying decisions shows us there are three groups of buyers:

- 15 percent always want to pay the lowest price.
- 5 percent always want to pay the highest price.
- 80 percent always want the best value.

LOWEST PRICE

These customers buy based on lowest price—period. It will not matter how much value you add. They don't care. They are going to hire the cheapest Realtor or buy the cheapest product. Price is the only factor for them.

Since the Ninja Selling approach is based on value-added services, we recommend you forsake this lowest-price group for three reasons:

1. You cannot have a high income per hour by being a discount broker. You will wake up one day and realize you are working harder than anyone for less. There are plenty of brokers to work

this niche. Let them do it. Focus on the other 85 percent who value what you have.

2. You cannot be all things to all people. You cannot position yourself as a value-added, quality Realtor and then cut your price to appeal to this 15 percent. It is not fair to the other customers who are paying your normal fee. If you want to build a relationship and referral business, you need to have consistency in your service and your fee.

3. People in this group are often called *grinders*. Their goal is to suck every penny out of a transaction. In the process, they often suck every ounce of energy out of you as well. Real estate ceases to be fun. Focus on the 85 percent of customers who relate to quality and value, appreciate what you do for them, and are happy to pay your fee when you demonstrate your value.

HIGHEST PRICE

Some people—about 5 percent—always prefer to pay the highest price. They may crave the status of having the best, or they might feel "I get what I pay for" or "I'm worth it." If your fee is too low, this group will not hire you. Their perception is that you are not very good.

I was teaching Ninja Selling to a group of bank officers. We were discussing this highest-price group, and one of the officers said that before starting his banking career, he and a partner owned a butler and household staff placement service for wealthy families in a major US city. The going rate for these services was 20 percent of the first year's salary. He and his partner decided to enter the market by offering their services at a discount—15 percent. To their surprise, very few families engaged them, and they were going broke. Then they had an "aha!" moment. Wealthy families don't want to hire the cheapest placement service. They worry they'll end up with an inferior butler, housekeeper, or nanny. They want the best and believe they need to pay the highest price to get it. He and his partner raised their rates to 25 percent; upgraded their brochure, office, and service; and within two years, became the top butler placement service in the city.

VALUE

Most people (80 percent) make their buying decisions based on value, which is the relationship between price and perceived quality. Their goal is to get the most quality for their money.

Survey of Buying Decisions

15% LOWEST PRICE
5% HIGHEST PRICE
80% VALUE

PRICE   QUALITY

The business term for this price/quality relationship is called the *value proposition*. Smart businesspeople know they need to figure out how to add value—that is, create more in value than they receive in payment.

Smart buyers are going to make buying decisions based on your value proposition—how much quality you're offering for the price, compared to other Realtors.

ARE ALL REAL ESTATE SERVICES THE SAME?

Research shows the public perceives the *quality* of real estate services to be the same, regardless of the Realtor they use. This is especially true for sellers who are hiring a Realtor to sell their house. Regardless of whom they use, they assume the services will be pretty much the same—a yard sign, multiple listing service (MLS), Internet, brochure, print advertising, and so on.

If the quality of the service is seen as the same, how will sellers make a decision on which Realtor to use? Price! They will select the cheapest Realtor. They have to. They make their buying decisions based on value—the relationship of quality and price.

Realtors misinterpret this price focus to mean that the seller is primarily interested in selecting the Realtor with the lowest fees. But that is true only with the 15 percent lowest-price sellers. The 80 percent who make buying decisions based on *value* will pay your fee if you can demonstrate that your quality is higher.

> "Smart buyers are going to make buying decisions based on how much quality you're offering for the price, compared to other Realtors."

Standing in front of our sales meeting with about two hundred of the sharpest Ninjas in the nation, I asked this question: "How many of you are frequently asked to lower your fee?" I was surprised that quite a few hands went up. Then I asked, "How many of you are seldom or never asked to lower your fee?" Again, quite a few hands went up.

What I noticed was that the people who offered a very basic level of service were the ones being asked to lower their fees. In most cases, they had been offering these basic services for years. Back in the day, their service was worth the fee they were asking. Today, those same services have a street value of 1 to 2 percent less. These Realtors simply need to raise the level of their game. I tease them that they are offering a black-and-white television in a color world.

The Ninjas who raised their hands and said they were seldom or never asked about their fees provide an amazing level of service. They are doing things that no one else in our market is doing—pre-inspections, staging, home detailing, sophisticated target marketing, individual property websites, counter displays, contract writing packets, state-of-the-art pricing systems, and market analyses. What they bring to the game is clearly a higher quality set of services. They are clearly differentiated from their competitors. Sellers quickly perceive this and want to hire them. The message: If you are being asked about your fee more than 15 percent of the time, raise your game by offering more and higher-quality services. Most of your sellers (85 percent) are willing to pay for it.

THE WINNING BUSINESS STRATEGY

In his book *Give & Take*, Professor Adam Grant at the Wharton School of Business summarizes his research on winning business strategies. Adam found three distinct strategies:

1. Givers (create value)
2. Takers (extract value)
3. Matchers (exchange value)

Which was the winning strategy? In the short run, takers who are good at extracting value did the best—but not in the long run. Over time, takers develop a reputation for extracting value and people shy away from them. It's difficult for them to form relationships. They need a continuous supply of strangers to make their extraction strategy work.

Matchers also struggle to build relationships because people feel they are always keeping score. In the longer run, the Givers did the best. They build a relationship business which results in referrals. They practice *The Law of Value* from the book *The Go-Giver*: "Your true worth is determined by how much more you create in value than you take in payment."

INCREASING YOUR INCOME PER HOUR

Several years ago, I was teaching a Ninja Retreat, and we were covering this topic of seller services and their pricing. At the break, Joe and Estelle Redd came up to me and said, "Larry, you commented that it would be very difficult to have high income per hour as a discount broker. We agree with that." Estelle said, "I *am* a discount broker. In fact, I am *the* discount broker in my market of Grants Pass, Oregon."

Estelle was the owner of one of the national franchise discount brokerages for that town. She was also one of the top-producing real estate people in her market.

Estelle went on, "I work harder than anyone, and I work for less. I'm on a treadmill, and I want to get off. But I've been a discount broker in my market for years. I've built an image and a brand. I have hundreds of clients who have worked with me at a discount. How do I suddenly change all of that?"

I suggested to Estelle that she offer a menu of services. When one of her clients calls her to list their house, she could say, "I really appreciate the opportunity to work with you again. I've now got two programs for you to choose from. We still offer our reduced fee/reduced service program that you used last time. We also offer an enhanced services program at a higher fee. Is it OK if I show you both programs and then you can decide?" More than 80 percent chose the enhanced service/higher fee program.

The enhanced program was so successful for Estelle that she later dropped the discount brokerage franchise, changed the name of her company to Redd McCarty Real Estate, and only offers her enhanced service package. Her firm—formed with her daughter Andrea McCarty—is thriving. More importantly, Estelle is happier and earning more per hour. She's now a Ninja!

A number of our Ninjas use menu pricing. They offer the seller a basic service at a lower fee and a "wow!" service at a higher fee. As the research suggests, between 75 and 80 percent of their customers select the higher service and higher fee.

Chapter 19

CREATING YOUR VALUE PROPOSITION

How do you create a real estate service that is so valuable that people will beat a path to your door? That they will pay you a premium for your services—and feel good about it because you delivered far more value than you received in payment?

We start with a process we call the *onion*. This is a great exercise for sales meetings in which you break into small teams and brainstorm the four categories of service.

Building Your Brand

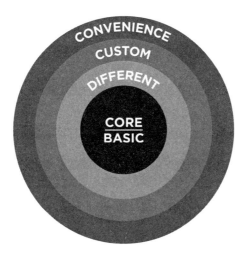

CORE/BASIC SERVICES

Start by listing the core services offered by virtually every real estate firm in your market. Here's a list of the basic eight:

1. Price opinion
2. Yard sign
3. Lock box
4. Multiple Listing Service (MLS) and upload to the Internet
5. Property brochure
6. Advertising—print and/or electronic
7. Scheduling showing appointments
8. Settlement services

Once these were considered full service. Today, they are seen as basic or even discount service. Most people expect more for their money.

DIFFERENTIATED SERVICES

Now, list the services you offer that are different from your competitors. Here are some examples:

1. A prelisting packet giving market statistics, background on you and your company, and an explanation of the selling process
2. A detailed, written marketing plan
3. Professional photography that is more appealing to buyers
4. Four-page, full-color property brochures, compared to your competitors' one-page or black-and-white brochures

5. Enhanced Internet listings with more photos, virtual tours, and higher search engine results
6. An individual property website
7. Visual-pricing tools to help sellers better understand the market (for example, www.focus1st.com)
8. Maximum Exposure marketing (as shown in the previous chapter)

CUSTOM SERVICES

List the services you provide that are customized for this particular property. Here are some examples:

- Pre-inspections to put the seller in a stronger negotiating position
- Staging services to enhance the home's appeal
- Professional measurement by an appraiser with a drawn floor plan
- Kitchen-counter display with information on pre-inspections as well as utilities, schools, and the neighborhood
- Contract-writing packet with everything required for a contract

CONVENIENCE SERVICES

What can you do to make the seller's life easier? Most are so busy they have little time to get the house ready to put on the market. Can you offer them handyman or cleaning services to help them? In our market, a cottage industry has grown up around home detailing, similar to that of the automobile industry.

COMMUNICATING YOUR DIFFERENCE

Once you have completed this exercise, the next step is to create a one-page document that communicates the extra value you bring to the game. At The Group, Inc. we have a simple brochure called "The Group Difference." Some of our Realtors also present a checklist format that lists their services on the left-hand side of the page with checks beside each service they offer. There are a couple of columns titled *Company B* and *Company C*, so the seller can compare what other firms offer.

The key is communication. Customers make their buying decisions based on perceived value. If you don't communicate it, they won't perceive it. The best way to let them see your value is to show them examples, rather than telling them about it. Talk less; show more.

EQUALIZE AND DIFFERENTIATE

Good Ninjas never bad mouth their competitors, instead they "equalize and differentiate." Here's an example. Jim Murray was competing for a listing with two iconic Realtors. Katie was the number one agent for her brand in the state of Colorado. Jan was number one for her brand in our city.

Here's Jim's dialogue.

"Thank you for inviting me in. I know you are talking to two of the top Realtors in our market and I'm honored to be a part of your consideration. (Equalize) One of the things that is different about me is that I live in Golden Meadows. (Opens a color-coded plat map of the neighborhood.) The houses with red dots are the ones that have sold over the past 17 years that I've lived here. The ones with both red and green dots are the houses I've sold. You have some great choices for who lists your house, but I will probably be the one who sells it because I know Golden Meadows better than anyone." (Differentiate) The sellers hired Jim to sell their house.

Chapter 20

BUILDING YOUR BRAND

You are a brand. People buy you first. Then they buy your services. What do your customers think of your brand and how do they decide to buy you?

The market research firm of Young and Rubicam specializes in analyzing brands and has shown that when a customer or a referral hears your name (your brand), the mind goes through a series of four steps. These are called the Four Pillars of Brand Building.

PILLAR 1: RECOGNITION

When you hear the names Ritz-Carlton, Walmart, or Starbucks, the first thing that goes through your mind is, *Have I heard of that brand before? Do I recognize that brand?* When people hear your name or the name of your company, is it an easily recognized brand? Effective marketing builds brand recognition.

PILLAR 2: REPUTATION

After customers do a quick mind scan to see if they recognize the brand name, they ask themselves, *How do I feel about this brand? What is its reputation?* A brand can rank high in recognition and low in reputation. A good example is British Petroleum (BP). Many people recognize the brand, and yet they don't feel good about the company after its Gulf Coast oil well leaked.

What is your reputation? What are you known for? At Ninja Selling, we have built a reputation for results.

PILLAR 3: RELEVANCE
How is this brand relevant to me? Relevance is important in two ways:

1. Do I need the product or service? Real estate services may not be relevant if the customer is not in the market to buy or sell.
2. If I need the product or service, am I getting what I wanted? Generally, as an industry, the answer is no. In many cases, as we'll see later, we are offering the customer the services we want to provide rather than the services they want and consider relevant. Ninja Selling has a strategy to change that.

PILLAR 4: DIFFERENTIATION
How is this product or service different from that of competitors? While real estate people come in all shapes and sizes, customers view their services as basically the same, as a commodity like electricity, gasoline, or toilet paper. Most real estate salespeople provide only basic or core services. If they were to provide the additional differentiated, customized, and convenience services, they would be differentiated in customers' minds and would command a higher fee.

THE NINJA DIFFERENCE
Most real estate salespeople and their companies focus only on the first two pillars: recognition and reputation. Ninjas focus on all four pillars, and it is pillars 3 (relevance) and 4 (differentiation) that really make the Ninja difference. The Ninja strategy is simply to be more relevant, more customer centric, and to give customers what they want.

Based on our own research as well as industry surveys, here are the top six services that are most relevant to buyers and sellers today.

For Sellers

1. **Access to Current Active and Sold Data.** By withholding sold data, the established real estate industry has driven consumers to non-Realtor websites such as www.zillow.com, which do provide this data. After two decades, this is only now starting to change. Our company, The Group, Inc. Real Estate, has provided sold data on our website for years, as this is the number-one service both sellers and buyers want. It helps make us more relevant and differentiated.

2. **A Prelisting Packet.** Sellers want information about the market, sales process, and salesperson's qualifications, so they can do their due diligence. Sellers want this information *before* being asked to sign a listing agreement. (Note: A national survey of Realtors conducted by Real Trends and Harris Interactive found that only about 20 percent of Realtors provide their sellers a prelisting packet. As an industry, we have an 80 percent failure rate on the second most important service a seller wants. The good news: Ninjas who provide a prelisting packet are differentiated from 80 percent of other Realtors.)

3. **A Pricing and Marketing System with Predictable Results.** Ninjas use Absorption Rate Pricing and the Focus 1st (www.focus1st.com) Visual Pricing Tools to clearly show a seller their odds of selling, as well as the absorption rate and the buying pattern in their neighborhood.

4. **A Proactive, Competent Realtor They Can Trust.** Sellers want someone who will look out for their interests and help them navigate the process. Unfortunately, customers often feel the Realtor is only concerned with making the sale.

5. **A Smooth Transaction.** Sellers want to close on time with no or few surprises.

6. **Consistent Communication.** Poor or no communication from their Realtor is a frequent complaint heard from sellers. Ninjas have a set time and system each week for communicating with their sellers that will be discussed in Principle 3.

For Buyers

1. **Access To Current Active and Sold Data.**

2. **A Buyer Packet.** The packet contains information about the buyer process, including contracts and the Realtor's qualifications, so that the buyer can do his due diligence.

3. **A Process for Finding the Right House.** The process should also help them find it at the right price and without missing anything.

4. **A Proactive, Competent Realtor They Can Trust.** They want someone who will look out for their interests and help them navigate the process.

5. **A Smooth Transaction.** They want to close on time with no or few surprises.

6. **Consistent Communication.**

Notice the similarity of the services requested by both sellers and buyers.

DIFFERENTIATE OR DIE

"Differentiate or Die" is a famous mantra from marketing guru Jack Trout, and it is a Ninja mantra as well. Our strategy is simple: To be more differentiated, simply be more relevant. Give customers what they want. This is not rocket science. Just deliver on the six services listed above, and you will be creating great value in your customers' lives.

> **"*The Ninja strategy is simply to be more relevant, more customer centric, and to give customers what they want.*"**

When you build your brand around being so relevant, so differentiated, and so "wow!" in your level of service, people will begin to talk. This word-of-mouth advocacy is priceless. We call it *fabled service*.

Here's an example: Three Ninjas had been out on the town in Fort Collins, Colorado. Bud George, Terri Johnson, and Garrett Frey were heading back to the hotel. Bud was driving and in the left-turn lane, when he realized his turn was farther up the street, and he swerved back into traffic. A policeman was behind him and pulled the car over.

After checking Bud's license, the police officer asked, "Mr. George, you are from Murfreesboro, Tennessee. What brings you to Fort Collins?"

Bud responded, "We are here for a seminar at The Group Real Estate Company."

"The Group!" said the officer excitedly. "Do you know Tami Spaulding? She sold our house for us. What an amazing job she did, and she helped us buy another one too."

The officer launched into a five-minute testimonial on the details of Tami's service.

Then he handed Bud his driver's license back and said, "You all take care tonight, and tell Tami hi for me when you see her tomorrow. Here's my card as a reminder."

When your level of service is so incredible (fabled) that it causes a police officer to stop what he is doing to tell you about it, you have built an amazing brand.

Chapter 21

A PROACTIVE TRUSTED ADVISOR

As a Ninja, you want to reposition yourself with your friends and customers *not* as a salesperson, but rather as a Proactive Trusted Advisor. Let's examine these three words:

PROACTIVE

One of the basics of customer service is being proactive. Ninjas call the customer first. We are the cause of what is happening, not the effect. We anticipate what needs to happen and take action. If a buyer or seller ever calls us first during a transaction and says, "Hey, what's going on with my contract or my listing?" we are failing.

TRUSTED

Ninjas put the customer's interests first. Most customers perceive that salespeople put their own interest first, that their goal is to make a sale—not look out for the customer. As a result, they don't trust salespeople. In contrast, the Ninja's goal is to provide a solution to the customer's pain and pleasure, to solve not sell, to help them get more life.

For years, we offered a free monthly workshop at our company to teach investors the fundamentals of how to analyze real estate investments. These workshops were very profitable for both our customers and for us. We had a very loyal following of hundreds of investors.

In January 2006, at the peak of the market frenzy and just before the financial meltdown of the Great Recession, we announced to our investor clients that we were discontinuing the investment workshops until further notice. We told them the fundamentals no longer made sense, and we were recommending that they take a time out.

I teach real estate market cycles as an adjunct professor in the College of Business at Colorado State University, and we could see the meltdown coming. Our goal was to help our investors to get in front of the inevitable.

Our investors were shocked. The media was shouting, "Buy! Buy! Buy!" Magazine covers screamed "Get Rich Buying Real Estate." Why would a real estate company not take advantage of this frenzy? Why were we saying, "Go to the sidelines until further notice"? Because we were looking out for our customers' interests.

We all know what happened next. The financial crisis was followed by a dramatic drop in real estate values. Over the next few years, we received many cards and emails from our clients thanking us for our advice. We restarted our monthly investor workshops in 2010, when the fundamentals returned.

ADVISOR

Customers want to work with somebody who has both deep smarts and street smarts, who really knows the market and where it is headed, knows how to negotiate, and knows how to manage a transaction.

I was attending a meeting at Colorado State University where it was mentioned that the school would be building a new seven-hundred-bed dormitory on campus. There had been no new dormitory construction on campus in more than forty years. As a result, the private properties right around campus rented for a premium.

I proactively called a friend who owns one of the largest apartment neighborhoods next to campus to let him know what I had heard. I mentioned that this new dorm could cause vacancy rates to jump from about 3 percent to double digits for a year or two, till the market adjusted, and that he should prepare to weather the storm.

He said, "I can't believe you just called me. I was just about ready to refinance my project, pull money out, and buy another apartment complex. I'll put that on hold till this blows over."

Vacancy rates later hit 30 percent right around campus, and my friend said my phone call saved his project and his net worth.

PROACTIVE VERSUS PURSUER

In an earlier chapter, we said, "Stop pursuing." Now we are saying, "Be proactive." What is the distinction? In my mind, it comes down to one word: value. If you call your friends and customers or send them something to create value, they see you as their proactive trusted advisor. If you don't have a reason to call, or you send them annoying mail or email that doesn't make them feel good or solve a problem, you become a pursuing salesperson, and they emotionally distance themselves.

You will build your relationships as a proactive trusted advisor if you follow the Five Rules of Ninja Selling:

- **Rule 1: Show up!** Show up for work. Show up on time for your customers. Be visible, and be there for your customers.
- **Rule 2: Pay attention.** Be present with your customers. Listen carefully. What they don't say is often as important as what they do say. Watch their body language. Notice the subtle and the hidden. Wherever you are, be there.
- **Rule 3: Tell the truth and keep your commitments.** Sometimes it's tough to tell a seller the truth about the market for their home or to tell an investor that now is not the right time to invest. Keep your commitments. Do what you say.
- **Rule 4: Create value for your customers.** Look for ways to solve their problems and make them feel good. Put their interests first.
- **Rule 5: Don't get attached to the outcome.** Follow the first four rules, and let the money take care of itself. When a

salesperson starts focusing on the commission, customers can sense "commission breath," and that changes the dynamics of the relationship. Customers pick up bad vibes. Trust evaporates, and you are no longer their proactive trusted advisor. You are a salesperson.

Principle 3

NINJA BUSINESS STRATEGY

Now that you have your Ninja vibe on, and you know how to create value for customers, how do you generate business? Principle 3 will give you the step-by-step process.

We'll start by showing the size of the market available to you and how to access these customers by becoming their Realtor of choice. We'll show you the simple formula for generating a continuous flow of buyers, so that you actually have overflow—too many buyers and sellers—and then how to handle that volume.

THE SCIENCE OF ABUNDANT REAL ESTATE TRANSACTIONS

Did you know that 11 to 14 percent of all households in the United States move every year? This is based on information from the Internal Revenue Service, which tracks changes of address on tax returns. If every one of these households was owned, and the residents had to sell their home and buy a home every time they moved, the transaction rate would be 22 to 28 percent. (Every move would entail two transactions—one to sell and one to buy.)

However, about a third of the households are renters, so the national transaction rate is closer to 15 percent. Here are the figures:

- 124 million = Approximate number of US households

- 80 million = Approximate number of US owner-occupied households
- 6 million = Average annual number of residential sales*
- 12 million = Average number of annual real estate transactions**
- 15 percent = US average transaction rate (12M ÷ 80M)

  * Six million is the average annual number of residential sales (including new home sales) each year. In hot markets, the figure will be higher. In recessions it will be lower.

  ** Every home sale involves a seller side and a buyer side, so each home sale creates two transactions.

With an average of twelve million transactions each year and approximately two million real estate licensees in the US, the average transaction rate per licensee is six.

The national transaction rate is approximately 15 percent; however, the transaction rate can vary from market to market. I've seen resort and retirement markets with transaction rates as low as 7 to 9 percent, and other markets with transaction rates more than 30 percent. The fact is, there is always a market, and you will see it when you have an abundance mind-set.

You can calculate the transaction rate for your specific market by multiplying total residential sales from your MLS times two (buyer sides plus seller sides), then dividing total transactions by the number of owner-occupied households in your market (available from census data or your local planning office).

SWIMMING IN ABUNDANCE

The 15 percent transaction rate means that there are approximately fifteen real estate transactions each year for every one hundred owner households who know you. This does not necessarily mean that fifteen of these one hundred owners will do a real estate transaction this year. It means that, collectively, the one hundred owners will do fifteen transactions. One owner may sell a home, buy a home, and also buy an investment property. That is three transactions for one owner.

Having done your homework, you know there are people who want to buy and sell everywhere. You are swimming in abundance.

Most Realtors tell me they know at least two hundred owners. That means they are surrounded by thirty transactions a year. Since real estate licensees average just six transactions a year, and yet they are surrounded by five times that many transactions, the Realtors can increase their sales by 500 percent just with the people who know them. Why don't they see it? Why are they constantly out pursuing new business or chasing strangers on the Internet? It's because they don't see the opportunities all around them.

I have worked with many salespeople over the years who come to us with scarcity thinking. Once they break through that, their sales soar. A Ninja with an abundance mind-set is like a bird on a wire above a parking lot full of cars saying, "So many cars, so little time!" Here's your mind-set: *I am swimming in abundance. On average, there are thirty transactions for every two hundred owner households who know me. My mission is to find and do those transactions.*

GETTING OUT OF A SALES SLUMP

One of our sales partners was in a slump, and we were looking for ways to help her get back on track. After she had spent several minutes whining about the bad market and how slow her business was, I asked her, "How many people do you have in your database?"

She replied, "About two hundred."

I had just calculated the transaction rate for our market and found it to be 19.6 percent, so I said, "You know there are about forty transactions a year being done by those two hundred people in your database."

She replied, "I don't believe that! Not with my people. That may be the market average, but my people are hunkered down. They aren't doing anything!"

"Well," I said, "why don't we find out? Let's take your database and give it to the title company and have them do a title search to see how many title transfers (transactions) your group did. To make it fun, why don't we bet? I bet it will be thirty or more (the national average)."

"I don't want to bet with you!" she retorted.

"Why not?" I asked.

"Because you always win," she said.

We found out that "her people" had done forty-three transactions the previous year. Unfortunately, they had not done them primarily with her. Why? Two reasons:

1. Her belief that the market was bad and her scarcity mindset kept her from seeing the opportunities and abundance all around her.

2. Believing the market was bad, she cut back on her expenses, which included the mailings and activities that kept her in flow with her database. As a result, her people got in flow with somebody else and did their transactions with them.

Flow is frequency of interaction with your people—face-to-face, phone, email, text, snail mail, and social media. Flow is what builds relationships. Flow is like oxygen to your business. When you cut it off, your business starts to die. Keep the oxygen flowing, and your business will thrive. When we simply helped this Realtor re-establish her flow systems, her business re-energized, and she was out of her sales slump. As Master Ninja coach Clara Capano says, "Flow fixes everything!"

Chapter 22

WORKING SMART

Because of our mobile society and the high 15 percent transaction rate on average, we know we are surrounded by an abundance of real estate transactions. Our goal is simply to find and do those transactions.

Following are some of the most popular business strategies for finding and doing business. As you can see from the conversion ratios, some strategies are more effective than others.

Conversion Ratios

Cold direct mail	2,000:1
Cold internet lead generation	1,600:1
Cold phone solicitation (illegal)	500:1
Door knocking	100:1
Personal contact with friends	50:1
Ad calls	25:1
Sign calls	20:1
Open houses	15:1
Walk-ins	10:1
Past buyers	9:1
Past sellers	4:1
Referrals	3:2

Source: National Association of Realtors®

While all of these strategies work, Ninjas are focused on the vital few that give the biggest return for their investment of time and money. Ninja Selling focuses on everything below the line in the chart—beginning with personal contact with friends.

THE CORE NINJA STRATEGY: BUILDING RELATIONSHIPS

Ninja Selling is relationship selling. It is based on the belief that people prefer to buy from someone they know, like, trust, and are in flow with. All four of these elements are essential.

Customers may know you, but not like you. They may know and like you, but not trust you. They may know, like, and trust you, but are not in flow with you. If they are in flow with someone else that they know, like, and trust, they will buy from them, not you. To be a Ninja, you must be in all four of these areas.

KNOW

You are either visible, or you are invisible. You decide. People need to see you to get to know you. I've never met a successful salesperson who was a hermit!

Your goal is to be at the top of mind when a customer is asked by a friend to refer someone who sells what you sell. For this to happen, they need to know three things:

1. Who you are (name recognition and someone they like and trust)?
2. What you do (list and sell real estate)?
3. Where you do it (name of your company)?

This seems simple. In fact, it is so simple that many salespeople take it for granted and fail to cover the basics. For example, people may know you but forget what you do. This is especially a problem if you have switched careers. They still think of you in your old career—not in real estate.

Wynn Washle, one of our partners at The Group, Inc., made a career change. He was well known in the community as a family therapist, not as a Realtor. So our first challenge was to rebrand Wynn as a Realtor. One of the methods we used to do this was a system we call *8 in 8*, which is a systematized way of keeping in touch with potential clients. We will explain 8 in 8 in depth in a later chapter.

If you are in the same career but have changed companies, you still need to rebrand yourself. Otherwise, customers will know who you are and what you do, but they will send referrals to your old company. Again, the 8 in 8 system is effective for this.

What's important is that your friends and customers think of you *first* for real estate service and instantly know where to find you or refer you.

LIKE

Have you ever known someone who had magnetic energy? You were drawn to them, and they had a relaxed, nonanxious presence that made you feel good just by being with them. What are the personality traits of these people?

Generally, I've observed that likable people tend to be positive: They have a positive outlook on life, and they emanate a positive vibe. They are also genuine—comfortable with themselves and not trying to be somebody they're not. They are confident but not cocky. They express a genuine interest in others. They would rather ask the FORD questions than talk about themselves. They make sure others have time of possession in the conversation. And their friends love them for it.

Relationship selling is a 24/7 career. You cannot be a loudmouthed jerk on the sidelines at your son's soccer game one day and Mr. Nicey Nice the next, when you are working in your sales career with one of the other soccer parents. Your ability to demonstrate emotional maturity is a key to being liked.

TRUST

Research from author and consultant James Kane indicates there are four keys to trust:

1. **Character. Can I count on you?** We trust people who do what they say, deliver on what they promise, and keep their commitments. Customers look for even the smallest evidence that you can be trusted. Did you show up for the appointment on time? Did you do what you promised? How much do you care?

2. **Competence. Do you know what you are doing?** You may be the nicest, most honest person in the world, but are you also competent? Do you demonstrate mastery in your chosen field? Customers want someone who has character but who also can deliver the goods.

3. **Capacity. Do you have the time and resources to solve my problem?** How do customers feel when they hear their Realtor talk about being busy and overwhelmed?

4. **Consistency. Are you consistent in your look and behavior?** Consistency is a key to trust and also to referrals, especially when it comes to look and demeanor. If you are continuously changing your dress or hairstyle, or your behavior is volatile, your customers begin to wonder what's going on with you. They won't trust you. They are looking for someone who is rock solid.

A good rule of thumb is *not* to dress like your clients. Instead, emulate the people whom your clients go to for advice. In some markets, especially resorts, a coat and tie would be inappropriate, but you still want to look polished and dressed slightly better than your customer. For women, especially young women, dressing up means professional attire—not something you'd wear to the nightclub.

Consistency is the key to referrals. Why do people refer? According to research in *The New Art and Science of Referral Marketing*, by Scott Degraffenreid and Donna Blandford, people refer if they believe it will make them look good. That's true of recommendations for restaurants, books, movies, and Realtors. If they feel the Realtor might make them look bad, they won't refer him or her. They will only refer salespeople with a consistent, likeable personality who can deliver consistent results.

FLOW

What is flow? At Ninja, we define flow as "frequency of interaction," which can mean by mail, email/text message, social media, phone, or face-to-face (which is the highest-quality flow).

As a Ninja, your mission is to find ways to increase the quality and quantity of your flow with the people who know you. One rule: All flow must be perceived as valuable to your customers. That is, it must either solve a problem or make them feel good.

Any mail must contain something of value to your customers. Otherwise, it is considered junk mail. All phone calls must end with the customer hanging up the phone and thinking, *That was really good. I'm sure glad (Ninja) called.*

If you can't find a reason to call that excites and adds value to your customer, don't do it. Your creativity in coming up with value-added reasons to be in flow with people who know you will be a key to your success.

People love to do business with people they know, like, trust, and are in flow with, especially if they feel people care. They also love to refer them. Once you have these keys in place, you will have a continuous flow of customers coming toward you. In fact, you will have overflow—more business than you can handle.

Chapter 23

THE POWER OF FLOW

As we've seen, customers prefer to work with a Realtor they know, like, trust, and are in flow with. But here's the challenge: According to the National Association of Realtors (NAR), most Americans know an average of twelve Realtors. How do you become their Realtor of choice?

Most Realtors believe if they do a great job for their customers (i.e., provide fantastic service), those customers will come back to them on their next transaction, as well as refer new business to them. Nothing could be further from the truth. Believe it or not, doing a great job is a great start, but it is not the key to getting repeat and referral business. Here are the facts based on an NAR "Profile of Buyers and Sellers." When home sellers were asked if they were satisfied with their Realtor to the point that they would use them again on their next transaction as well as refer their Realtor to friends, here were the sellers' responses:

- 74 percent said they would definitely use the Realtor again, as well as refer them to friends.
- 15 percent said they would probably use the Realtor again, as well as refer them to friends.
- A total of 89 percent said they would definitely or probably use and refer their Realtor.

On their next transaction, how many actually used their Realtor again? Just 29 percent!

With home buyers, the results are even more shocking:

- 75 percent said they would definitely use the Realtor again, as well as refer them to friends.
- 15 percent said they would probably use the Realtor again, as well as refer them to friends.
- A total of 90 percent said they would definitely or probably use and refer their Realtor.

This time, only 13 percent used their Realtor on their next transaction!

WHAT HAPPENED?

Buying or selling a home is an infrequent event. The time between transactions is measured in years or even decades. Customers can forget the Realtor they worked with (especially if the Realtor doesn't stay in touch), or they meet new Realtors. On average, customers know twelve Realtors, so they have a lot of choices. How do they pick their Realtor?

Various studies on the home-buying process provide some answers. First of all, the home-buying and selling process takes longer than we thought. From the time buyers and sellers first get the inspiration to do something until they have a closing takes from 9.3 to 21 months.

During this 9.3 to 21-month process, they select a Realtor in just seventy-two hours. Their choice is quick and arbitrary, based primarily on flow. The Realtor they were most recently in flow with during this seventy-two hours is the Realtor who has their top-of-mind awareness. That Realtor becomes their Realtor of choice.

John and Mary Smith go to a party at a friend's home. Their friends have just purchased a new home and are very excited to show it off.

On the way home, John says to Mary, "What do you think of the

Jones's new home?" Mary says, "Maybe we should think about doing something like that."

So they start discussing the idea. The spark is lit, and both John's and Mary's RAS are now engaged.

The next morning, as they drive to work, they notice yard signs in front of properties for sale for the first time in years. John has a breakfast meeting, and as he walks into the restaurant, he picks up a homes-for-sale magazine. (Their RAS is really working.) Now John and Mary are surfing the Internet and scoping out neighborhoods.

Buyers like John and Mary go through four stages of the buying process: curiosity, interest, desire, and commitment. In this case, John and Mary have moved from curiosity to serious interest. At this point, they have some questions and feel they need to talk to a Realtor. But who should they call? Who is the first Realtor to pop into their mind? It will be the Realtor who was most recently in flow.

John may say, "I'll call Justin. I just talked with him at Rotary." Or Mary may remark, "I can call Heather. She'll know the answers. I just saw her at the health club." Or they may decide to call Tim, because that day they received his real estate newsletter. Those are the Realtors they are in flow with right now, and those are the Realtors they will consider calling. Unfortunately, they are not thinking about the Realtor they worked with nine years ago (who did a great job for them), unless that Realtor has stayed in flow.

GOOD NEWS. BAD NEWS.

The fact that most customers select their Realtor based on flow is really good news for rookies. As a rookie, you can drop into this business, set up a good flow system, and be successful your very first year (as long as people like you and trust you).

Unfortunately, this is bad news for the old pro who thinks that because he did a great job for his customers nine years ago they will stay loyal to him. Have you ever heard an old pro say "those are my people," as if they were branded cattle? He figures they carry his brand and, as they roam around the marketplace, they will return to his corral. This is not reality. Customers don't see it that way. In contrast, the productive old pro Ninja knows he has to earn his business every day. And the way he earns it is with flow.

RELATIONSHIPS & REFERRALS

I was teaching an early morning session to mangers at the Colorado Real Estate Convention. We were discussing two studies. One said that each American adult knows an average of four people who will be moving this year. What an opportunity for referrals if you stay in flow!

In the other study, 74 percent of homebuyers said they never heard from their real estate agent again after the closing. These agents did not stay in flow and were not interested in building a relationship and earning referrals. They were only interested in the transaction. Just 6 percent heard from their agent on a consistent basis (once a month or more). A manager raised his hand and stated that he didn't believe the study. "We aren't that bad!" he snorted.

Fast forward two hours later. On the main stage, in front of 5,000 Realtors, Lee Cockerell, retired Executive Vice-President of Disney was giving a wonderful speech on customer service when he paused and asked, "Can I share an observation on your industry? My wife and I have purchased and sold 11 homes in our lifetime. We've never once had the real estate agent connect with us after closing." He went on to say, "I'm interviewing two or three executives a week who are looking for multimillion dollar housing. If my agent had stayed in touch, I could have made their career." I was looking for that manager!

Chapter 24

YOU ARE EITHER VISIBLE OR INVISIBLE

Flow builds relationships. Think about your best friends or your kids. The more you interact with them, the stronger the bond, the stronger the relationship. The same is true with your customers. Flow is the lifeblood and the oxygen of your relationships—and your business. Flow is what makes you visible and keeps you top of mind. There are two kinds of flow: *auto-flow* and *live flow*.

> *"Flow is the lifeblood and oxygen of your relationships—and your business. Flow is what makes you visible and keeps you top of mind."*

AUTO-FLOW—YOUR THREE PER MONTH

How much flow do I need to become the Realtor of choice? Our research of top producers indicates you need a minimum of three auto-flow touches per month. The days of sending one mailing a month are over. People live in a media swirl, and to be heard above the noise takes three touches a month. Many top-producing Ninjas average one touch a week.

We recommend these touches be a combination of mail and email and that you set them up on a calendar for the entire year. That way, you aren't spending your time trying to figure out what to send each month. Set it and forget it. It's automatic!

Auto-flow keeps you visible even when you are invisible (on vacation, for example). Your customers are still getting your newsletters, market updates, and so on.

One of the top Realtors in Denver shared with me that, after taking a Ninja Selling class, she began her three-per-month flow program with her database, as well as in the neighborhood where she lived. Within a year, her business went to an even higher level, plus she was capturing more than 50 percent of all the new listings in her neighborhood.

After several years of success, she thought maybe she could cut back on her flow (and her expenses). She kept her three per month for her friends and customers but reduced her flow to once a month for her neighborhood. The next year, her share of neighborhood listings fell to less than 12 percent. It proved to her that the system works, but you have to work the system. She went back to her three-per-month flow system, and immediately, she was again capturing 50 percent or more of the listings in her neighborhood.

LIVE FLOW—YOUR MAGIC FIFTY

In addition to the three mailings or emails per month (auto-flow), we recommend a minimum of fifty live interactions per week—face-to-face or on the phone. When I suggest this at a workshop, there is usually a gasp in the room. How will I ever find fifty people to interact with live every week? It's easy.

Every person you interact with counts, as long as you ask the FORD questions and listen for change. So at your weekly service club meeting, you sit at round tables of ten. When you ask the other people at your table about their family, occupation, recreation, and dreams, and you listen for change, that counts as nine. When you call your three sellers to give them their weekly update, that counts as three. When you call your four buyers to give them their weekly update, that counts as four. If seven people come to your open house, that counts as seven. You are visiting with parents at a soccer game, back-to-school night, or church: That counts. If you are in flow, you will easily have fifty live interactions a week.

I was teaching a Ninja Installation session in Seattle, and a student asked if we could meet after class. He said he had taken the basic one-day Ninja Selling class a year ago and had been working the system, but the system didn't seem to be working for him. Specifically, he said he had been tracking the fifty people per week that he was talking to. I asked him to describe his business and what he was saying when he met people. The gentleman proceeded to talk nonstop for twenty minutes.

I quickly realized his problem. He was doing all the talking and controlling time of possession. He was not asking FORD questions and listening.

I called time out to get him to stop talking. Then, we reviewed how Ninjas ask questions and listen for change, and how the customer or friend has time of possession. I then suggested that he stop talking to fifty people a week and instead start *interviewing* fifty people per week. He made this correction, and his business took off.

FLOW QUALITY

When we suggest three mailings or emails a month (auto-flow), plus fifty live interviews per week (live flow), we are often asked, "Is this too much?" It *is* too much if your flow is of low quality. Your friends and customers do not like receiving annoying Realtor junk mail and emails. You want your touches to create value—to solve a problem or make the receiver feel good. If they don't do that, don't send them. If your calls don't create value, don't make them.

The art in Ninja Selling is to come up with meaningful, value-added flow. When you solve people's problems and make them feel good, they want more of that kind of value. You can't send enough of this kind of flow.

When designing a powerful program for the best flow, here are four criteria:

1. **Valuable.** The best flow offers value (solves a problem or feels good).
2. **Customized.** The more customized a flow item is, the more powerful it is. Making the item unique to the receiver is the key. For example, nearly everyone values market statistics; people want to know what is going on in the market. Market statistics solve a problem. They're even more valuable when the statistics are customized for a particular neighborhood or home.
3. **Personalized.** Make these market statistics even more powerful by writing the receiver a personal note and including it with the statistics.
4. **Combination of Art and Science.** Art is the heart. Science is the head. Your flow system should combine items from each of these two areas. Here are some examples:

    Art:
    - Personal notes (including relevant news articles)
    - Tickets and giveaways
    - Calendars—including sports and entertainment
    - Notepads
    - Ice cream coupons for the kids
    - Happy birthday and happy anniversary cards
    - Coupons and gift certificates
    - Invitations to events

Science:

- Neighborhood locator maps
- Quarterly neighborhood statistics
- Newsletters about the market
- How to invest in real estate brochures
- Financing and refinancing information
- Just listed/just sold cards
- Annual real estate review
- Classes and events—investment classes, new home design classes, and so on

Many Realtors tend to send out the type of items they enjoy. If they are relationship oriented (art), they'll give birthday cards, calendars, and personal notes. If they are more analytical (science), they tend toward market statistics, financing information, and investment information. The fact is, your clients need both art and science; sending a combination of these items is most powerful.

TIPS FOR FLOW SUCCESS

- Mail tends to be more effective than email—but is more expensive. Direct mail is making a comeback, because there is less of it today than ten years ago. Today, it is junk email that is filling everyone's inbox. You are actually more differentiated with snail mail today. We recommend you use a combination of mail and email in your flow system.

- Only 18 percent of real estate emails are ever opened, so make sure your message is prominent in the subject line and the preview window. Avoid attachments whenever possible.

- With direct mail, other than personal notes, design your mailings as postcards. Avoid envelopes whenever possible. When your friends and customers go to their mailbox, and they see your face, name, and company, you have made an impression. You are in flow, even if you only make it from the mailbox to the recycle bin.

BUDGETING

You can operate an effective three-per-month flow program for as little as $2 per name per month or less. If you have 200 people in your database, that would be about $400 per month or $4,800 a year. When we start talking about this investment of time and money, we often get pushback. New people just getting started in the business say they don't have the money, and old-timers say they don't need it.

Our experience with more than 50,000 Ninjas throughout the US and Canada shows that when you work the Ninja System, you will generally earn $1,000 or more in gross commission income for every household in your database. If that includes 200 households, and you work the Ninja System, you'll earn $200,000 in gross commission income per year. A key part of working the Ninja System is your flow. If you could earn $1,000 for every $24 ($2/month) you invest in your business, how much would you invest? The answer: *All you have.*

If you are an old-timer, remember your future business is not based on your past. It is based on your current flow. Most people choose their Realtor based on flow. I see long-time Realtors who think they have a "book of business," and they stop or cut back on their investment in flow. Their business starts a long, slow downward spiral. They don't have a blowout; they just have a slow leak.

What if you are new in the business and don't have the money? Let me ask you this: If you just bought a farm and buying it took all your money so that you didn't have any cash for seed, what would you do? You would borrow the money. You can't have a harvest unless you plant! I see new Realtors trying to have a harvest without planting.

They turn into hunters and gatherers—chasing customers and deals, constantly in pursuit, hoping to find a transaction. Ninja Selling is a system that will give you predictable results, but you have to invest the time and the money.

JON'S STORY

Helen Gray is our marketing director at The Group, Inc. Every newbie has to check in with her. She sets them up with their business cards, their personal brochure, their website, and so on. She also gives them a menu of items they can choose from for their flow system, and she can predict their success based on their commitment to flow.

One day Helen came by my office and said, "Watch Jon Holsten. He's going to be a superstar."

I said, "How do you know?"

Helen replied, "He's a great guy, and he went all in on his flow program."

She was right. Jon, a former police officer with six kids, did forty-eight transactions and earned $345,000 his first year in real estate!

Your flow program is not an expense. It is an investment in your friends, customers, and relationships. I watch Realtors blowing their money on advertising and buying Internet leads, yet they won't invest two dollars a month in the people who know, like, and trust them. There are fifteen transactions waiting for you each year for every one hundred households you know. Flow is the key to accessing those transactions.

Most Realtors talk about building a business based on relationships, yet they invest very little in them. They have good intentions to follow-up, to stay in touch to stay in flow, but they get busy chasing the next transaction. They are not relationship driven; they are transaction driven. They talk a lot about relationships and "my people," but they run their business like a series of one-night stands.

SYSTEM OVERRIDE

There is one way Ninjas can be successful without doing the three mailings or emails per month. They override the system with more powerful flow—more live interviews, either face-to-face or on the phone. Live flow is more powerful than auto-flow. Here is the pecking order of flow:

1. Face-to-face (most powerful)
2. Voice-to-voice (phone)
3. Text
4. Mail
5. Email/Social media
6. Advertising (least powerful)

The Ninjas who don't do the three mailings/emails per month override the system by doing something far more dramatic—making typically fifty to one hundred live calls a day. My experience is that most Ninjas are not dedicated enough to conduct one hundred live interviews a day. Our system asks them to have fifty live interviews a *week* and augment that with three mailings/emails per month. This approach is very doable and more user friendly for most Realtors.

Chapter 25

THE POWER OF 8 IN 8

To demonstrate the power of flow, the Hobbs/Herder marketing firm did a research study on a neighborhood in Southern California. They surveyed homeowners by phone and asked one question: "If you were to sell your home, what Realtor would you call?" They then recorded the responses and rank-ordered the Realtors based on this top-of-mind awareness.

Next, they began mailing into this neighborhood one piece of mail each week for eight weeks (8 in 8) to the residents of this neighborhood. The mail was something that would be perceived as valuable by the homeowners and was sent from a fictitious Realtor. This Realtor did not exist. Hobbs/Herder created the face, name, and company.

After the eight weeks of mailings, Hobbs/Herder conducted the same phone survey a second time asking the same question. Now which Realtor do you think was the most mentioned? The fictitious Realtor. The top-ranked Realtor from the first survey was sometimes still mentioned, but the *most* mentioned Realtor was the made-up one. This study demonstrates once again the power of flow.

After hearing about the 8 in 8 study, I was eager to try it out. About a week later, I was at a chamber of commerce breakfast, where I met a young man named Greg. We were seated at the same round table, and I introduced myself by asking Greg the FORD questions.

I discovered Greg was new in town, having moved here from California. He was married with two young boys, one of whom was ten years old (same age as our son) and a soccer player (same as our son).

Since we had this in common, we talked about the boys and soccer for a bit.

I asked him if he had purchased a home yet. He said they had bought a home in Village West, a great family neighborhood with a community pool. I asked if he had used a Realtor. He said he did, mentioned the Realtor's name and company, and proceeded to give a glowing testimonial of her service. I recognized the name but did not know the Realtor very well.

When I asked, "What brought you to Fort Collins?" Greg replied, "My company brought me here to build this division."

We talked for a while about his company and his work, and then the meeting started. Afterward, we exchanged business cards, and I said to myself, "I'm going to do an 8 in 8 with Greg and see what happens." Here were my eight contacts:

- **Week 1.** I sent a personal note: "Hi, Greg. Great to meet you. Welcome to Fort Collins. Hope to see you on the sidelines at a soccer game soon. Best regards, Larry"

- **Week 2.** I sent Greg a city map with all the new streets on it and a personal note: "Greg, I thought you would like a new map for your new city. Again, welcome to Fort Collins. Hope to see you soon. All the best, Larry"

- **Week 3.** I sent a high-altitude baking book, written by my wife, Pat, who is a professor of nutrition at Colorado State University. With it, I sent a note that read, "Hi, Greg, I was just thinking of you and Suzanne. Thought you might be able to use this. Shows you how to bake at 5,000 feet. Welcome to Colorado! Larry"

- **Week 4.** This week, I sent Greg a newsletter from The Group. "Hi, Greg, I thought you might like a copy of our newsletter. It's full of information on the local real estate market. If you don't want to receive this, please let me know. All the best! Larry"

- **Week 5.** I sent a brochure on how property taxes work in Larimer County. "Greg, I was just thinking of you and thought you would like to see how property taxes work here. You'll be getting a property tax notice soon. This brochure will explain it. Call me if you have any questions. Larry"

- **Week 6.** I sent Greg a summary of home sales in Village West for the past twelve months with a personal note. "Hi, Greg, When you get your tax notice, if you want to protest your taxes, you'll need this information. Let me know if you need any help. All the best for you and your family, Larry"

- **Week 7.** When I got to week 7, I made a phone call. I'll never forget Greg's first response when I called him: "My wife, Suzanne, wants to meet you. She wants to meet this guy who is sending us all this good stuff." I said, "Well, I would like to meet Suzanne and the boys as well. In fact, the purpose of my call is to invite you to lunch. I felt we had a great connection at the chamber breakfast, and I would like to get to know you better."

- **Week 8.** We went to lunch. We were sitting in Bisetti's Italian Restaurant talking about his boys, soccer, and how his family is adjusting to life in a new town. Here's our conversation:

  Larry: "How's business?"

  Greg: "We are really busy right now. We just bought a small company in Anaheim and need to move forty-seven people to Fort Collins."

  Larry: "Do you need any help with that move?"

  Greg: "What do you mean help?"

  Larry: "Do you need maps, relocation kits, information on Fort Collins, job opportunities for spouses, and so on?"

  Greg: "I never even thought about that. I don't know where to begin. I'm brand new here."

Larry: "I can help you put all of that together." After a brief discussion of what we needed to gather for Greg, he asked a question.

Greg: "Larry, I know this is a lot to ask, but would you consider going with me to Anaheim and helping me do the in-plant presentation. I'll talk about their jobs, and you can talk about the Fort Collins community. Together, I think we have a good chance of convincing them to make this move."

Forty-three of the forty-seven eligible employees for this corporate move chose to come to Fort Collins, and we helped them find housing. Later, we went with Greg to Buffalo, New York, and to Chicago, Illinois, where they also had bought small companies and needed to move people to Fort Collins. In that first year Greg was in town, we moved more than 120 employees to Fort Collins. All because of 8 in 8.

Epilogue: Near the end of that lunch at Bisetti's I asked Greg how the house was working out. He talked about how the neighborhood was great, the boys had made friends, and the family loved it. I then said, "Greg, I was thinking the other day and trying to remember who you bought your house from."

Greg rolled his eyes up (performing a mental search), "It was a woman"—he no longer remembered her name—"at XYZ Realty." It was a woman all right, but she worked at ABC Realty. Greg had forgotten her name and had the wrong company.

Interestingly, the company he mentioned, XYZ, was the listing company, and he probably remembered their listing brochure and their sign in the front yard (which was probably in his garage). Less than four months after buying his home (and giving me a testimonial for his Realtor), Greg couldn't remember her name or company.

Like most Realtors, she never followed up with Greg after closing or built a relationship with him. Now he is in flow with someone else. Greg and his family were just a transaction to her, and she has moved on to find another transaction.

A national survey by Quality Service Certified (QSC) found that only 18 percent of Realtors follow-up live (phone or face-to-face) after closing. A study conducted by Colorado State University College of Business for The Group, Inc. Real Estate found that in Larimer County, Colorado, more than 50 percent of buyers and sellers could not accurately identify their Realtor's name and company thirty days after closing. Flow is the key to maintaining your relationship.

> "A national survey found that only 18 percent of Realtors follow-up live . . . after closing. . . . Flow is the key to maintaining your relationship."

PUTTING 8 IN 8 TO WORK

Here are five ways to use 8 in 8 to build your business:

1. **Build a New Relationship.** Use 8 in 8 to build new relationships, just as I did with Greg. When I meet a key person who is in a position of leadership and influence, I always do an 8 in 8 with them. It really works.

2. **Rebrand Yourself.** If you are new in real estate, or if you have recently switched companies, your friends and customers are still thinking of you in your old profession or at your old company. You need to rebrand yourself at your new profession or your new company, and 8 in 8 will do just that. We recommend that all new people who join our company do an 8 in 8 with their database.

3. **Rejuvenate a Stale Database.** Are there people in your database whom you haven't talked with in years? Would you like to

reconnect with them but feel it would be awkward to just call them up after all these years? Start them on an 8 in 8 first, then call them.

4. **Annual Refresher.** Many of the top-selling Ninjas do an annual 8 in 8 with their database just to keep it fresh.

5. **Geographical Farming.** Obviously the 8 in 8 system was first perfected for geographical farming—working a neighborhood. As a Ninja, we recommend you put your time and energy into people who know you versus strangers. The 8 in 8 is a good way to introduce your name to strangers in a geographical farm; however, to be the most effective, you need to actually meet the people in the farm face-to-face and start building a relationship.

After the initial burst of 8 in 8, put your new potential customers into the normal three-per-month auto-flow program.

LOGISTICS

To set up and run an 8 in 8 program:

1. Simply create six flow items (a combination of art and science) to send once a week.

2. Your seventh week will be a phone call, and your eighth week will be a face-to-face meeting (lunch, breakfast, or coffee).

3. If you are doing an 8 in 8 with a large database, stagger your mailings so you start about five new people each week. That way, on the seventh week, you only have to call five people, and on the eighth week, you only have to meet with five. Can you imagine running through all two hundred people in your database at the same time? Yikes! On week eight, you'd have to have two hundred lunches.

Chapter 26

HOW DO YOU GENERATE BUSINESS?

How do you generate a continuous flow of customers coming to you? Is this one of your challenges? The key to solving this challenge and turning it into an opportunity comes with your awareness that there are two parts to the sales business:

- **Part 1: Doing the Business.** Most Realtors are pretty good at *doing the business*. If you give them a buyer, they know how to show property and write a contract. Give them a seller, and they will list the house.

- **Part 2: Generating the Business.** Generating business is the area where most Realtors are weak. This skill is what separates Ninjas and star salespeople from the rest. Generating business is simply a matter of focus and daily habits. Follow the Ninja Daily Routine and you will have a continuous flow of business coming to you.

THE NINJA DAILY ROUTINE

1. **Show Up for Work.** Come to work in the morning dressed and prepared to make money. When I walk into the office between 8:00 and 9:00 a.m., the top-selling Ninjas are already there, ready for showtime. Struggling salespeople tend to not show up,

show up late in the day, or show up in their sweats to hang out in the office and do paperwork.

2. **Work *on* Your Business in the Morning. Work *in* Your Business in the Afternoon.** Research shows that most property showings occur in the afternoon. There are exceptions, but overwhelmingly, it seems buyers prefer to look at homes after noon. Similarly, most listings are taken either in the afternoon or the evening. It just seems that the natural flow of the marketplace is for the afternoon to be the time to list and sell real estate—to be working *in* your business. That leaves the mornings to work *on* your business, that is, to generate the business and run your flow systems. This is the part of the business many Realtors leave out and is one of the reasons they don't show up for work in the morning. Running your flow systems is the most important activity you can do—and it's easier to have a set time to do that.

Realtors who don't run their flow systems tend to not have enough business and develop a scarcity mind-set. Or they work with anybody, even pretend customers—those who are not really serious about buying or selling real estate. The result is a waste of time.

Ninjas who work on their flow systems in the morning have an abundance of business in the afternoon. In fact, they typically have an overflow. This is a great problem to have. They can now work with the A Clients—those most serious about buying or selling—and refer the B and C clients to other Realtors. Or they can form a small team and hand off the extra business to other team members. By working on your business in the morning, you become a *rainmaker*.

If for some reason you don't have business in the afternoon, take the afternoon off. Play golf, go to your kids' games, do something for yourself. The system works, and you will have plenty of business most afternoons.

> *"Work on your business in the morning. Work in your business in the afternoon."*

We have documented the work habits of top-selling Ninjas and have identified nine activities they do every day or every week. We call these the *Ninja Nine*. They are habits anyone can do and, when done consistently, will cause a dramatic increase in your income per hour. Aristotle said it best, "We become what we do repeatedly. Excellence, therefore, is not an act. It is a habit." Make the Ninja Nine your Habit!

The Ninja Nine are easy to accomplish. The first five activities are *daily* habits and will only take about fifteen to thirty minutes each morning. The next four activities are *weekly* habits and will take several hours a week. Each habit will be discussed more fully in the next two chapters. It works best if you schedule a set time each day and week to do your Ninja Nine. Here's a summary.

Daily Habits

1. Daily gratitude: Get up in the morning and give thanks.
2. Show up for work, and stop opening your email first. Stay on your agenda.
3. Write two personal notes each day.
4. Focus on your hot list daily.
5. Focus on your warm list daily.

Weekly Habits

1. Make your weekly customer service calls.
2. Schedule two live real estate reviews.
3. Have fifty live interviews.
4. Update your database.

Let's look at each one of the Ninja Nine in detail.

CLIENT OR CUSTOMER

In our Ninja Installation workshops, the discussion often comes up about whether we are working with a client or a customer. In real estate, the difference is sometimes determined by state law regarding agency. Each state may have a different law and definition. For the purposes of this book, feel free to use whichever term you are comfortable with in accordance with your state laws.

Chapter 27

THE NINJA NINE—
YOUR FIVE DAILY HABITS

"People do not decide their futures. They decide their habits and their habits decide their futures."
—**F.M. Alexander**

SUCCESS HABIT 1: START WITH DAILY GRATITUDES.

Start your day by getting your energy into the positive quadrants. This is not only important for your personal health, but you will also broadcast a positive energy vibe to those around you.

SUCCESS HABIT 2: SHOW UP! DON'T OPEN YOUR EMAIL FIRST! STAY ON YOUR AGENDA!

What happens when you open your email? You are suddenly on someone else's agenda. Distractions destroy excellence. Resist the temptation. Do your first five daily habits before opening your email. Those emails can wait fifteen minutes. "Time Block" your day and your week. Schedule your to-do list.

SUCCESS HABIT 3: WRITE TWO PERSONAL NOTES.

The most powerful thing you can send to another human being is a handwritten, personal note. Have you received one? How did it make you feel? Did you save it? Personal notes make people feel good, creating value in their life. There is another benefit of writing the notes: It makes you feel great as well. What a great way to start your day—making yourself and others feel great.

Writing notes is easy. There are three magic phrases you can use to start your notes: 1. Thank you, 2. Congratulations, and 3. I was just thinking of you and . . . Start your notes with one of these phrases, and you are off and running. Notes only take a few minutes to write and cost very little to send. Done consistently, they will transform your business. If you write just two a day, ten a week, five hundred a year, what will happen to your business?

Nolan Matthias was just twenty-seven when he and his wife, Jen—two of the top mortgage lenders in Calgary, Canada—came to a Ninja Installation in Colorado. Three months after the class, a very excited Nolan called to tell me their lending business was soaring to even higher levels as a result of their Ninja training. He and Jen wanted to say thank you.

I asked him, "What was the one thing that helped you the most?" Nolan laughed and said, "It was the thing I thought during class that was the most silly—those crazy little personal notes. I already used text and email, but I decided to try the notes. Those crazy little notes have transformed our business!"

Start writing notes, and your business will be transformed as well. You don't have to limit yourself to just two a day. Tami Spaulding writes ten a day, including her birthday and anniversary cards. For a great example of the power of personal notes, read the inspirational book *365 Thank Yous: The Year a Simple Act of Daily Gratitude Changed My Life* by John Kralik.

SUCCESS HABIT 4: FOCUS ON YOUR HOT LIST DAILY.

A hot list is a list of people who want to buy or sell, know they want to buy or sell, want to buy or sell with you, and want to buy or sell soon (typically in the next ninety days). Pull out this list and ask yourself this question: "Who on this list wants to write a contract this week?"

Because of the reticular formation of your brain (RAS), when you focus on "Who on this list wants to write a contract this week?" you will start to see contracts that you were not seeing before. I watch top-selling Ninjas carry their hot list with them on home tours and pull it out to see who might want to buy the house they just toured. I also watch them with their hot list at sales meetings, intently listening to the pitches and looking at their hot list for a match. Create and focus on your hot list, and you will sell more real estate.

SUCCESS HABIT 5: FOCUS ON YOUR WARM LIST DAILY.

A warm list is a list of people who want to buy or sell but may not know they want to buy or sell. However, you know they want to buy or sell, because you are observing their current situation or life changes and they probably will want to buy or sell sometime during the next year.

Here's how it works. I'm sitting at a round table of ten at our weekly Rotary meeting. Next to me is a friend named Russ. I ask him, "How's business?" (FORD questions).

Russ lights up at my asking and tells me how he just got the promotion he has worked his entire career for. He's going to be vice president of the western US region for his company. This is a really big deal, and I congratulate him.

Later, Russ says the only downside to the promotion is that he will have to work out of the Denver office. I ask him what his plans are, and he says he'll continue to live in Fort Collins because of his family, and he'll commute to Denver—about an hour each way.

In my head, I do the math: one hour each way, each day. That's two hours a day times five days a week—ten hours a week. Assuming Russ gets four weeks of vacation each year, forty-eight workweeks times ten hours a week of drive time equals 480 hours a year on I-25. That's twelve forty-hour workweeks a year!

I say to myself: "Russ is in pain. Russ is moving. Russ doesn't know he is moving. Russ is euphoric about the promotion and in denial about the commute." That day, Russ went on my warm list.

I would see Russ on weekends at our kids' soccer games, and I would simply monitor his pain.

One day, I asked him, "Hey Russ, how's it going?"

Russ replied with a question, "Larry, how's the market?"

I knew what he was thinking and replied, "You mean the market in The Landings?" (That was Russ's neighborhood.) Russ got a funny grin on his face, realizing I knew why he asked the question.

"How's the commute?" I asked.

"It's killing me!" Russ exclaimed.

"What do you want to do?" was my next question.

"Kathy and I have talked it over, and when school's out this spring, we want you to sell our home and help us find a Realtor in Denver. We need to move there. I never see my kids. I'm spending all my free time in the car."

That day, Russ went from my warm list to my hot list.

Here's a simple exercise that will help you build your warm list. This exercise involves sixteen life changes that can motivate someone to move. The more of these changes someone has going on, the higher their move score. A good rule of thumb is that about 20 percent of your database should end up on your warm list.

Take out your database of people you know. Go through the names one at a time. Bring the person/family into your consciousness. Think about them and ask yourself the following questions regarding their situation. If they fit a particular question, write the number of that question next to their name. The names with the most numbers have the most changes going on in their lives and the highest move score. They go on your warm list.

After going through your entire list, you will have a clear picture of the potential real estate needs and wants of your customers—and the start of a warm list for yourself.

How many of the people you know:

1. Have had an increase in family size in the past year?
2. Have children age ten and under?
3. Have teenage children?
4. Have children who have left home recently?
5. Are living below or above their means?
6. Have lived in their same house seven years or more?
7. Have had their employer/company expand in the past year?
8. Have had their employer/company downsize in the past year?
9. Have a commute of one hour or more?
10. Have received a substantial inheritance?
11. Own a building lot?
12. Are getting married or are recently married?
13. Are getting divorced or are recently divorced?
14. Are getting divorced and remarried?
15. Have a dream for investment property?
16. Have a dream to live in a particular place or area?

DEBBIE'S STORY

Debbie Hansen was a nine-year veteran with a consistent track record of $125,000 a year in gross commission income. Suddenly, during the Great Recession her income doubled to more than $250,000 a year. The market went down, yet Debbie's income doubled. I had to find out why.

"What are you doing differently?" I asked.

Debbie blushed and said, "I finally created that warm list you've been talking about for the last nine years!"

"Can I see it?" I asked. Debbie's warm list had fifty names on it. I noticed thirty-two of them had check marks beside their names.

"What are the check marks?" I asked.

"Those are the people who had a closing this past year," Debbie said. So thirty-two of the fifty people on her warm list bought or sold something in the past year.

"I'm not quite sure how it works," Debbie explained. "I don't know if it's what you focus on expands, or possibly the Law of Attraction, or maybe I just put more focus and energy into those people. But it definitely works. It's almost like magic."

Debbie's doubled income was not just a one-year event. It has become permanent. She shifted to a new level, and her income stabilized at a new high of $250,000 per year or more.

As a side note, when I saw Debbie's income and warm list, I said, "You must have about 250 people in your database."

She gave me a curious look and said, "I do! How do you know that?"

I said, "When you work the Ninja System, you will generally earn $1,000 or more per year per name in your database, and you earned $250,000. Plus, you typically will have about 20 percent of your database on your warm list, and you had fifty on your warm list. It's a formula. TSW!"

YOUR BUSINESS TRACKER

What you focus on expands, so it is good to have a system to keep your hot and warm lists in front of you. This system is called the *Business Tracker* and can be downloaded by going to www.NinjaSelling.com. Here's what it looks like:

Ninja Business Tracker as Predictor

6 months
90 days
30 days

Ninja Business Tracker

"Warm" List	"Hot" List	Under Contract (Pending)	Closed
Name	Buy/Sell	Possible Price	Comm %	Gross Inc.	Name	Buy/Sell	Target Price	Comm %	Gross Inc.	Name	Buy/Sell	Price	Comm %	Gross Inc.	Name	Buy/Sell	Price	Comm %	Gross Income

Four buckets

Each predicts future income.

Ninja Nine is what fills the "Warm" bucket!

The Business Tracker is designed to do just that—track your business. We call each of the columns *buckets*. Your customers start in the warm list bucket. This is where Russ started. When he told me that he and Kathy were ready to move, they moved to the hot list bucket. When we listed Russ and Kathy's house, we could either keep them in the hot list bucket or we could add them to another bucket called *listings*. Some Ninjas also like to create special buckets to track a builder or relocation account. Next, the customers move to the *under contract bucket* and finally to the *closed bucket*.

Customers simply move across the page from bucket to bucket. It's a great way to track your business at a glance. Most Ninjas have this spreadsheet in their computers, but they also print a hard copy each week to carry with them and refer to it multiple times each day.

A quick glance at your Business Tracker will help you forecast your business. Empty warm list or hot list buckets are an ominous forecast of your financial future. I watch Realtors focusing primarily on their under contract bucket, "nursemaiding" those customers to the closing table. But they are not refilling their hot and warm list buckets. The result is their income becomes erratic. They have a big closing month, and then they have months of nothing, while they refill their warm and hot list buckets. The drama of this erratic income can cause burnout in the business.

You want to keep your buckets full at all times. How? One word: *Flow*. Flow solves everything. Flow will not only increase your income but will stabilize it as well.

The first five Success Habits of the Ninja Nine are daily activities. The next four Success Habits are weekly activities.

Chapter 28

THE NINJA NINE— YOUR FOUR WEEKLY HABITS

SUCCESS HABIT 6: FOCUS ON YOUR CUSTOMER SERVICE CALLS.

We recommend you have a set time each week (preferably in the morning) when you make your weekly customer service calls. These customer service calls serve two purposes:

1. Your goal is fabled service, and one of your measures is whether you're calling your buyers and sellers first. If they call you first during a transaction, you are failing. You need to be proactive. One of the biggest complaints buyers and sellers have about their Realtor is their lack of communication: "They never followed up," "I always had to call them to find out anything," and "We listed our house and never heard from them again" are typical complaints.

2. Customer service calls are a key part of your flow system. Your current active customers are your very best source of referrals. Why? Because their RAS is fully engaged in the process of buying and selling. They notice everyone else who is also interested in buying or selling and will refer them to you if you are in flow. The Ninja mind-set and expectation is: *My next transaction is embedded in this transaction.* I just need to discover it. I do that with flow, and it starts with my weekly customer service calls.

One of the Ninja philosophies is to only make calls that create value. As a result, you will never put yourself in the position of being rejected by making these calls. They are very user friendly. Here are eight calls that create value:

1. **Current Customers, Sellers, Under Contract Buyers, and Active Buyers.** These important players should be called regularly with updates.
2. **Recently Closed Customers.** Reach out to see if they need anything.
3. **Referral Sources.** Say thank you and update sources on referral progress.
4. **Home Purchase Anniversaries, Wedding Anniversaries, and Birthdays.** Congratulate past customers and wish them well on special days.
5. **8 in 8 System.** Call on week seven to set up a face-to-face on week eight.
6. **Tickets and Giveaways.** Offer your customers tickets to sports and entertainment events, as well as product or service giveaways.
7. **Annual Real Estate Review.** This is explained in Success Habit 7.
8. **Thank yous, Congratulations, Thinking of You.** This is the same idea as the personal note, except by phone.

The Five-Step Calling Process

Ninja has a system for everything, including how to make your customer service calls. Here's the five-step process:

1. **Salutation.** "Hi, Don, this is Larry at ABC real estate. How's your day going so far? Is this an OK time? Great."

2. **Common Ground (FORD).** "First of all, congratulations to Heather (daughter) on her scholarship to CSU. I just read about her in the paper. What a great honor! What are her plans? Major?" And so on.

3. **Purpose of the Call.** "Well, the purpose of my call is to give you an update on your referral of Bill and Susan Jones. Again, I want to thank you for your confidence in me to help Bill and Susan. What a great couple and a great family. They told me some stories about you guys in the old days. Bill and Susan arrived in town this week. We have them settled in an executive rental while they look for a home. They seem really happy about the move, and we looked at homes yesterday. Bill said he was going to give you a call to get together."

4. **Common Ground (FORD).** "By the way, I was at the United Way luncheon yesterday, and Randy said you guys (Don's company) are buying XYZ Corp. What does that mean for you?" Discuss the impact, growth, potential relocation, and so on.

5. **Length—Two to Three Minutes at Most.** "Don, thanks for your time today. I'll give you another update when Bill and Susan find a home. Meanwhile, say, hello to Mary (Don's wife) and congratulations to Heather. Goodbye."

Key Points

First of all, customer service calls are fun and easy to make. You just need to make them. And you will, if you have a set time for them. Schedule about two hours from 9:00 to 11:00 a.m. once a week to make the calls.

Steps 1, 3, and 5 are the customer service parts of the call. Steps 2 and 4 (common ground) are where the relationship is built and the referrals are generated. Listen for change.

It's important to keep the calls short and sweet. Avoid getting bogged down in long visits, or your customer will avoid your call the next time. If you are making your calls frequently and consistently (every week), they will be short and sweet. It is when you haven't talked to somebody for months that the calls will take longer.

You may get voice mail; this happens quite a bit. Stick to your five-step process. Read the dialogue above again, and notice how it would be virtually the same if you were leaving a voice mail. There would only be a few modifications in what you say.

Avoid using email for your customer service calls whenever possible. If your customer prefers email communication, honor that request. However, most customers prefer a call on the phone.

Here are five reasons to use the phone versus email:

1. **Customer Preference.** The annual Profile of Buyers & Sellers survey conducted by the National Association of Realtors indicates that 78 percent of buyers and sellers prefer phone communication from their Realtor when they are involved in a real estate transaction.

2. **It's Faster.** The average person speaks at a rate of 150 to 180 words a minute and types (or texts) at an average rate of 30 to 40 words a minute. You communicate 500 percent faster by phone. You can make more calls in less time. Ninja is about increasing your income per hour.

3. **It's Better.** Through phone calls, you pick up the subtle and hidden nuances of voice tone. A Harris Interactive Survey of 2,395 adults showed that 82 percent of emails are misinterpreted regarding tone, not content. Also, when talking with a person on the phone, you have more of that person's attention. The quality of the communication is much higher.

4. **Referrals.** When you are communicating by phone, Steps 2 and 4 of the five-step calling process are where you discover the referrals. This doesn't happen with email or text.

5. **It Works.** In training and coaching thousands of salespeople over the past forty-plus years, I've observed that, with a very few exceptions, those salespeople who primarily use the phone are far more productive than those who primarily use email.

Avoiding the Nasties

In a Ninja Selling class, we often practice the five-step calling process. I'll usually start with a demonstration where I'm the salesperson, and one of the students plays the role of a buyer or seller. Often, the Realtor who is playing the role of the seller will get nasty, yelling, "Why haven't you sold my house!" They later say they were venting their frustration, because they have been treated that way by sellers.

I have asked our Ninjas and our instructors if they have ever been treated with disrespect or in a nasty way by a buyer or seller on one of these calls. The answers are universally "no" or "very seldom." The reason, we believe, is because these Ninjas are making the calls consistently every week. When they have a consistent frequency of interaction, the relationships are built and unpleasant confrontations never materialize. The nasties are usually caused by frustrated buyers and sellers who haven't heard from their Realtor in a long time. The Realtor doesn't have a consistent customer service program for making these calls. As a result, when customers finally hear from their Realtor, they unload with the nasties. When the Realtor does call, it is usually because of some crisis in the transaction. Now there is lots of drama, emotions are high, and the situation starts to spiral out of control. No foundation of trust has been built. As a result, the Realtor becomes afraid of the situation and starts emailing rather than picking up the phone. The situation deteriorates further.

Be a Ninja! Schedule a set time each week to make your customer service calls. Build a platform of trust and confidence. When you do, you will have fun making money and helping people.

SUCCESS HABIT 7: SCHEDULE TWO LIVE REAL ESTATE REVIEWS WEEKLY.

As a Ninja, your relationship with your customers and friends is that of a proactive trusted advisor. As such, your responsibility is to offer them an annual review of their real estate holdings, which are typically one of their largest financial as well as emotional assets. They receive monthly statements for their bank and brokerage accounts. They want at least an annual update on their real estate.

People see their accountant, doctor, dentist, banker, and attorney on a regular basis. These are their trusted advisors. You, too, should offer an annual sit-down to review their real estate holdings. You will review the values, current market conditions, refinancing options, and answer any questions they may have. This is *not* a disguised listing pitch. Resist the temptation to act like a salesman.

If you sold them their properties, I recommend you bring their closed files to the meeting. When they go to their accountant, doctor, or dentist, these professionals pull out their file. Their closed file similarly positions you as a professional trusted advisor. If you did not sell them their home, don't worry. You can do real estate reviews for your friends—or anyone really.

You do not need to do a full-blown market analysis. Typically, you just need to know what has sold and what is for sale in their neighborhood, or the type of property (golf course or lakefront property, for example). Your multiple listing service (MLS) or Realtors Property Resource (RPR) probably has what you need with just a few keystrokes. Many Ninjas like to use the charts and graphs from Focus 1st (www.focus1st.com) and the House Price Index for their area from www.fhfa.gov. You should be able to prepare this information in five minutes or less.

Whom do you call first to provide a real estate review? Start with your warm list. Call your clients and, using the five-step calling process, invite them to lunch, breakfast, or coffee. Here's how it sounds:

- **Step 1.** "Hi, John, this is Larry Kendall over at The Group. How are you today? Great to hear that. Is this an OK time?"

- **Step 2.** "Well, before we get to the purpose of my call, how are Mary and the kids? I've been thinking about you lately." (FORD)

- **Step 3.** (Purpose of the call) "John, as part of my service to you and Mary, I offer the opportunity to sit down once a year and review your real estate holdings. They are some of your most valuable assets. I've prepared a report for you and would like to come by your home to go over it. Or would you prefer to get together for lunch, breakfast, or coffee? What works best for you? (Make the appointment.) Note: We have found nearly 100% will agree to the appointment if you offer to come to their home. They also like to show you their home and ask you questions about it.

    If John is too busy to meet, say, "That's OK. I know you and Mary have a lot on your plate right now, so I'll drop this in the mail to you. It will give you a good idea of the market and the value of your properties. If you have any questions, will you please give me a call?" Note: Do not email the packet. Send it by snail mail. We have tracked the results, and you will get a much better response.

- **Step 4.** "By the way, what are your plans for the summer? Are you doing anything fun? Any trips?" (FORD)

- **Step 5.** "Great, John. I look forward to seeing you for lunch at Bisetti's on the twenty-fourth."

Continue calling clients and offering the real estate review until you have two live appointments this week. Even those who can't meet will appreciate your taking the time to do something valuable for them.

At the appointment, start with FORD. "It's been a year since I've seen you. How's the family? Work?" It is all about them first. We'll get to the real estate later. Listen carefully for change. Here are some magic questions that stimulate their thoughts:

- "What are your long-term plans for this house?"
- "With some of the lowest interest rates in our lifetime, are you living in the home you want to be in?" (If you are not in a low-interest rate environment, you can leave off the first part of this question.)
- "If you could wave a magic wand and live anywhere, where would that be?"

Our Ninja coaches track metrics on all Ninjas in the various coaching programs. What are the results for real estate reviews? For face-to-face or Zoom reviews, 33 percent of the time, they result in some form of business—listing, sale, or referral. If you mail the review, it results in some business 15 percent of the time.

Each year, we interview our top-selling Ninjas and ask this question: "If you had to eliminate everything you do to generate business, except for *just one thing*, what would you hold on to? What is the one thing that most drives your business?" For years, the answer has been the same: fifty live interviews a week. (See Success Habit 8, which follows.) However, because of the 33 percent conversion rate, real estate reviews have become the just one thing, with Success Habit 8 a close second.

SUCCESS HABIT 8: SCHEDULE FIFTY LIVE INTERVIEWS WEEKLY.

There is no substitute for live interaction—face-to-face or voice-to-voice is the most powerful. We say these should be interviews, because your friends and customers should have time of possession. You are asking them questions and listening for change. And they love it, because they get to talk about themselves.

Your customer service calls in Habit 6 count in your fifty live weekly interviews, but these interviews do not *have* to be customer service or prospecting calls. Any live interaction where you ask the FORD questions and listen for change counts. Here are some examples: having fun with your friends at a party, visiting with people after church or at the ball game, calling someone to wish them happy birthday, meeting people coming through an open house, calling your sellers and buyers to give them weekly updates, and conversations at committee meetings.

One of the simplest and most powerful systems I've ever seen is from Ninja Dave Trujillo, who works with us at The Group. Dave carries a notebook with several stapled sheets that have the names and contact information of the people in his database. (He basically photocopies his sheets of mailing labels.) Dave's goal is simply to have a live interaction (face-to-face or on the phone) with everybody in his database (about five hundred people) every quarter. He writes notes beside their names and codes each name for whether the interaction was face-to-face or by phone and whether he interacted with them multiple times. What a simple visible system, and yet so powerful! At the end of the quarter, Dave archives this set, makes a fresh set of sheets, and starts over. His simple system gives him one of the highest incomes per hour of anyone I know.

THE MISSOURI MOM

Several years ago at a Ninja training in Fort Collins, Colorado, Wynn Washle—whose nickname is *Dr. Flow*—had just shared how he makes his morning customer service calls and was reviewing the importance of at least fifty calls a week.

A young woman in the class raised her hand and said that she really didn't like using the phone and that if Ninja Selling was about making these calls, count her out. I was immediately curious about her comment and asked her if she would share a little about herself and where she was from.

She said she was from a small town in Missouri, was married, had two young children, and had been in the real estate business about five years. I asked if I could question her a little about her business, and she said yes. Here's the conversation:

"What is the average sales price in your market?"

"About $137,000."

"Are you a stronger listing Realtor or buying Realtor, or are you pretty balanced in your business?"

"I'm probably stronger on the listing side."

"About how many listings do you have right now?"

"Thirty-five."

"Do you mind sharing what your gross commission income was last year?"

"Sure. It was a little over $250,000."

At this point, I was thinking to myself, *This young woman is amazing! How does she make that kind of income in a small town with a relatively low average sales price? Plus, she has a husband and two kids. And, she just called out the instructor to say she's not going to make calls.*

What was she doing that was driving her business? She was doing *something*. I needed to figure out what it was. As it turned out, the answer lay in her routine—how she spent her time.

"So, if it is all right with you, I would like for you to flow through a typical week with us. Let's start on Monday morning."

"Sure. I get up early (usually about 5:00 a.m.) and go to the health club. I like to work out early, so I can get home in time to get the kids ready for school."

"Tell me about the health club."

"Well, I meet my girlfriends there. A group of us work out together."

"Tell me about your girlfriends."

"My best friend is Julie. Her husband is our city manager. Sarah is a really good friend, too. Her husband is the minister of our church." (She goes through the friends she meets every morning, and they represent the human infrastructure of this small town!)

"What do you do after the health club?"

"Well, we stop at Starbucks. We just got one in our town. It is so cool! The girls who didn't get up early enough that day stop by and have coffee with the rest of us." (She then lists more of the human infrastructure of the town.)

This young Missouri mom continues to describe her week: church committees, kids' soccer games, fundraisers, meeting her buyers and sellers, and so on. By Tuesday night, she already has her fifty live interviews, and they have all been face-to-face. She is in live flow with more than a hundred people per week in the most powerful way possible. This is what is driving her business. In fact, her form of flow is a system override. This is all she needs to do. It's her *one thing*!

SUCCESS HABIT 9: UPDATE YOUR DATABASE WEEKLY.

Your database is the central nervous system of your business. It represents your relationships and is your most important business asset. You need to take care of it and update it weekly. Take care of your relationships, and they will take care of you.

Your database is dynamic, and it needs weekly attention at least. By the end of the week, you've accumulated a stack of notes, scraps of paper, phone numbers, and business cards that need to be processed and loaded into it. Again, do this in the morning, when you are working on your business. If you don't have a scheduled time each week for this activity, you start to get behind, and the stack gets bigger. Before long, you find yourself missing phone numbers and important contacts that are still lying in the stack.

As a minimum, here are the things you need to do weekly with your database. If you have an assistant, he or she can help you keep your database up to date and fresh.

1. **Update.** Make everything current—especially your hot and warm lists. We live in a mobile society. People are continuously changing addresses, jobs, and spouses. (How embarrassing to send something to a couple who have been divorced for a year.)
2. **Add.** Enter new contacts you have met and new information that you have learned about existing ones.
3. **Delete.** Your database depreciates at a rate of about 15 percent a year. If you have two hundred names in your database, about thirty of them will die, move away, get into real estate, or choose another Realtor each year. If you are not updating, adding, and deleting, your database gets stale and irrelevant.
4. **Back up.** The database is your most valuable asset. Back it up.
5. **Print.** Every week, print an updated hard copy of your hot list and warm list (or your Business Tracker) to carry with you. If you are following Dave Trujillo's system, you will make a hard copy of your entire database at the start of every quarter.

FOCUS ON PRODUCTIVE ACTIVITIES AND PRODUCTION TAKES CARE OF ITSELF.

Focus on the daily activities that cause your success. These activities are auto-flow (three different ways of reaching out a month) and the Ninja Nine. This is a very simple business when you work the Ninja System.

Tami Spaulding is one of the top Realtors in the United States. I remember when she was starting out. She had just been named Rookie of the Year by the Fort Collins Board of Realtors. She had proven she could do it, and now she wanted to show that she could run with the big dogs—the elite Realtors in our market. She set some really big goals for her next year.

Tami started the next year in a deep slump, however, going weeks without writing a contract or taking a listing. She was distraught. She pulled out her sheet of goals and started reviewing them with me. "I want to prove that I can be with the best," she said.

"Can I see those goals?" I asked.

Tami handed me her sheet of written goals.

I said, "Tami, you don't have goals. Your goals have you. They are stressing you out. Your customers can feel it. I can feel it. You are not acting like your natural self. Let's forget about the goals for a while. Instead, I want you to focus on your activities of creating value for people. Your new goals are activity goals (not income or transaction goals)." We laid out a plan for how many personal notes she was to write each day, how many live interviews each day, and her mailing program. Tami had a new list of activity goals rather than production goals.

"When you have achieved these activity numbers each day, celebrate!" I told her. "You have hit your goal for the day. Go home and relax. The production will take care of itself."

And it did—in a big way. Within a week, Tami was listing and selling again. Despite her slow start, Tami ended the year having doubled her income from the previous year. She was definitely running with the big dogs.

Chapter 29

WHAT HOLDS YOU BACK?

If the Ninja Nine are so easy to do, what holds you back? When I ask this question in a class, the first response is usually "fear." When I ask, "Fear of what?" someone usually answers, "Fear of rejection."

"The Ninja Nine is designed to never put you in the position of being rejected," I answer. And when we review the list, we agree that nothing there would cause the least bit of rejection. So it is something else.

Someone pipes up, "What holds me back is lack of time."

"Lack of time?" I ask.

"Well, I tend to procrastinate," someone says sheepishly. "I tend to do other things instead of the Ninja Nine."

"Why do you procrastinate?" I ask. And the answer comes back to "fear."

Are the Ninja Nine activities easy to do? How hard is it to do the following?

Ninja Nine

1. Get up in the morning and give thanks.

2. Show up for work and stay on your agenda.

3. Write two personal notes each day.

4. Focus on your hot list daily.

> 5. Focus on your warm list daily.
>
> 6. Make your weekly customer service calls.
>
> 7. Schedule two real estate reviews this week.
>
> 8. Have fifty live interviews this week.
>
> 9. Update your database this week.

The Ninja Nine create value (solve problems and make people feel good). They never put you in the position of being rejected. As a result, they are user friendly and easy to do. Unfortunately, they are also easy *not* to do.

ARE YOU IN THE GAME OR ARE YOU IN YOUR HEAD?

Richard asked if I would come in his office for a minute.

I sat down, and Richard said, "I'm frozen."

"What do you mean you're frozen?" I asked.

"I'm ready to do my Ninja Nine, and I can't pick up the phone. I'm afraid my friends will think I'm a salesperson. I'm afraid I'll come off like a telemarketer. I'm afraid it will hurt my relationship with them."

"Richard, you have used the word *afraid* three times. What is fear?"

Richard thought about it for a moment and then said, "That's a good question. What is fear?"

"Fear is the absence of love," I said. "The reticular formation of the brain has two pathways—love and fear. It can only focus on one or the other. Therefore, fear is the absence of love." (Marianne Williamson describes this beautifully in her book *A Return to Love*.)

"And Richard, when you are afraid, it is because you are thinking about yourself. Listen to your language: '*I'm afraid* they will think *I'm* a salesman. *I'm afraid* they will think *I'm* a telemarketer. *I'm afraid I* will hurt *my* relationship with them, Who are you focusing on? Yourself![1]

"You are in your head, instead of in the game. In your mind, you have a program running that somehow you think the Ninja Nine is like traditional sales, and it is scaring you. You are afraid, because you are focused on yourself and your imagined fears.

"When you are in your head, you are not in the game. You are disconnected. Start focusing on your customers, and your fears will go away. Get into love and out of fear. Start asking yourself, how can I make someone's life better? How can I make them feel good? How can I help them solve a problem? Focus on *them* and your fears will go away."

---

1 The concept that says if you are afraid, you are thinking of yourself comes from *Go-Givers Sell More* by Bob Burg and John David Mann.

Chapter 30

BUILDING YOUR DATABASE

A survey[1] of twenty thousand Realtors showed that fewer than 40 percent had any kind of a database. Even scraps of paper and business cards in a shoebox counted. Yet 60 percent had nothing. The 40 percent with at least some semblance of a database earned 251 percent more income than the 60 percent without a database. Your database is your most important business asset and is the central nervous system of your business. If you don't have a database, you are not serious about this career, you are a hobbyist.

> *"Your database is your most important business asset and is the central nervous system of your business. If you don't have a database, you are not serious about this career, you are a hobbyist."*

---

1 Real estate class with Darice Johnston, author of *Efficiency by Design*.

THE THREE LAWS OF REAL ESTATE

You have probably heard that the three laws of real estate are location, location, location. Actually, location is only the first law of real estate. Here are all three:

1. **Location.** Clearly the location of a property is important. Also, real estate markets are very local, so each one is unique. Location matters.

2. **Timing.** Real estate markets are cyclical. Knowing how to surf the various market waves, or cycles, is a key skill. I've seen builders who have the right product at the right price in the right location but are at the wrong time in the market and therefore lose everything. I've also seen marginal products in marginal locations sell well at high prices because they are offered at the right time. Timing matters.

3. **Relationship.** People prefer to work with Realtors they know, like, trust, and are in the flow with; that is, they prefer to work with someone they have a relationship with. Relationship matters.

SCALABILITY

Scalability—the ability to deliver high quality at high volume—is important if you want a high level of income and to still have a life. And you really can't achieve scalability without a database.

There are on-accident Realtors who are able to create value and do a reasonably good job for their customers without one. They survive because they are only doing a few transactions a year.

But when low-volume Realtors try to grow their business without a database, they often become overwhelmed and burn out. They are trying to drive seventy miles an hour in first gear. Their health and their family start to pay the price. They need to shift. The only way to do that is by having a database and the systems to properly use it.

I often see this pattern with Realtors who are in their second or third year of the business. There are also Realtors who have been in the business a decade or more and are still on accident for the same reason. They don't have ten years in the business, they have one year in the business ten times.

These Realtors look at Ninjas who are closing fifty or a hundred transactions a year and say to themselves, "I don't want to work that hard." I have news for them. The Ninjas are working fewer hours than they are. How? By building a scalable business with Ninja systems and a database.

As you build your database you need two things:

1. **Intention.** Set a time on your calendar to get started with your initial setup and loading of names. Assemble your scraps of paper, files, business cards, Facebook contacts, committee rosters, directories, and so on. Review the "150 Ways to Build Your Database" by Walt Frey at www.NinjaSelling.com, and make a list of people who know you. If you need help with this, hire someone. Not having a database is not an option if you want to be a Ninja.

2. **Patience.** Databases are built incrementally, so be patient and relentless in your focus and commitment to start it and maintain it. We recommend you set a goal to add two to three households per week. This is an achievable goal for most people—yet it amounts to 100 to 150 people added to your database in a year. At $1,000 per name, you are adding $100,000 to $150,000 a year to your income.

THE DATABASE DIALOGUE

When Pat and I first moved to Fort Collins, we did not know a single person. My database was zero. My goal was to meet and add two to three people per week in a very incremental approach. We got involved in various organizations—United Way, chamber of commerce, church, playing on a city league basketball team, the Fort Collins Newcomers organization for people new to town, among others.

I could have simply loaded the rosters from these organizations into my database and started blasting them with my flow. Somehow, that didn't feel right to me. It seemed like I would come off as the new salesman in town. Instead, I wanted to at least start a relationship before adding flow.

So I chose to only add people I had connected with, and in most cases, they asked me if they could receive something from me (that is, be on my database). Our dialogue went like this:

- **Step 1: Introduction.** I would introduce myself and then start asking folks the FORD questions. People loved to talk about their family, occupation, recreation, and the rapport/relationship started easily.

- **Step 2: Reciprocity.** After a period of time, people would realize they were doing all of the talking, and they would start asking me the FORD questions.

- **Step 3: Offer Value.** Eventually, they would wonder what business I was in, and when I told them I was a real estate broker with The Group, they almost always asked this question: "How's the market?"

I would respond, "The market is very interesting right now. It depends on the market segment you're in. Which part of the market most interests you? Residential, commercial, a new home, investments, or a particular neighborhood?"

Often, they were interested in a specific neighborhood or even a specific home. I would answer their questions, and then, as if a lightbulb went off in my head, I would snap my fingers and say, "You know, I have something I could send you on that."

Then, I would briefly describe what that something was and ask if they would like to receive it. They almost always very enthusiastically said yes. I would get their contact information, load it into my database, and send them the information along with a personal note thanking them for the opportunity to get acquainted and looking forward to getting to know them better.

They would now go into my normal three-per-month auto-flow program. On the first several mailings, I would write them a personal note and mention, "I was thinking of you and thought you would like to see this. If for any reason you don't want to receive this information, please let me know. All the best, Larry."

I used this simple three-step process to add people to my database one at a time. It was slower, but the quality of each relationship was much stronger.

HOW'S THE MARKET?

All Realtors are asked, "How's the market?" Be careful how you respond. I frequently see Realtors make three mistakes in answering this question. Don't give these wrong answers:

- **Mistake 1.** "I'm so busy right now." Realtors love to talk about themselves, and customers get bored hearing how busy they are. More importantly, if the customer is asking this question because they are interested in buying or selling, they are going to think, *I guess this Realtor is too busy to work with me.*

- **Mistake 2.** "There's no inventory." If the customer is asking this question because they want to buy, they are going to imagine, *I guess I missed it. There's no inventory left.*

Sadly, I watched a Realtor offer the "there's no inventory" answer to someone at a party. I heard the Realtor ramble on about being busy, how there was no inventory, how many multiple offers there had been, blah, blah, blah. The conversation was all about the Realtor, who was dominating time of possession.

Later, at the same party, I followed up with the person who had asked about the market, posing my favorite question: "Which part of the market are you interested in?"

He responded, "The upper end. Generally homes over $1 million." Interestingly, that market segment was very slow, with abundant inventory. In fact, there was a twenty-seven-month supply of homes. It was an upper-end buyer's dream market. The lesson: Stop talking. Ninjas ask good questions and listen.

- **Mistake 3.** "There's no market." Fact: 11 to 14 percent of all US households move each year. There is always some market somewhere. Your mission is to find it.

FINDING AND ADDING CONTACTS

In addition to organizations, here are five other great ways to find and meet people. Use the three-step database dialogue to build rapport and add them to your database.

1. Meetings, Events, and Parties

Get there early. Most of the networking occurs *before* the meeting starts. Make sure you meet the people sitting at your table. Ask the FORD questions and listen.

2. Working the Room

Be serious about meeting and connecting with people. The best places to stand where you will be in the flow with the most people are the entrance, bar, food table, name tag table, and kitchen (if in a private home). Avoid the temptation to just hang out with your closest friends—especially if they are other Realtors. Make it a point to meet new people and to reinforce your relationship with others. Be in flow!

3. Name Tag Table

Have you ever gone to an event where they have the name tag table at the entrance? Instead of just looking for your own tag, take a few moments to browse the names and see who is going to attend this event. Who do you know that you want to make sure and connect with at this event?

Mel C. was named the new president of one of Fort Collins's largest employers. I saw the story and his picture in the newspaper and made a mental note to meet him. A few weeks later, at a Chamber of Commerce event, I noticed Mel's name at the name tag table. I told myself, "I'm going to meet Mel C. tonight!" And I did. I stood by the entrance and waited for him. (I guess some might say I was stalking.) I recognized him immediately from the photo.

Once he had his name tag and was looking around the room, I went up and introduced myself: "Hello Mel. Welcome to Fort Collins. My name is Larry Kendall. I recognized you from the article in the paper. Congratulations on being named president of your company." I then asked him the FORD questions, a rapport was established, and our relationship was launched. The simple act of intentionally meeting him started a twenty-five-year friendship.

4. Open Houses

Your open-house strategy is like the rest of your Ninja strategies: Offer something of value. We have found open-house buyers love market information—statistics, maps, and sold data, among others. Have this kind of information available to them (on the kitchen counter or table) as they come through your open house. When you see someone eagerly looking through the material, ask, "Would you like me to send you this information? We update it every quarter." Most of the time, you won't even have to ask them. They will ask you!

Jessica Tate is a young rookie in our company. She typically holds one open house a week and uses our company newsletter, which is packed with market information, as her item of value. Virtually every open-house visitor asked her if they could receive it monthly. Jessica added 102 people to her database in her first sixty days in the business. She did twenty-one transactions her first year in real estate—a great career start for a young single mom beginning her career with a small database.

5. Social Media

People voluntarily share their FORD information, as well as their pain and pleasure, on their social media pages. Rather than using social media as a marketing channel to push out their flow, smart Ninjas spend most of their time *pulling* FORD information from social media. Ninjas then follow-up by phone, text, or personal note rather than on social media. Why? Because it differentiates you from the two hundred "friends" who respond on Facebook.

Josh is a twenty-four-year-old from Michigan who showed up in our Ninja Installation class in Colorado. There is a point in the class where we give students the opportunity to practice their Ninja Nine—specifically, Success Habit 6: Customer Service Calls. We give them thirty minutes to make telephone calls using the five-step calling process. We encourage them to use the eight calls that create value, mentioned in Chapter 28.

Josh came up to me and said, "Mr. Kendall, I'm brand new in the business. I just got my real estate license three days before I got on the plane to come out here. I don't have any customers to call. In fact, I don't even have a database. How am I supposed to do this exercise?"

I said, "Josh, do you have Facebook?"

Josh said, "Sure."

"Then you have a database," I said. "Here's what I want you to do. I want you to go back to your seat and start looking through your Facebook contacts. I want you to look for pain and pleasure. Whenever you see a person posting about pain and pleasure, jot it down on your notepad. Then, I want you to physically call the person and talk to them. Do not respond on Facebook. I want you to call them on the phone using the five-step calling process. Can you do that?"

"Of course, that will be easy," Josh said. He headed back to his seat with a sense of mission and focus. Later, I saw him making calls with a big smile on his face.

Within twenty minutes, Josh came up to me and said, "Mr. Kendall, this stuff works! I just got my first buyer appointment!"

Josh noticed a friend was about to have a birthday and called to wish him happy birthday. When the friend asked Josh what he was up to, Josh responded that he was in Colorado taking a real estate sales course. His friend said, "Josh, I didn't know you were getting into real estate. When you get back to Michigan, can we get together and look at houses?"

Three days in real estate, and Josh had his first buyer appointment using Facebook and the five-step calling process.

Chapter 31

FORMATTING AND USING YOUR DATABASE

Your database is the central nervous system of your business. You can't run your Ninja systems without it. With so many database products available, how do you choose the right one for you? Here are a few criteria we recommend:

- **Digital and mobile.** Today you really need an electronic database that works with your smartphone. The old-fashioned 3-by-5-inch card file, rolodex, or notebook systems are antiquated in today's digital environment (but are better than nothing).

- **Calendar.** Your database needs to sync with your calendar. This is a very important feature. Part of your Ninja system will be to load important dates into your calendar, so you will automatically be reminded to contact your friends and customers. It is this calendar feature that helps turn your basic database into a customer relationship management (CRM) tool.

    Many new Realtors often show up with their database in an Excel spreadsheet. This is a great start. At least they have a database. But Excel is not mobile friendly, and it doesn't have a calendar. Fortunately, we can export Excel into mobile-friendly databases that do have a calendar.

- **Simpler is better.** I find that if the system is too complicated to set up, load, and use, most Realtors won't maintain it. Keep it simple.

- **Relational?** You will have to make this decision depending on how important simplicity is to you. Relational databases are more powerful, but unfortunately, they are also more complicated.

A relational database gives you the ability to search for names that have similar attributes. For example, you could ask your database to give you a list of everyone who has children under a certain age. If you want to sponsor a family day at a local movie theater with the latest Disney movie, this would be a valuable feature to have. Another example would be to ask your database for a list of people who own a specific type of property, because you have a buyer looking for that.

A simple database that is popular with many Realtors is Outlook. It is easy to set up, load, and use. It syncs with their phone and calendar. Unfortunately, it is not relational.

FORMATTING YOUR DATABASE

A very simple way to organize your database with your client's information is to use the following six categories:

1. **Contact Information.** Include addresses (home and work), phone numbers, email addresses, Facebook.
2. **Family.** Include his name, her name, kids' names, pets' names, birthdays, anniversaries, and so on.
3. **Occupation.** Include where he/she works, titles, responsibilities, longevity, company information.
4. **Recreation.** Include favorite hobbies, sports teams, restaurants, vacation spots, wine preferences, and so on.

5. **Dreams.** Include any goals they have shared—kids attending college, house on water, ten rental houses by age forty, for example.

6. **Real Estate.** Include detailed information on their real estate holdings.

If you are using a simple database such as Outlook, the FORD and Real Estate categories can be organized in the notes section.

CATEGORIZING YOUR DATABASE

You categorize your database both by relationship status and their urgency to buy or sell.

Relationship Status

A

Your *As* are your advocates. They are your raving fans. They proactively refer you. At a party, if they hear someone from across the room mention buying or selling real estate, your *As* will make it a point to go across the room, find that person, and refer them to you.

Flow Frequency: *As* receive the three auto-flow items each month plus phone calls, cards, gifts, and invitations to events. Their flow averages one contact per week (fifty a year). Spend most of your time and your money on your *As*.

B

Your *Bs* are your fans. They will refer you if asked but are not as proactive as your *As*.

Flow Frequency: *Bs* receive the three auto-flow items each month, plus a fair amount of your attention with cards, phone calls, and the occasional gift of a bottle of wine, gift certificate, or tickets to an event. Their flow averages forty to fifty a year.

C

Your *C*s know you, like you, trust you, and will do business with you if you stay in flow with them. For whatever reason, their RAS is not engaged enough to refer you. However, they will work with you when they are ready to buy or sell. They tend to be the largest group in your database and can easily slip away to the other eleven Realtors they know if you don't have a good flow system with them.

Flow Frequency: *C*s receive the three auto-flow items each month plus a live interaction (face-to-face or on the phone) once a quarter.

D

Your *D*s are the people you want to meet and develop a relationship with. For example, Mel C. was on my *D* list. After I met him, he became a *C* and, ultimately, an *A*, one of my greatest advocates. People move from *D* to *A* based on flow. Frequency of interaction and the creation of value build a relationship.

Flow Frequency: After the initial contact, put *D*s on an 8 in 8 program with the seventh contact being a phone call and the eighth a face-to-face meeting for coffee, lunch, or breakfast. They have now moved up to *C* status—with the *C* flow frequency, until they move up to a *B* and later, hopefully *A*.

Urgency

- **Hot List.** This list is comprised of people who want to buy or sell, know they want to buy or sell, want to buy or sell with you, and want to buy or sell soon—within the next three months.

- **Warm List.** These are people who want to buy or sell but may not know they want to buy or sell. However, you know they want to buy or sell because you are observing their current life changes. They probably will want to buy or sell within the next year.

Again, we recommend you carry a hard copy of your hot and warm lists with you (use your Business Tracker) and focus on them daily.

Load your electronic calendar with the important dates in the lives of your friends and customers (birthdays, anniversaries, and contract dates). You want these dates to pop up automatically as a reminder to you. Then you can call or write them a note.

FIFTEEN POST-CLOSING CONTACTS

Customer surveys show that hearing from their Realtor live after closing is a top priority for real estate buyers. They have come to expect this kind of follow-up, because they experience it in other areas of their life—for example, after car service or a doctor's appointment. They expect that after purchasing a product worth hundreds of thousands (or millions) of dollars that their Realtor will at least make a phone call after closing to make sure everything is OK. As we learned earlier, only 18 percent of them do. Why? They are out hunting and gathering their next customer, instead of taking care of their current customer and building a relationship.

Most Realtors have the best of intentions to follow-up after closing, but they don't have a system to help them stay on track. The best system I've ever seen was developed by Wynn Washle of The Group, Inc. He calls it *Fifteen Post-Closing Contacts*. Wynn personally contacts his customers fifteen times in the first year after closing. Here is his list:

1. Two-day follow-up. (Are there any surprises or unmet expectations in the house?)

2. Two-week follow-up. (Are they starting to get unpacked/getting pictures up on the walls?)

3. One-month follow-up. (Have they met their neighbors yet?)

4. Three-month follow-up. (How is the home working out?)

5. Six-month follow-up. (This becomes an annual call.)
6. Anniversary of closing. (This becomes an annual call.)
7. Her birthday. (Call to remind *him* three days prior to her birthday.)
8. Her birthday. (Call to wish her happy birthday.)
9. His birthday. (Call to remind *her* three days prior to his birthday.)
10. His birthday. (Call to wish him happy birthday.)
11. Wedding anniversary. (Call to remind *him* three days prior to the anniversary.)
12. Wedding anniversary. (Call to wish her happy wedding anniversary.)
13. Children's birthdays. (Mail a birthday card to each child on his or her birthday, along with a note and gift certificate to a local ice cream shop.)
14. Tickets. (Call to give away tickets to sporting events, plays, and upcoming activities.)
15. Home visit. (Call three to five months after closing to set up a home visit.)

Wynn loads these reminders into his calendar, and they automatically pop-up, letting him know what he needs to do that day or week. He has a system. Is it any wonder that he is one of the top Realtors in the nation?

Wynn also has the highest income per hour of anyone I know. He consistently cranks fifty to seventy-five transactions a year with just himself and a part-time assistant, works very few nights and weekends, and takes nine to twelve weeks a year off. What's his secret? Flow! His flow system delivers him an abundance of buyers and sellers. In fact, Wynn has overflow. With more than he can handle, he takes those customers who are ready to buy and are willing to work with him on his schedule. He refers the rest to other Realtors and takes a referral fee. Most of his customers are willing to fit into Wynn's schedule, because his customer service is off the chart. He's a Ninja! Follow Wynn's simple system, and you will be as well.

What happens if, on the very first call (where Wynn asks if there are any surprises or unmet expectations with the house), the buyer says there is a problem with some small item? Say the dishwasher doesn't work or one of the garage door openers is missing. Wynn's response: "I'll take care of it for you" (at his expense). If it is a larger item, say water in the basement, Wynn says, "I'll be right over to help you figure out what we need to do." Wynn is totally committed to customer satisfaction, and it shows in his repeat and referral business.

How does Wynn get the information for his post-closing calls? He simply asks for it, either at the closing or sometime during the buying or selling process using a simple form called *Fun Facts*.

FUN FACTS

Names: _____

Birthdates: _____

Children: _____

Children's Birthdates: _____

Wedding Anniversary: _____

Email: _____

Favorite Local Restaurant: _____

Favorite Sport Team: _____

YOUR FILE VERSUS YOUR DATABASE

Language is important. When you are updating your database and you are visiting with your friends and customers, never use the word *database*. Nobody wants to be in a database. Instead say, "John, I was just updating your file and wanted to make sure I had Heather's (their daughter's) birthday."

Chapter 32

THE POWER OF PIE TIME

The goal of Ninja Selling is to help you increase your income per hour, so you can have a life. To do this, you must focus your time and your energy on the vital few—those activities that give you the biggest return for your investment. How do we help you do that specifically?

Have you ever tracked your time to see how you're investing it? Notice that I say invest, not spend. One of the best systems for doing this was developed by Ninja master instructor Walt Frey. Here's how it works.

THREE CATEGORIES OF TIME

P Time—Productive Time

There are three ingredients to P time—you, a customer, and a contract or strong potential for a contract. Here are some examples of P time:

- You are sitting in a listing appointment with a seller.
- You are presenting a contract to a seller.
- You have a qualified, motivated buyer in the car, and you are showing houses.
- You are negotiating a contract between a buyer and a seller.

What *does not* count as P time is preparing for the listing appointment or setting up showings on the houses you will see with a buyer.

These are important activities, but they technically don't count as P time, because the customer is not with you.

I Time—Indirectly Productive Time

I time is what creates P time. Another word for I time is flow time. This is the time invested in—

- Making your customer service calls and your fifteen post-closing calls
- Real estate reviews
- Fifty live interviews
- Personal notes
- Running your three-per-month auto-flow system

Basically, I time is the time you invest each week in your Ninja Nine activities and that generates P time.

Here's a secret: If you want to increase P time, you have to increase your I time. You cannot control P time. You can only control what controls it, which is I time. If you want more time with customers in a contract situation, increase your I time, That is, increase your flow time.

E Time—Everything Else

Here's a simple way to look at your time. Generally P and I time require a real estate license. E time can generally be handled by an assistant. It is not unusual to find Ninjas earning several thousand dollars an hour when they are in P time. They can hire someone to do the E time for a lot less.

For the next thirty days, fill out the simple time log at the end of this chapter. It is easy to do: At the end of each day, simply record your total hours worked that day and how much of it was P or I time. After about thirty days, you'll start to see a pattern and be able to correlate your P and I times: The more I time you have, the more P time you will have.

You will also probably notice that a tremendous amount of your time is going into E time. Some of that is critical, such as sleep, family time, and skill development (training), but notice how much seems to be wasted. This is an opportunity. When you shift more of your E time into I time, you'll see your income rise.

Here are some ways to do this:

- **Whenever possible, blend your daily activities into I time.** Remember how Mike Malvey converted E time at the soccer games into I time by simply getting to know the parents and asking them the FORD questions? Mike was able to blend his kids' soccer game with generating I time in his business. Remember the Missouri Mom? She was a master of this.
- **Increase Your I Time by Scheduling and Doing Your Daily and Weekly Ninja Nine Activities.** You will see an increase in your business within forty-five days.
- **Hire Someone to Help You with Your E Time.** You can delegate much of your real estate E time.

There's another advantage besides raising your income, and that is increasing the harmony in your life. One of the biggest "ahas!" for Mike Malvey was discovering that he no longer felt that his life was an impossible either/or choice. By following the Ninja Way, he found harmony. Life and business were fun again. As Lawrence Pearsall Jacks wrote: "People who are masters in the art of living make little distinction between their work and their play, their labor and their leisure, their mind and their body, their information and their recreation, their love and their religion. . . . They simply pursue their vision of excellence at whatever they do, leaving others to decide whether they are working or playing. To them they are always doing both. Enough for him that he does it well."

CHASING THE TEAM IN WHITE

In our Ninja Installation class, we show a short, one-minute video of two basketball teams. One team is dressed in black and the other team is dressed in white. The commentator in the video says, "How many passes does the team in white make?" The two teams start passing their balls, and your eyes are fixed on the team in white, as you count their passes.

At the end, the commentator says, "The answer is thirteen." At that point, the students in the class cheer, because they got the right answer. Then the commentator asks, "But did you see the moonwalking bear?" The video rewinds, and this time, right in the middle of the two teams passing their balls, you see someone in a bear costume doing the moonwalk.

I then ask the students, "How many of you saw the moonwalking bear the first time?" Few or none of the students raise their hands. "How many of you saw him the second time?" I ask. Virtually every hand flies up.

"Why didn't you see him the first time?" I ask.

They respond that they were focused on the team in white and counting the passes. "Why did you see him the second time?" I ask.

"Well, we were told to look for him. Once we focused on him, we saw him."

My point is the power of the RAS and how what we focus on expands. Then I ask, "What does the moonwalking bear represent?"

The answers range from "opportunity" to "the contract that wants to be written" to "what's important" to "the vital few."

And what does the team in white represent? Typically, the answers are "distractions," "the daily swirl of our lives," "meetings," "email," and "Facebook."

Basically, the moonwalking bear is P and I time—these are the vital few. The team in white is E time.

What do Wynn Washle, Tami Spaulding, Jon Holsten, and top-performing Ninjas have in common? They focus more of their attention and their time on the moonwalking bear (P and I time) and invest limited time chasing the team in white (E time).

Unfortunately, many Realtors, when given the chance, will chase the team in white every time. They are very easily distracted and invest their time in unproductive activities, often without realizing it. They come home exhausted at the end of the day, thinking they have worked hard in meetings, on their email, and so on, but they were really just chasing the team in white. Keep the thirty-day PIE log, and you will discover how you are investing your life.

Here's an example of Ninja, Paul Schnaitter's PIE analysis for March. Note that Paul earned $75, 675 for the month working 40.88 hours per week.

His "P" time was worth $2,609 per hour.

He needs 1.97 hours of "I" to generate 1.0 hour of "P" time.

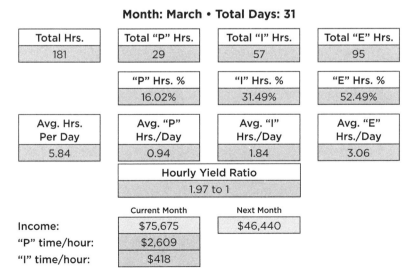

For PIE Time Tracker, go to www.NinjaSelling.com/Resources

PIE Time Log

P time = Three ingredients: you, a customer, a contract.
I time = Time you invest creating P time. Flow activities.
E time = Everything else.

Gather your data at the end of EACH day . . . enter it in this format:

Date	Total Hours Worked	"I" Hours	"P" Hours
Totals:			

Principle 4

CONNECT AND COMMUNICATE

Principle 4 is where it all begins to come together. Here's where you put your mind-set and skill set into action to help customers make good decisions. We will start with the science of the customer, learning about their personalities, how they think, how they make decisions, and what they value. Ninja Selling's research into the science of the customer is one of our unique principles.

In this section, you'll learn the Four-Step Ninja Consultation, and in the appendices, you will be able to apply your skills with the Ten-Step Buyer Process and the Sixteen-Step Seller Process. These processes are scientifically organized to help your customers make good decisions and deliver predictable results for you.

Chapter 33

THE PLATINUM RULE AND PERSONALITIES

Have you heard of the Golden Rule? Treat others the way you want to be treated. It's a pretty good philosophy for business and for life. Ninjas go a step further and practice the Platinum Rule: Treat others the way *they* want to be treated. Fit into *their* personality, *their* decision strategy, *their* learning modality, and *their* preferred communication style—not your own. It's not about you. It's about them.

WORKING WITH DIFFERENT PERSONALITIES

Customers come in all shapes and sizes. They each are unique. In order to connect with them and treat them the way they want to be treated, you will need to understand their personalities. The Ninja System uses the four basic personality types identified in the DISC personality profile assessment (discprofile.com).

> *" In order to connect with customers and treat them the way they want to be treated, you will need to understand their personalities. "*

We have found that many salespeople cannot remember what the DISC stands for, so we prefer to use the definitions provided by Chris Helder in his excellent book, *Stop Selling, The Art of Reading the Client and Winning the Business*. Chris Helder is, in my opinion, one of the top speaker/trainers in the United States and Australia, and a personal friend. I shared the FORD questions with Chris, and he shared Power, Party, Peace, and Perfection People with me. They are categorized as follows:

Power People (15 percent to 20 percent of the US population)

- **Time Frame.** They are focused on the future. How fast can they get to the future? Can you help them get to the future, or are you in their way?
- **Motivator.** They are motivated by their goals. They have a sense of urgency about them, and that urgency is to get to their goals in the future.
- **Focus.** They are task and bottom-line oriented.
- **Energy.** They are outgoing and energetic.
- **Decision Speed.** They are fast decision-makers. They need just a few pieces of key data, and they make a decision. They will not give you much time unless they are doing the talking. When you talk, they get restless.
- **Decision Strategy.** They are risk takers. They make decisions to move toward what they want and are willing to take risks to get there. They focus on winning.
- **Your Materials.** They won't take the time to read your materials other than perhaps an executive summary. They want the highlights, and they want them quick. They look at charts and graphs. They want to get the big ideas in a hurry, make a decision, and move on.

- **Recognizing Them.** They tend to talk fast and move fast. They are often fidgety. They write short, cryptic emails and have a take-charge attitude. Often, they walk with a forward lean, as if they can't wait to get to the future. Their cars are big and fast, preferably in black or white, because their world is black or white.
- **Careers.** They are usually CEOs, entrepreneurs, and sometimes salespeople.

Party People (25 percent to 30 percent of the US population)

- **Time Frame.** They focus on the present. They are very much in the now.
- **Motivator.** Having fun is important to them. Will you be fun to work with? Will this be a fun process? They like recognition and dislike being ignored.
- **Focus.** They focus on others and are team players.
- **Energy.** They are outgoing and optimistic.
- **Decision Speed.** They are impulsive and make fast decisions. As a result, they often have buyer's remorse and change their minds.
- **Decision Strategy.** They are risk takers. They are *go-for-it* people who will take a chance. They focus on winning.
- **Your Materials.** They like color, photos, and anything fun or whimsical. They will look at your testimonials to see if there is anybody they know.
- **Recognizing Them.** They like fashion, dressing up, and parties. They are talkative, positive, and fun to be with. Relationships are important to them. They like to talk on the phone

and face-to-face versus email, although they like Facebook. They like any car that is fun.
- **Careers.** They are usually salespeople or people in the hospitality and entertainment industries.

Peace People (35 percent to 40 percent of the US population)

- **Time Frame.** They focus on the past and present. They like the status quo, keeping things the way they are. They don't like upset or change.
- **Motivator.** Peace is their motivator. They dislike conflict, drama, or change and just want everybody to get along.
- **Focus.** They focus on others and are team players.
- **Energy.** They are reserved, patient, and empathetic.
- **Decision Speed.** They make decisions very slowly. Your normal one-hour listing consultation might take several hours (or even several days) with them. They will not make a decision until they get comfortable with trust. Do they trust you? Do they trust the process? Do they trust themselves?
- **Your Materials.** Do you have a process? They like process. They don't want to be your science project. Testimonials from people they trust are huge for them.
- **Decision Strategy.** They are risk avoiders. They move away from what they don't want and focus on not losing.
- **Recognizing Them.** They are soft spoken, write lengthy emails, and have lengthy conversations. Relationships are important. They wear conservative and/or relaxed clothes. They drive Subarus, minivans, and other practical cars.

- **Careers.** Their careers are in helping professions, such as nurses, schoolteachers, or therapists.

Perfection People (15 percent to 20 percent of the US population)

- **Time Frame.** They are focused on the past. They ask a lot of questions about the past—market statistics, your sales statistics. They want data and believe data from the past will help them make a good decision about the future.
- **Motivator.** They are motivated by perfection and data.
- **Focus.** They are task oriented and have high standards. They like to be in control and enjoy working alone.
- **Energy.** They are reserved, thoughtful, and can be perceived as pessimistic.
- **Decision Speed.** They make decisions very slowly. They may have to build a spreadsheet. They request so much data that they can sometimes become overwhelmed and suffer paralysis analysis.
- **Your Materials.** They will read everything you give them and correct any spelling or grammatical errors. They will recalculate your charts and graphs to see if there are mistakes. They will ask for more data. You can't give them enough.
- **Decision Strategy.** They are risk avoiders.
- **Recognizing Them.** They are very methodical and ask for a lot of data. Their personal attire, home, and car are immaculate. A place for everything and everything in its place—unless they have a bit of Power Person in them and they take on too many tasks, in which case, they have piles of unfinished projects. Their emails are perfect, with no misspellings or errors.

- **Careers.** They are accountants, bankers, engineers, and some are doctors.

Can a person have multiple personalities or traits from all of them? Absolutely. But most tend to have a single personality trait that is stronger and dominates the others. They can also have different personalities in their different roles. For example, they can be a Party Person at home with the kids and a Power Person at work.

The following chart from Ninja instructor John Brewer summarizes the four personalities.

Four Personalities

```
              OUTGOING
                 ↑
          Power  |  Party
TASK  ←----------+----------→  PEOPLE
       Perfection | Peace
                 ↓
             RESERVED
```

In our Ninja workshops, we invite our students to stand up, and we ask them several questions to determine if they are outgoing or more reserved. The outgoing people are invited to come to the front of the room, the more reserved to the back. If they are unsure where to go, they are reserved. Outgoing people clearly know it, and some of them even start heading to the front before I finish my instructions.

Once they have sorted themselves into these two groups, we ask them a series of questions to determine if their priorities are tasks or people, and we separate them again based on their answers. So they end up in four groups, as shown on the chart. Interestingly, the size of each group generally fits the national averages: Power (15–20 percent); Party (25–30 percent); Peace (35–40 percent); and Perfection (15–20 percent).

Here's where it gets interesting: We ask, "If you could choose to be with one of the other groups, point at your favorite choice." Nearly everyone will point to the group next to them: Power People point at Party or Perfection, Peace People point at Party or Perfection, and so on. What this points out is that the majority of us are most comfortable with the personalities most like our own.

Only a few people will point diagonally across the room, and they have an advantage in communication. For most of us, the biggest challenge will be communicating with a person who has a diagonally opposed personality—Power and Peace, Party and Perfection.

Power People are quick decision makers and get impatient with Peace People who like to take their time. Power People need to slow it down and Peace People need to speed it up when working with each other.

Perfection People are detail oriented and need to "mellow out" when working with Party People who are more interested in relationships. Likewise, Party People need to be more focused on data and details when working with a Perfection customer. If your customer is the diagonal opposite of you, adjust to their personality and practice *the platinum rule.*

Chapter 34

DECISION STRATEGIES

Customers have two basic decision strategies: *toward* and *from*. Think of two tennis players in a match. One player is on the offense, trying to overpower the other and taking risks to try and win the match. This player has a toward strategy. The other player is more conservative, tends to play defense, and is a risk avoider who focuses on not making mistakes (not losing). Either strategy can work.

When it comes to real estate, it helps if you know how your customers make decisions. Here's an example of how your questions will change, based upon your customer's decision strategy: You are showing a home, and your customer gives you strong buying signals. They go through the home more than once, they sit down in the home, and they start mentally moving into it. At this point, you feel it is appropriate to ask a soft closing question, "Can you see yourself living in this home?" They answer, "Yes." You go a step further and ask, "Can you see yourself owning this home?" They answer, "Absolutely." Now, here is where your next question will vary depending on the customer's personality and decision strategy:

- Power and Party People (risk takers—toward strategy): "Shall we see if you can buy this property?"

- Peace and Perfection People (risk avoiders—from strategy): "Shall we make sure you don't lose this property?"

EXTERNAL AND INTERNAL DIALOGUES

All of us have both external and internal dialogues: what we say to others versus what we say to ourselves. Throughout the sales process, customers are talking to us (external dialogues) and, at the same time, talking to themselves (internal dialogues).

Have you ever had a buyer say, "We want to think about it"? That is their external dialogue. Wouldn't it be great if we knew what they just said to themselves (their internal dialogue)?

In our experience, whenever buyers say they want to "think about it," it is usually because they are either confused or they are afraid. They don't want to say they are confused or afraid, so they will just say they are going to *think about it*.

Part of the Ninja Selling process is to help customers become clear and confident. When they are clear and confident, they are ready to commit.

You may wonder why we ask a particular question or why we ask it at a certain time or in a certain order. These questions and processes are designed to speak to the customer's internal dialogue—to start a movie in their mind.

> "*Part of the Ninja Selling process is to help customers become clear and confident.*"

Chapter 35

THE POWER OF PRETEND

One way to access a customer's internal dialogue and to help them become clear is through the use of "pretend states," where we put the customer in a make-believe frame of mind. The reason many customers are afraid to tell you what they are really thinking is because they are afraid of making a mistake or giving the wrong answer. This comes from our schooling, where we always wanted to have the right answer.

A state of pretend is a kind of game where the answers don't really count. Customers then feel more confident to open up about how they really feel. One of the favorite ways Ninjas put their customers in a pretend state is to ask them to wave their magic wand. It sounds like this: "Just for fun, if you could wave a magic wand and have this sale go perfectly for you, what would that look like?" Now, the seller opens up and starts dreaming about a perfect sale and what is most important to them.

Sometimes, their answer is buried in their nonconscious. Through the magic wand exercise, and what we call an "aha!" experience, they discover clarity.

"I LOVE MY HOUSE!"

Here's an example of the power of pretend states: Pat and I had just finished a bicycle ride and were sitting on our deck having brunch. It was a beautiful Colorado morning with a clear blue sky, and our flowers were in full bloom. We were enjoying the setting, when Pat said, "I just love this house."

I acknowledged her and said, "I love this house too."

Then she emphatically went on, "I *really* love this house!"

I always pay attention when somebody repeats a comment. Obviously, it is important to them, and I'm curious about what is driving the comment. What is their internal dialogue? What was Pat really thinking? We had lived in this house twenty-three years, had raised two kids in it, and our son was graduating high school in a few weeks. We would be empty nesters, and this house was a perfect empty-nester home—main floor master suite, and so on. Was she thinking she wanted to stay here permanently? What was her internal dialogue? I decided to probe.

Larry: "Are you saying you love this house enough that you want to stay here after Matt graduates?"

Pat (rather noncommittally): "Probably."

Larry: "Then, are you thinking this is our forever house, our terminal house, our final resting place?"

Pat: "Well, I wouldn't go that far. I think we have at least one more house in us."

Larry: "Really? Where would that be?"

Pat (disinterestedly): "Oh, I don't know."

Larry (putting her in a pretend state): "Well, if you could wave a magic wand and live anywhere, where would that be?"

Pat (after thinking a bit): "It would be Fort Collins. Definitely Fort Collins."

Larry: "Why Fort Collins?"

Pat: "Our friends are here, our kids are here, our properties are here, and I like living here."

Larry: "Great! Got it. Fort Collins. Where in Fort Collins?"

Pat: "Well, I like running around Warren Lake every morning, so I would like to stay in the Warren Lake area."

Larry: "Got it. Fort Collins. Warren Lake area. Pat, we live in the Warren Lake area. We've lived here twenty-three years. You say you love your house here in the Warren Lake area. Are you saying this is where you want to live?"

Pat: "Well, if I could live anywhere, I would want to live on the lake."

(We lived two blocks off the lake.)

Larry: "Where on the lake?"

Pat: "If I could live anywhere, I would want to live on the east side of the lake, so I could look across the lake at the mountains."

(Now she is really into it!)

Larry (summarizing): "OK. Fort Collins. Warren Lake. East side. That's Harbor Walk Lane. There are only fourteen houses there. Which house?"

Pat: "I don't know. Let's go over there and look!"

(She starts sliding back from the table to go.)

Larry (laughing): "Can we finish brunch first? We can look at them tomorrow when we run around the lake."

Isn't it interesting that five minutes earlier, Pat was saying, "I *really* love my house." And then suddenly, she was ready to jump up from brunch and go look at houses? What happened? The "magic wand" question opened up her nonconscious to possibilities that she got excited about.

The next morning, we were running around Warren Lake and heading down Harbor Walk Lane. Pat was checking out each of the fourteen houses and making a list of her three favorites. Two weeks later, Bobbie Cook, a partner of mine at The Group, Inc., called and said, "Larry, I'm listing a house on Harbor Walk Lane and thought you might be interested in it."

I'm sure I was on Bobbie's warm list.

"What's the address?" I asked. When Bobbie told me, I said, "Uh oh, that's one of Pat's three favorites." And, yes, we are living in that home today!

Would we have bought that home anyway? I doubt it. The combination of a pretend state opening Pat's mind to the possibilities and Bobbie having us on her warm list were the keys.

Chapter 36

GIVING PERMISSION

Sometimes, customers just need permission to make a decision they really want to make but, for whatever reason, are afraid of making. Again, it gets back to clarity and confidence. The psychologist Georgi Lozanov, author of *Suggestology* and *Outlines of Suggestopedia*, points out that people are very open to suggestion. Your suggestions speak to their internal dialogue. Here's an example of suggesting to buyers that it is OK to buy a home that's not perfect.

THE 85 PERCENT PERFECT HOME

After the buyers have told you what they are looking for in a home and before you start looking at homes, have this dialogue:

Summarize what they are looking for in a home. Then say, "Our goal is to help you find a home that is as close to meeting these features as possible and, most importantly, finding a home you will be happy living in."

Look at them and nod. They will nod back. You have just confirmed agreement on this.

Then say, "You know, so far I've never had a customer who found the perfect home. We've been close to perfect a few times, but there is always something that isn't exactly perfect."

Share a story: "Sometimes, buyers get frustrated and feel the only way they will get a perfect home is to build it. So they buy land, get an architect and a builder, and take the time to build their dream home.

Then they invite Pat and me over for dinner. As they are taking us on a tour of their dream home, guess what they do? They pick it apart, talking about what they would do differently or how something didn't turn out as expected. Even their dream home is not perfect."

After sharing the story, say: "So, here's my recommendation. When we are out looking at homes, and you find a home you really like but it is not perfect—perhaps it's 85 percent perfect or 90 percent perfect. If you can see yourself living there and being happy, I would recommend you seriously consider it. OK?"

What just happened? First of all, you spoke the truth. There is no such thing as a perfect home. Second, you gave them permission to buy a home that's not perfect. Third, you will now hear them using this language as they look at homes. John will say, "What do you think, Mary?" And Mary will say, "I'll give it an 85." And John will say, "I was going to give it a 90."

The Ninja Selling System is designed around the science of how customers think: their internal and external dialogues; their decision strategies (toward/from); the dreams buried in their nonconscious that are accessed with your "magic wand"; and suggestions we make that they either take or leave to help them make decisions.

Chapter 37

THE NINJA CONSULTATION

Most salespeople have been taught the traditional three-step sales presentation: 1. Make a connection (build some rapport), 2. Make a presentation of features and benefits, and 3. Close. It looks like this:

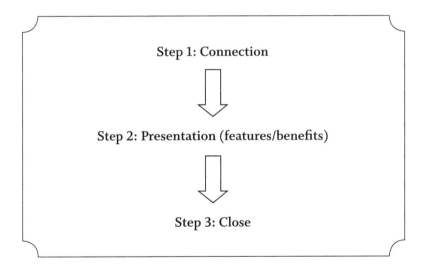

Today, most sales presentations still follow this classic three-step process. The Ninja Consultation is a four-step process. Only the first step (Connection) is the same as the traditional three-step sales presentation. Here's how the four-step process works:

STEP 1: CONNECTION

Customers want to work with someone they like and trust. They decide this in the first two minutes. Do they feel a connection with you? Do they like you, trust you, and want to go down this path with you, or do they want to escape from you?

STEP 2: INFORMATION (PAIN/PLEASURE)

This is a critical transition step. In the traditional three-step sales process, you would now be at the presentation stage, where you launch into your pitch of features and benefits. Most salespeople love this step, because they get a chance to strut their stuff. They're on stage and loving it.

There are two problems with this approach: First, you are trying to be the answer to your customers' prayers without knowing what they are praying for; and second, you have time of possession. After a few minutes, the customer stops paying attention to you, drifts off, and you lose connection. Because the traditional three-step process is so ingrained in our industry, this step is the hardest habit for us to break in Ninja Selling.

As a Ninja, instead of launching into your spiel, you start gathering information via a planned set of questions that we will teach you. These questions are designed to keep the customer connected (they have time of possession), build a platform of trust and confidence, and discover pain and pleasure (find out what they are praying for). Then, you can begin to formulate potential solutions in your mind.

STEP 3: SOLUTION (CREATE POTENTIAL SOLUTIONS)

There is science behind how customers decide that a solution is right for them. We will show you what makes it easier for them to decide. Two of the keys are for them to be clear (not confused) and confident (not afraid). The Four-Step Ninja Consultation and our series of questions help them do that.

STEP 4: PROPOSAL (CUSTOMER MAKES DECISION)

As a Ninja, you simply propose potential solutions. You don't sell. You solve. Knowing the science of how people process and store information is a key to being able to have a powerful consultation.

Once again, here's what the Four-Step Ninja Consultation Process looks like:

Step 1: Connection

Step 2: Information (pain/pleasure)

Step 3: Solution (create potential solutions)

Step 4: Proposal (customer makes decision)

THE FOUR-STEP NINJA CONSULTATION IN ACTION

Several years ago, one of my good friends and a successful developer, Chad McWhinney, called and asked if I would help him convince a commercial tenant to locate in a new regional shopping center Chad was building. The prospective tenant was a women's clothing store.

We would be meeting with the CEO of the company, and I asked Chad what I could do to help.

Chad said, "Bring all your maps and statistics. He'll want to see population counts, demographics, household incomes, and drive counts." So I packed my briefcase and showed up at Chad's office.

I remember walking into Chad's conference room and seeing this beautiful couple, who looked like they had just stepped off the cover of a magazine. The executive—I'll call him *Mr. CEO*—was tall, handsome, with dark hair, and all dressed in black. His vice president was a woman who looked like a supermodel—perfect makeup, hair, clothes, and jewelry. These two had just flown in from California.

Chad did a great job warming up the conversation with the connection step. He sensed that we were connected and the timing was right to move to the next step, so he said, "I've invited Larry in, because he really knows the area. I believe when he is done with his presentation, you'll realize this area will be a great place for you to put a store."

Then Chad tossed me the ball.

The typical salesperson, using the traditional three-step process, would now launch into a presentation—out with the maps and the statistics. Start "tellin' and sellin'." But I'm a Ninja. My next step is *not* presentation; it is information. Here's what happened next:

Larry: "Sir, I brought quite a bit of information for us to look at, but before we go there, could I ask you a couple of questions?"

Mr. CEO: "Sure."

Larry: "If it is all right with you, I would love for you to take a few minutes and share the story of how you built this company."

Mr. CEO had been sitting back from the conference table with his legs crossed, a bit slouched, and somewhat disengaged. When I asked this question, however, he uncrossed his legs, sat up, and leaned forward. "Larry, let me tell you how it started," he said and began to recount the history of his company.

Larry: "Amazing! How many stores do you have now?"

Mr. CEO: "Hundreds of them."

Larry: "How many stores do you have in Colorado?"

Mr. CEO: "Eleven."

Larry: "What's your process for deciding where to open your stores?"

Mr. CEO: "Well, it starts with my people. They do an environmental scan. They look at population, demographics, and household incomes. If it looks good on paper, then we come out and do a site visit."

Obviously, Mr. CEO's people have already seen what is in my briefcase. If I had started with a presentation of that stuff, Mr. CEO, who was already disengaged, would have disconnected completely.

Larry: "What do you look for on a site visit?"

Mr. CEO: "We look for two things. The first thing we look for are the women."

Larry: "I bet that is fun and interesting. What are you looking for in our women?"

Ms. Vice President pulled out two sheets of paper with a line down the middle and tick marks on each side of the line.

She said, "We look for two things. Yesterday, we spent the day sitting at Austin's Restaurant in Old Town and simply watched women coming down the sidewalk. Each woman was rated on two criteria: 1) Can that woman wear our clothes—yes or no? and 2) By looking at the way that woman is dressed, does it look like she would spend the money for our clothes—yes or no?"

The two sheets of paper with the tick marks for yes and no told the story.

Larry: "And what is your opinion of our women so far?"

Mr. CEO: "We love your women!"

Both Mr. CEO and his vice president smile broadly. We have obviously found a point of pleasure.

Larry: "Is there any particular group of women that prefers your clothes?"

Ms. Vice President: "Yes. Our stores do very well with Asian and Hispanic women."

Larry: "Are you aware that Greeley, Colorado, is 35 percent Hispanic?" I pulled out the demographic profile for Greeley and showed the statistics. This was the only paper I pulled out of my briefcase. Mr. CEO's people must have missed this fact, because he snatched the paper out of my hand and circled the Hispanic population numbers.

Mr. CEO: "How far is Greeley from this store?"

Larry: "About fifteen to twenty minutes."

Mr. CEO wrote "fifteen to twenty minutes" on the demographic profile, underlined it, and added three exclamation points. We obviously had found another point of pleasure. At this point, it was looking really good for us, but I remembered something else Mr. CEO had said.

Larry: "You mentioned you look for two things on your site visits. One is the women. What is the other thing?"

Mr. CEO: "We look for cows."

Larry: "Cows?"

Mr. CEO: "Yeah, cows. If we see a lot of cows, we know the area is too rural. There's not enough population to support our stores or the population is too spread out. Our stores have not done well in rural areas. And, Larry, when we drove up here from the airport, we saw a lot of cows."

At this point, Mr. CEO leaned back from the table, crossed his legs, and folded his arms. He was no longer smiling. I believed Mr. CEO had made up his mind. He loved our women (pleasure) but hated our cows (pain). It seemed pretty clear he was not putting a store in the area. I had to handle the cows for us to stand a chance.

Larry: "When you drove up from the airport, did you take E-470? It's a toll road."

Ms. Vice President: "Yes, that's the one. The toll road."

Larry: "You know that is a fairly new road. They built it out in the middle of nowhere. That's why you saw all those cows. Would you do me a favor and go back to the airport by a different route? Take I-25 to Denver and then I-70 over to the airport. Going that way, I believe you will see we are much more connected to the Denver metro area, and I don't think you'll see as many cows."

Mr. CEO: "You're on! We'll go that way and see what happens."

They drove to the airport by the route I'd suggested and didn't see the terrible cows. He put a store in the shopping center, and it was his top store in Colorado in sales per square foot its first year. Simply suggesting a different route was the solution.

Would Mr. CEO have put a store in the shopping center if I had used the traditional three-step sales process? I don't think so. It was the Four-Step Ninja Consultation that worked. Notice that I was asking rather than telling. Mr. CEO had time of possession and loved it. Notice how I discovered his process for opening a store as well as his pain and pleasure. As a result, I knew what to do to offer him a solution. My goal was to solve not sell.

And our entire conversation took less than ten minutes (perfect timing for a power person like Mr. CEO).

> **" *In Ninja Selling, you control the process, and your customer controls the decisions.* "**

PROCESS AND DECISIONS

In Ninja Selling, you control the process, and your customer controls the decisions. It is their decision. Don't try to talk (sell) them into something they don't want. Simply have a process that helps them clarify their pain and pleasure and their potential solutions.

For you to control the process, of course, you need to have one! Unfortunately, most Realtors don't have a process. They wing it. They are on-accident and get on-accident results. They often try to make up for this lack of process by being a stronger closer. Yet the stronger they close, the more it feels like they are trying to make the decision for the customer. This kind of pressure usually backfires, as the customer starts to distance.

Ninjas use the soft Ninja Four-Step Consultation as the framework for their Ten-Step Buyer Process and Sixteen-Step Seller Process, which are discussed in appendices A and E. Their customers like the process and are comfortable making decisions because there is no pressure. And the Ninjas get predictable results.

BE A NINJA

Let's summarize our approach with customers.

- **Ask Don't Tell.** Stop tellin' and sellin' and start asking questions. Let customers have time of possession. You will stay more connected to them, and they will love you for it.

- **Pull Don't Push.** Stop pushing your message, and start pulling information from your customer. Find out what they are praying for.

- **Probe Don't Pitch.** Nobody likes to be "pitched." What is the pitch of Ninja Selling? That there is no pitch. Probe for pain and pleasure, so you can offer a solution.

- **Consult Don't Present.** Be their consultant, their trusted advisor, not a salesperson who's presenting. Ninjas don't have listing presentations; we have listing consultations.
- **Solve Don't Sell.** Ninjas don't sell. We provide solutions.
- **Serve Don't Sell.** Ninjas have a servant's heart. We are here to serve not to sell.

Look at the two columns of words in the following illustration. The words on the left describe a Ninja. The words on the right describe a salesperson.

Be a Ninja

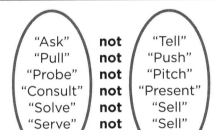

Now let's look at the four steps in The Ninja Consultation in greater detail.

Chapter 38

NINJA CONSULTATION STEP 1: CONNECTION

Early sales training taught us that the most important step in the sales process was the closing. Modern sales research says the critical step is not the closing; it is the opening. The first step is the connection.

Customers decide in the first two minutes whether they like you, trust you, and want to work with you. If they don't feel the connection, they will either move away from you, or if they stay, the relationship will be strained. There is no second chance at a first impression. Your first two minutes are critical.

We have found the Ninja Three-Step Greeting will help you get off on the right foot. It is specifically designed to help you connect and build rapport with the customer.

THE THREE-STEP GREETING

Step 1: Enroll

You enroll the customer by asking them a simple question, such as, "Hello. How are you today?" or, "Hi, how's it going?"

Asking these simple, low-key questions requires an answer from the customer, and you have immediately connected. These questions are also nonthreatening to customers, so they are very comfortable answering.

Listen carefully to how they answer this simple question, and they will give you early clues about their decision strategy. Listen for the subtle and the hidden.

When you ask, "How are you today?" and the customer responds with, "Doin' great!" or "Super!" this is an early indication that their decision strategy may be *toward* or risk taker. They are optimistic and move toward what they want.

If they answer your question with, "Not bad," or "Can't complain," this is an early indication that their decision strategy may be *from* or risk avoider.

Step 2: Acknowledge

After you have asked the enrolling question, acknowledge your customers. There are some good ways to do this:

- **Thank you.** A simple "thank you for meeting me" or "thank you for your time" is enough.
- **Welcome.** If they are from out of town, I'll say, "Welcome to Fort Collins." If you are a new-home salesperson at Harmony Club, and a customer comes into your sales center, your acknowledgment could be "Welcome to Harmony Club."
- **Compliment.** Giving an appropriate compliment is a form of acknowledgment. This needs to be done naturally and received as genuine. Here are some examples: "Great outfit!" "Great tie!" "You look great. You're really tan. Have you been on vacation?"

Step 3: Who You Are

You say your name *last*. Most people, especially salespeople, have been taught to say their name first. When they meet someone for the first time, they are very quick to extend their hand for a handshake and say, "Hi. My name is Jason Burns. How are you today? Thanks for coming in."

Jason just did the three steps, but he did them in the wrong order. Plus, most of the time, he never even gives the customer a chance to answer the question "How are you today?" This fast-talking approach is a turnoff to the customer and positions you as a typical salesperson.

MELT THE SHIELD!

What is the greatest fear of customers as they approach an open house or a new home sales center? That there's a salesperson in there! Their protective shield goes up as they approach the front door. If you follow the simple three-step greeting, the shield will go down. The process *melts* the shield! Here's how it sounds at an open house:

Ninja: "Hi, how are you folks today?"

Customers: "We're doing good."

Ninja: "Great. Thanks for coming in today. My name is _____. Here's some information on the property. Please make yourself at home. If you have any questions, I'll be here for you."

Pause for an instant after saying your name, and many times customers will give you their names, because they can already feel the connection, and they want to reciprocate. Notice how much softer this approach is by doing the three steps and putting your name last? When you put the customer first and yourself last, the customer feels safe and feels a connection. You are somehow different from what they expected, especially compared to the typical salesperson, who lunges at them with his hand extended. With that traditional approach, the customer's natural reaction is to move away—to distance. And the salesperson's natural instinct is to pursue. The "Pursuer-Distancer Dance" begins.

> **"** *Modern sales research says the critical step is not the closing; it is the opening.* **"**

THE FIRST TWO MINUTES

In your first two minutes with a customer, you have two goals:

1. **Connection.** You start with your three-step greeting, and then work your way into the FORD questions as you build rapport. How can you tell when you are connected? You can usually feel it. If you're not quite sure, just start gently nodding. Your customer will involuntarily start nodding back. The guitars are in tune. You are connected.

2. **Take Control of the Process.** Now that you are in rapport with your customer, you are ready to take control of the process. Here's what that sounds like:

Pat and Chris Smith are relocating to Fort Collins, Colorado. You have emailed each other and visited on the phone, but you have not met each other face-to-face. They are coming into the office at 2:00 p.m. to start the process of looking for a home. You are waiting for them in the lobby of your office.

You: "Hi, Pat and Chris. How are you doing today?" (Step 1.)

Pat: "We're doin' fine." Chris nods.

You: "Welcome to Colorado." (Step 2.) "My name is Larry, and it's great to finally meet you two face-to-face." (Step 3.)

Chris: "It's great to meet you as well."

You: "How was your trip?"

Pat and Chris talk about their flight, checking into the hotel, leaving their kids with friends in California, and so on. (FORD.)

You ask about their kids and confirm that they are here for a four-day house-hunting trip. You start nodding gently, as Pat and Chris answer, and you notice that Pat and Chris start nodding back. (Connection.)

You (taking control of the process): "If it's all right with you, what I would recommend we do first is sit down and take a few minutes to review everything we've talked about over the phone. I have a few additional questions I would like to ask that will help me help you find the right home. Will that work for you?"

You have just taken control of the process. Further, you asked their permission to take control of the process when you said, "If it's all right with you. . . ." Remember, *you* control the process and *your customer* controls the decisions. It's like this ledger:

(You)	(Customer)
Control Process	Controls Decisions

You stay on your side of the ledger and your customer stays on his or her side. How does that work? By asking them questions that require them to make small decisions. You have already asked them their first decision-making question: "Will that work for you?" Pat and Chris have said yes, and you are now ready for the next step.

Chapter 39

NINJA CONSULTATION STEP 2: INFORMATION

The information step is perhaps the most important step in Ninja Selling. Unfortunately, most salespeople skip this step. They have been taught to immediately go from Connection to Presentation. They lose their connection and try to make up for it with a stronger close, which alienates the customer.

Once you learn the new habit of going from Connection to Information, you start to discover your customer's pain and pleasure and what you need to do to provide a solution. Your customer satisfaction rates, referrals, odds of selling, and income per hour will start to soar.

THREE GOALS

1. **Clarity.** Your series of questions are designed to help your customer become clear—not confused.

2. **Confidence.** Your questions also help your customer build a foundation of trust and confidence—not fear.

3. **Comfortable to Commit (Make a Decision).** When your customers are clear and confident, they are comfortable to make a decision. If they are confused or afraid, they will "think about it."

Part of helping your customer to get comfortable making decisions is to control the process and first ask questions that require small decisions. For example, we are now seated in the conference room with John and Mary, and I have a series of questions to ask them. They will have time of possession, and as they become comfortable making small decisions, they will get into a decision-making pattern. Later, when we are in a home they like, it will be easy for them to make a decision on whether to buy it.

Contrast this approach with the typical salesperson, who launches into a spiel about the market and financing and takes time of possession away from the buyer. The buyer starts to disconnect. The first real decision the buyers face comes when they find a home they like. Since they are not in a decision-making pattern, they usually say they will think about it.

THE QUESTION SEQUENCE

It is not enough to ask the right questions at the right time; science shows we need to also ask them in the right *sequence* for the customer to become clear, confident, and comfortable committing.

Several years ago, I was teaching a Ninja Selling class, and a student said to me, "You've obviously read Thomas Freese's classic book, *Secrets of Question-Based Selling*." I said, "No, I haven't heard of the book."

"Well, you are teaching it!" replied the student.

I figured I better read the book, and after I did, I realized why Ninja Selling is so effective. We are asking the right questions in the right sequence. We stumbled onto this order through years of trial and error. Now, we had the science to know why it works!

There are four basic types of questions. Here they are in their proper order:

1. Rapport/Connection Questions

These are asked first. Most salespeople know this and are pretty good about beginning with these questions. Step 1 of the Ninja Selling System covers this—the three-step connection and the FORD questions.

2. Foundational Questions (Access Prior Learning)

These are called foundational questions because they are the key to building a foundation of trust and confidence. Since we have learned that it is good to have the right answers, we want to begin with easy-to-answer questions, especially those that access a customer's prior learning.

Here's where most salespeople fall down. They skip this step and either jump into a presentation or pose diagnostic questions.

Here's what happens when you skip this step. Say you ask a diagnostic question like "What price range of home are you interested in?" Your customer's internal dialogue goes like this: *How do I answer this question? I just got in town two hours ago. I've looked online, but I haven't looked at any houses. What if I say a number, and then I realize it's wrong? That the price doesn't get us what we want?*

The customer starts to get confused and nervous—not the way you want to start your buyer interview. Your goal is clarity and confidence. Not confusion and fear.

Instead, start out by asking easy questions your customer can easily answer. For example, "Tell me a little bit about the house you're living in now. How many bedrooms does it have? What do you like the best about it?"

Think about the dialogue I had with Mr. CEO. After connecting, what was my first question? "If it is all right with you, I would love for you to take a few minutes and share the story of how you built this company."

What was I doing? I was accessing his prior learning. Think about the questions I asked in the foundational sequence: "How many stores do you have now?" "How many stores do you have in Colorado?" "What is your process for deciding to open a store?" All of these questions are simple and access his prior learning; he knew the answers cold.

Two things happen when you ask prior learning questions: 1. You begin to learn about the customers—their process as well as their pain and pleasure. 2. They start to open up. Their confidence builds, and so does their trust in you. These are key ingredients to a successful sale as well as to a relationship.

3. Diagnostic Questions

We can now start diving deeper into their situation. While the goal of foundational questions is to build trust and confidence, the goal of diagnostic questions is clarity. Customers have to achieve clarity in six areas, or they won't feel comfortable making a decision. These areas are: who, what, when, where, why, and how.

I was teaching a Ninja Installation class in Seattle. On the second day, a woman came up to me and asked for advice on how to handle a young unmarried couple she was working with. She had shown them more than forty homes and didn't seem to be making any progress. She was frustrated, and they probably were as well.

I asked her, "Who seems to be the one most interested in buying?"

She said, "Obviously, the girlfriend. Her boyfriend, Justin, doesn't seem to like any of the houses."

I suggested she visit with Justin privately and ask him how he thinks it's going, if they need to look at different types of houses, and so on. The next day, she came to class and said, "Guess what? I discovered the problem. Justin isn't sure if his girlfriend is *the one!*" Justin was confused about the *who*. As a result, he wasn't buying a home anytime soon. You could show him another forty houses, and it wouldn't matter. Justin and his girlfriend have issues that are beyond the scope of your Ninja consultation process to solve.

Confusion in any of these areas (who, what, when, where, why, and how) will cause customers to "think about it." Our questions in the Ten-Step Buyer Process and the Sixteen-Step Seller Process are designed to help customers become clear in these areas.

4. Solution or Closing Questions

Your role as a trusted advisor is to help your customer become clear and confident. When they are, they will often close you! They get it. They discover the solution. Control the process (your questions), offer solutions to their pain and pleasure, and let them make the decisions.

Chapter 40

NINJA CONSULTATION
STEP 3: SOLUTION

One November, I was asked to teach a Ninja Selling class in Hawaii. It was cold in Colorado at that time, so Pat and I went a few days early to enjoy some time in Maui. We checked into the beautiful Wailea Marriott Hotel and started planning our days in paradise. Pat said that she would like to play golf one of the days, so I headed to the concierge to check on tee times.

The concierge asked, "Would you like some free golf?"

"What's the catch?" I asked.

"You have to attend our ninety-minute time-share presentation," he explained.

"Sure!" I replied.

"Boy, that was easy," exclaimed the concierge. "Usually, I have to twist arms to get people to go."

"I would love to go," I repeated. "First of all, I'm a sales trainer, so I want to see the presentation. Second, Pat and I own Marriott time-shares and love them. In fact, we are staying at this hotel using our Marriott points. We might be a buyer. And third, I would like the free golf."

"You're on," said the concierge, and the next morning we headed to the 9:00 a.m. presentation.

Susan was our Marriott host, and she greeted us warmly. We liked her immediately. She really had the Connection step down. Once she could feel the connection, Susan launched her presentation. She was obviously old school and had been taught the traditional three-step sales process.

"Let me start by giving you a history of the Marriott time-share program," she began.

At this point, I made the time-out signal with my hands and said, "Susan, we are familiar with the Marriott time-share program, since we've owned them for seven years."

What do you think Susan did next? She went right on with her presentation. It was as if she didn't even hear me. She was sticking to her script, no matter what. So Pat and I sat there patiently, as Susan went through all the stuff we already knew. I checked out mentally and thought about the golf we were going to play that afternoon and where we wanted to have dinner that night.

When Susan finished her spiel, she said, "Let's go look at the property."

Pat and I followed her out of the room.

We looked at one-bedroom, two-bedroom, and three-bedroom condos. Then, we looked at a villa. After Susan had presented all of the products, she now moved to her third step, the close. "Well, what do you think?" she asked.

I turned to Pat and said, "What do you think?"

Pat looked at me and said, "I don't know."

At this point, Susan did the smartest thing of her entire presentation. She suggested we step out on the deck and talk it over. Standing on the deck with the sun, the palm trees, and the waves crashing onto the beach was very compelling—especially since we had just left a very cold Colorado. Evidently, it wasn't compelling enough for Pat, though, because she said, "I'm tired and confused. I'm not ready to buy anything. I want to leave."

We went back inside, and I gave Susan the classic buyer response: "Thank you so much. You've been absolutely great. We're not going to do anything right now. We are going to think about it."

Susan was very gracious, not hard sell at all. She said, "Let me put together a package of information for you to take with you. If you have any questions, my card is right here. Just give me a call." And she handed us an expensive package of beautiful materials.

We played golf that afternoon and enjoyed dinner as the sun set over the Pacific that evening. As we recapped the day, I said, "What a great day this was. I'm so happy we came here."

Pat replied, "Yeah, except for that time-share presentation this morning. That was really a waste of time. I wish we hadn't done that. It was not worth it for the free golf."

Now, Pat and I had been married for more than forty years. During my real estate career, she has often been one of my role-playing partners. I decided to try an experiment to see if the outcome would have been any different if Susan had used Ninja Selling. Pat would play herself, and I would be Susan as a Ninja.

We began at the point where Susan said, "Let me start by giving you a history of the Marriott time-share program." I asked Pat to say, "Susan, we are familiar with the Marriott time-share program, since we've owned them for seven years."

Larry (getting curious): "Really. Where do you own them?"

Pat: "The Desert Springs Marriott in Palm Desert, California."

Larry: "What a great resort! Do you use them or trade them or both?"

Pat: "We do both, but we always go every year. We love it there." (Pleasure.)

Larry: "What do you love about going there?"

Pat: "I always feel younger when I come home. It's a place of renewal for us." (More pleasure.)

Larry: "How many time-shares do you have there?"

Pat: "We have two. One wasn't enough, so we bought a second one." (More pleasure.)

Larry: "You say you go every year. Is there a particular time you like to go?"

Pat: "Yes. We always go in April. April is not a very good month in Colorado. The skiing is over, and the golfing and cycling aren't very good yet. It's a transition month, and a good time to get out of Colorado." (Pain.)

Larry: "Is there any other month that is a bad month in Colorado where you would like to go someplace?"

Pat: "Yes, November is a bad month as well, pretty much for the same reasons. The skiing hasn't started, and the golf and cycling are pretty much over." (More pain.)

Larry (noting that we are in Hawaii in November): "Pat, if you could wave your magic wand, how would you feel about spending April in Palm Desert and November in Hawaii each year?"

Pat (with a laugh): "I could handle that!"

Larry: "Well, if we were to do something like that (pretend state), would we invite our kids and make it an annual family gathering or would it just be a getaway for the two of us?"

Pat: "I was thinking about that. I would love to have an annual family gathering in Hawaii, but it's a long way to travel, and there are a lot of moving parts. I'm worried they would come the first year or two and then stop coming. I think it would be better if we had a retreat for just the two of us as an annual getaway."

At this point, Pat's eyes got huge, and she said, "We need the one-bedroom! We should buy the one-bedroom! I'll call Susan tomorrow, and tell her we'll take the one-bedroom!"

Larry: "Time out! This is an experiment! We are not buying the one-bedroom!"

Pat: "I can take care of it. You have to teach, but I can take care of the paperwork. I know how to do it!"

Larry: "Pat, we are not buying anything. This is a role-play. We can come to Hawaii with our Marriott points, just like we are doing right now."

When I share this story in my Ninja Selling classes, many of the female students feel I was a grinch for not letting Pat buy that timeshare. I'm really very supportive of her, though. Remember the house we are living in on Harbor Walk Lane?

The point of sharing this story is to point out the power of the Socratic approach and the Ninja Selling process of identifying pain and pleasure and then offering a solution. It also points out what can happen when the customer becomes clear and not confused. When they have answers for the six areas (who, what, when, where, why, and how), they often have an "aha!" or "oh, my gosh!" experience. They want to take action. They start closing you! This is exactly what happened with Pat.

Here's how she became clear on the six areas:

- **Who:** Just the two of us spending time at a retreat together (not the whole family).
- **What:** The one-bedroom works perfectly for two.
- **When:** November is a good time to leave Colorado (pain).
- **Where:** Maui.
- **Why:** It is a place of renewal. We will feel younger (pleasure).
- **How:** The Marriott time-share program works great for us. We are comfortable with it and can afford it.

Isn't it interesting that five minutes earlier Pat had said, "That time-share presentation was really a waste of time. I wish we hadn't done that." Now she was wild eyed and closing me on buying the one-bedroom.

What happened? She simply became clear and confident as I helped her find a solution. She presented the solution to me.

Chapter 41

NINJA CONSULTATION STEP 4: PROPOSAL

Once you have identified a customer's pain and pleasure and formulated some solutions, you need to be able to articulate your solutions in a way that your customer "gets it." What your customer "gets" or "doesn't get" is what you've communicated. There are six ways to increase the power of your communication. Here's the science.

1. MAXIMIZE THE QUALITY OF YOUR COMMUNICATION.

The quality of your communication depends on—

- Your words
- How you sound when you say your words—volume, pitch, tone, and tempo
- How you look when you say your words—body language, facial expression, hair, dress, and so on

When the game is on the line and you want the highest quality communication, do your best to get face-to-face. If this is not possible, the telephone is your next best option. Even though large numbers of people are moving to electronic communication, its popularity doesn't necessarily mean the communication is of high quality. It's generally not, which explains why so many emails and texts are misunderstood according to tone.

Here's a fun exercise that points out how live communication and tone convey meaning. Consider the witness on the stand who says, "I didn't say he shot his wife." Now say this phrase seven times, each time accentuating a different word.

If you have a choice of communicating with a customer via email text, phone, or face-to-face, which will provide the highest-quality communication? Face-to-face.

When a seller says, "I would prefer that we communicate by email," your response is: "Absolutely. Can I make one request? When we get a contract on your home and the game is on the line, we need to have the best possible communication. Would it be all right with you for us to sit down and go over the contract? If that is not feasible, would it be OK with you if I email you the contract, and we talk about it over the phone?"

Live communication, either face-to-face or on the phone, is critical in a negotiation. A study at Stanford University found that in electronic negotiations the success rate was only about 10 percent, because the parties become the "faceless other."

2. MATCH LEARNING MODALITIES.

Customers organize information in their brain and think in one of three modalities: sounds, pictures, and feelings (kinesthetics). They use all three modes but tend to have a favorite. Again, the rule of thumb is to *match* their modality. Practice the Platinum Rule.

Visual Thinkers

Most Americans (about 60 percent) think primarily in pictures. This is why television, YouTube, and selfies are so popular. If you want to communicate effectively with these folks, you need to *show* them stuff rather than just talking about it. Show them the graph of the statistics, rather than just telling them about it. Show them the picture of the house and its floor plan, rather than just describing it.

How do you recognize visual thinkers? They tend to talk fast (they are trying to describe what they see, and a picture is worth a thousand words). They access the hard drive of their brain by rolling their eyes up—pulling pictures off their mental hard drive. They use a lot of visual predicates and phrases such as: I see what you mean, I'm clear on that, or show me what you mean.

Auditory Thinkers

At the other extreme are the auditory thinkers. They think in language. They are very sensitive to sounds and tend not to like loud places. Many musicians are primarily auditory. They are very comfortable talking about the subject and don't need visual aids.

How do you recognize them? Their eyes seldom look up, because they don't need to access mental pictures. Moving their eyes from side to side is how they access sounds and language from their brain. They use a lot of auditory predicates and phrases such as: I hear what you mean, that sounds good to me, or tell me what you mean. This is the smallest percentage of the US population. Most people need to either see it (visual) or feel it (kinesthetic) to get it.

Kinesthetic Thinkers

These people need to touch it or feel it to really understand it. Visual thinkers can look at a photo of the home. Auditory thinkers can hear a description of the home. But kinesthetic thinkers need to actually go into the home to get a feel for it.

How do you recognize them? Those who enjoy nature and anything with the body—from sports to food—tend to be strongly kinesthetic.

To access their feelings, they tend to look down and to their right. They talk a bit slower and are very sensitive to touch. You are wise to give them a brochure, so they can hold it in their hands rather than just showing it to them. When they are in a home, they will feel the woodwork and sit down in the home. They use a lot of kinesthetic words and phrases such as: That feels good to me, this house has a good vibe, or I sense they won't take that offer.

Practice by watching and listening for the subtle and the hidden. When you give a customer a brochure, do they look at it (visual); do they start feeling the texture of the paper with their fingers (kinesthetic); or do they hand it back and say, "Just tell me about it" (auditory).

When you go to a restaurant, listen carefully to how people order: "That salad looks good to me" (visual); "I like the sounds of that special" (auditory); "I feel like a steak tonight" (kinesthetic).

While people tend to have a preferred mode of thinking and storing information, they use all three of their modalities. To present your message best, use all three modalities. Show them. Tell them. And let them feel it.

3. MATCH AND MIRROR YOUR CUSTOMER.

Since body language and voice volume, pitch, tone, and tempo are so important in communication, match your customer as much as you can without losing your authenticity. Practice the Platinum Rule. Treat others the way they want to be treated. They tend to like and trust people who are similar to them.

Voice

If customers are soft spoken, lower your voice. If they tend to talk faster than you, speed it up. If you are too slow, you will start to annoy them, and they will get impatient or check out.

Body Position

Match their body language. When Mr. CEO was sitting at the conference table leaning back with his legs crossed, I was sitting the same way across the table from him. When I asked if he would take a few minutes to share his story, he immediately put both feet on the floor and leaned forward. I did the same. Remember, your body emanates energy at a frequency. The frequency of your energy is a function of what you are thinking and feeling, and how you are positioning your body. Get in tune with your customer.

Gestures

Everyone has a natural gesture orbit. No orbit is represented when you have your arms crossed. A small orbit would be represented by small movements with just the hands. A large orbit is when you extend your arms and gesture emphatically.

A good rule of thumb is to keep your gesture orbit equal to or slightly smaller than that of your customers. They are comfortable with this. Having a gesture orbit larger than theirs makes them uncomfortable—and they start to distrust you. Picture the soft-spoken, deliberate customer with a small gesture orbit being overwhelmed by the loud, fast-talking, arm-waving salesperson. There will be no sale in that situation, no matter how good the product, service, or price.

4. GO FROM BIG PICTURE TO SMALL PICTURE.

It is easier for people to organize information in their brain if you present the information from the general to the specific, from big picture to details. For a seller, start with the general market in their town or city, then go to their price range, then go to their neighborhood, then go to their house. Too often, Realtors jump into an analysis of the specific property without putting it in the context of the bigger picture (market). When you go from big picture to small picture, you help your customer become clear.

5. MAINTAIN YOUR NONANXIOUS PRESENCE.

Whenever I role play with the students in our Ninja classes, they comment, "Larry, you seem so relaxed, yet attentive. You're confident, but not cocky or smug. How do you maintain your nonanxious presence when we turn up the heat?" (Realtors can be far tougher in role-play than real customers.)

There are two secrets to maintaining your cool under fire:

1. **Don't Get Attached to the Outcome.** Focusing on the outcome causes you to be tense and can lead to "commission breath." If you want the transaction more than your customer does, you are in trouble. I'm relaxed, because I'm not obsessed with winning the role-play or the transaction. I simply focus on my proven Ninja questions and let the outcomes take care of themselves.

2. **Focus on Your Process.** Just work the system (process) and TSW—The System Works.

Here's advice from two young people who focus on process.

"Miracles are not random. You are in charge of your destiny. Practice your process and the results take care of themselves."
—**Mikaela Shiffrin, age seventeen, youngest person to win an Olympic Gold Medal in Alpine skiing (slalom)**

"I just focus on my process and don't worry about the result. Just really get into the process."
—**Rory McIlroy, age twenty-five, after winning the British Open golf tournament**

When you have a relaxed, nonanxious presence, you show up differently to others. You have a calm, positive, focused energy that is magnetic. People are naturally drawn to you. You expect great results, but you aren't attached to them, and you don't need them. As a result, you shift the power-need dynamic in your favor.

Power-Need Dynamic

```
     NEED            POWER
      ↕                ↕
    POWER            NEED
```

The person with the highest need has the lowest power. When salespeople need a transaction, their power is reduced. As they become attached to the outcome, they unwittingly start to grovel or exert pressure. Customers sense the desperation and stop trusting the salesperson.

The person with the lowest need has the highest power. You expect positive results but don't need them. Instead, you focus on your process and let the results take care of themselves. You are more confident, have greater power, and your customer trusts you more. You are a trusted advisor rather than a salesperson.

6. PRACTICE THE THREE RULES OF COMMUNICATION.

Dave Dornan, one of my partners at The Group, Inc., came up with three rules for communication in sales. We have found if we follow these three rules, we will have very high quality communication with our customers.

- **Rule 1: Showing Is Better than Telling.** Most people are visual. They need to see it to get it. Even the auditory thinkers don't want a salesperson who is tellin' and sellin'. If someone is going to talk, they would prefer it be them. They want time of possession.

- **Rule 2: Asking Is Better than Telling.** By asking, we learn more about the customer's pain and pleasure and how we can provide a solution. It also keeps the customer connected and gives them time of possession.

- **Rule 3: It Matters Who Says It.** Is it more powerful if we tell the customer how great we are or if their friends on Facebook tell them how great we are? It matters who says it. Is it more powerful if we say the right price in a listing consultation or if the seller says the right price? Is it more powerful when our customer suddenly has an "aha!" experience and closes us on the home they want to buy? Our Ten-Step Buyer Process and Sixteen-Step Seller Process are designed to help the buyers and sellers say it rather than us.

Chapter 42

HELPING CUSTOMERS MAKE GOOD DECISIONS

When customers make good decisions, they are usually happy with their Realtor. When they make a decision they are unhappy with, they often blame their Realtor. So, it is in our best interests to help our customers make good decisions.

We have found that customers who make *balanced brain decisions*—those that combine the head and the heart—seem happiest with what they decided. A balanced brain decision is where the customer uses both their emotional (right brain) and analytical (left brain) in balance. Buyers often regret decisions that are too impulsive (emotional) and then suffer buyers' remorse. Or they often miss out if they are too analytical (paralysis analysis) and can't make a decision. Their *nondecision* becomes a *bad* decision.

> *" We have found that customers who make 'balanced brain decisions'—those that combine the head and the heart—seem happiest with what they decided. "*

THE ANALYTICAL BRAIN

Your customer's analytical brain (left hemisphere) is most powerful when it is focused on just three to five criteria. It can handle more variables than that, but with more than five variables, it slows down, and above nine variables it goes into paralysis analysis. Many Realtors unknowingly confuse their customers by giving them too much data. They force customers to "think about it." Here are some common examples of overtaxing the analytical brain:

With Buyers

Showing more than five homes in one showing sequence. After the fifth home, buyers can't remember the first home they looked at. If circumstances require that you show more than five homes in a day, make sure your buyers are ranking the homes and have their top three favorites. This can be a rolling top three, where they can take out a favorite and substitute a different one. This process focuses the buyers on just three houses at a time.

With Sellers

Realtors commonly confuse sellers by giving them a stack of multiple listing sheets. And when the seller gets confused, their emotional brain takes over, and they blurt out "Our house is nicer!" or "We need more money." In the seller process, we will show you how to focus sellers on the five determinants of value: price, location, size, condition, and amenities.

THE EMOTIONAL BRAIN

The emotional brain is creative and processes a massive amount of data at the nonconscious or intuitive level. Its decision is based on feeling. How does the house feel? How does the decision feel? This is a very important part of the decision.

The analytical brain sets the priorities, criteria, and boundaries around which the decision will be made. This is the *context* for the decision. Then the emotional brain (right hemisphere) can decide on the *content* of the decision. A balanced brain decision is a combination of the head and the heart. Here's the formula for a good balanced brain decision:

- Set the criteria of the three to five most important factors in the decision.
- Within these boundaries, if it feels good, do it!

If your customer finds a home that meets the criteria and it feels good, it is probably the right home for them. It's as simple as that.

NEXT STEPS

Now that you know the art and science of the Ninja Selling System, it is time to apply your knowledge with buyers and sellers. The appendices that follow give you the specific step-by-step processes to be a Ninja. The Ten-Step Buyer Process and the Sixteen-Step Seller Process have been field tested by thousands of Ninjas throughout the United States and Canada.

You have one more step, however. You will need to convert your knowledge of the Ninja Selling System into actual Ninja skills. How do you convert knowledge into skill? Practice! You will need to practice these processes with a partner or in a small group. We recommend you meet for at least one hour a week with your partner or skills group and rehearse.

You are not yet a Ninja. You're at the beginning of the Ninja Path.

Conclusion

THE NINJA PATH

The Ninja Path is more than a selling system. It is a path you walk every day and a way of being in the world. It is a lifestyle of gratitude and abundance, one of creating value, cultivating relationships, and focusing on life goals. It is about building a better life and making the world a better place.

Ninja is as simple as the goals Jack Fanning (age twelve) and his sister, Emerson (age nine), recite each morning on their way to school. Their father, Michael, is a Ninja instructor. Right before he drops them off, Michael asks, "OK, team, what are your goals for today?"

The kids reply with a shout, "To be awesome and help somebody!"

Ninja Selling is as simple as that. Just be awesome (the best you can be) and help somebody (create value).

One day after school, Jack said to his father, "Dad, I learned I only have to do one to do both. When I help somebody, I'm awesome!" Out of the mouths of children comes a simple, powerful philosophy of life.

The Ninja Path and the Ninja Selling System are built around the power of incremental change—doing small things each day that compound over time to give you big results in both your life and your career.

These Ninja activities are very easy to do. Unfortunately, they are also very easy *not* to do. Why would anyone not follow such a simple yet powerful system that improves their life and career? Over the years, I've observed three traps that hold people back.

1. **They Feel It Is Beneath Them.** They think Ninja Selling is

too basic and they need something more advanced. It has to be more complicated than this. Where's the magic dust? Guess what? This is not rocket science. Ninjas simply do the basics better than anyone. Ninja works!

2. **They Get in Their Own Way.** They overanalyze every detail, causing them to freeze up and not take action. Or they engage in creative avoidance. Ninjas simply "trust and embrace the dance."

3. **They Want Instant Results.** The Ninja Selling System is simple and easy to do, but it takes patience and discipline to see results. Whether you are lifting weights, following a diet, or planting a crop, it takes time before you start seeing results. Persist! As Jimmy D., the Original Ninja, says, "Don't quit right before the magic happens."

I'm often asked by managers of real estate companies, "How much time do you give a rookie to start producing income?" Six months? A year? My answer is, "There is no time limit!" Whether you are a rookie or an experienced Realtor, when you work the Ninja Selling System, I have complete confidence the system will ultimately work for you. TSW—the system works!

Rick Merrill, a Ninja in Hendersonville, North Carolina, once shared with me how following the Ninja Path had transformed his life and career in about nine months.

I asked Rick, "What was the key that motivated you to walk this path?"

Rick replied, "After all these years in real estate and all the classes I've taken, I finally chose to *submit* to the process. I didn't overanalyze it or think I needed to change it. I simply chose to submit to it."

So what will you do now? You are near the end of this book, but you are not near graduation from Ninja. You are at commencement. You are at the start, not the finish. You are at the trailhead to a better life and career.

The stack of balanced stones and butterfly on the cover represent your future. In the mountains, a stack of balanced stones, called a cairn, is used to show climbers the trail or path. Ninja Selling is your cairn showing you the path.

When a caterpillar spins its cocoon, it goes through a transformative process and then emerges as a butterfly. It takes time and work to make this transformation. Work the Ninja System and you will transform your business and your life.

We have shown you the Ninja Path, but only you can walk it. Begin it now. Be awesome and help somebody!

> *"Life happens at the level of movement—not words."*
> **—Jimmy D. (The Original Ninja)**

APPENDICES

Appendix A

THE TEN-STEP BUYER PROCESS

The goal of our process is to help buyers become clear and confident, so when they see a home they like, they will have the green light to buy it. If they are confused or afraid, they'll have a red or yellow light and will think about it.

This concept of Green Light Selling was created by psychologist Don Aspromonte and is described in his book (with Diane Austin) of the same name. Don used to live in Colorado and consulted with our company for two years. He is a master salesman and has influenced both our buyer and seller processes.

A BUYER'S FOUR GREATEST FEARS

Here are the four greatest fears you need to remove before your buyers will have the green light to buy a home.

1. **Losing the Home.** When a buyer steps across the threshold and emotionally falls in love with a home, the little voice inside says, *Oh, my gosh, this could be the one! I better buy this house before someone else gets it.*

2. **Missing Something.** The buyer's first fear of losing the home came from his or her emotional brain. Now, the analytical brain engages, and its little voice says, *Wait a minute. Not so fast. This is only the second house we've looked at. We may be missing something.*

3. **Paying Too Much.** The analytical brain starts to pile on by saying, *Besides, the reason this house is still available is because it is probably overpriced. Be careful!*

4. **Something Wrong with It.** To make sure the red light is on, the analytical voice says, *There is probably something wrong with this house. That's why it is still available.* This fear can usually be handled with either the inspection clause of a contract or with an enlightened listing Realtor who had the home pre-inspected, has the inspections on the kitchen counter, and offers a home warranty.

Of the buyer's four fears, their two biggest are missing something and paying too much. When they start hearing voices that are conflicting, they become confused. Confused buyers don't buy. They think about it.

As a Ninja, your mission is to help your customer become clear and confident. Your Ten-Step Buyer Process is designed to remove these fears *before* your customer starts looking at houses. Then they will have the green light to buy when they find something they like.

Here's a summary of the Ninja Ten-Step Buyer Process:

Step 1: Greeting

Step 2: Meeting

Step 3: Buyer Interview

Step 4: Buyer Packet

Step 5: Funnel Process

Step 6: Scale of 1 to 10

Step 7: Dream Home Exercise—Three Priorities

Step 8: Whats and Whys

Step 9: Cash or Loan?

Step 10: What Happens Next?

This is a ten-step process. Think of it like making a ten-digit, long-distance call. If you skip a digit or change the order, your call cannot go through. The same is true with your Ten-Step Buyer Process. Stick to the order. Don't leave steps out. Follow this process, and you will get predictable results. And your buyers will love you! Let's go through each step in detail.

STEP 1: GREETING

When you are meeting buyers at your office, prepare and coach your receptionist. Let's say that John and Mary Smith are relocating from California to Colorado. You've visited by phone and email but have not met each other face-to-face. They are coming to the office for a 2:00 p.m. appointment. Give your receptionist the Smiths' names in advance.

When John and Mary come to the front desk and say, "Hello, we have an appointment with Jessica Tate," Debbie, our receptionist, is prepared to reply, "You must be Mr. and Mrs. Smith. Welcome to The Group. We're glad you're here. Jessica is looking forward to meeting with you."

How does this make John and Mary Smith feel? It makes them feel special, and you have immediately created value. How does it make Jessica look? Prepared and professional. How does it make Debbie and your company look? Great! What did it cost? Nada!

Use the three-step greeting you learned in the Connection Step:

1. Enroll: "Hi, John and Mary. How are you doing today?"

2. Acknowledge: "Welcome to Colorado."

3. Who you are: "I'm Jessica. It's great to finally meet you face-to-face."

Then move into rapport-building (FORD) questions such as "How was your flight? When did you arrive in town? Have you checked into your hotel yet? How much time do we have together today?"

Your goal in this first two minutes is to connect and take control of the process. You can usually feel when you are connected. If you want to make sure, gently start nodding and see if your buyers nod back. It's an involuntary energy response, if you are connected. John and Mary start nodding, so you are ready to take control of the process.

Say, "If it's all right with you, what I recommend we do first is sit down and review everything we've talked about on the phone. Plus, I would like to ask you a few questions that will help me help you find the right home. Will that work for you?"

Notice you not only took control of the process, you also asked their permission.

STEP 2: MEETING

It is very important that you move to another space for the meeting. You greet in one space and meet in a separate space. This is all about energy. When strangers meet for the first time, they bring a nervous (negative) energy with them. As the nervousness subsides, there is still a residue of this negative energy in that space. You want to move to fresh energy.

This is easy in an office setting. You greet in the lobby and move to a conference room or office. In a new-home sales center or an open house, you should script out where you are going to greet (entrance or foyer) and where you are going to meet (such as a plat table, over an aerial photo of the property for new homes, or the kitchen for an open house).

If you are meeting buyers at the property, get there early and prepare the house. (Make sure the lights are on, and so forth.) When you see the buyers arrive, come out of the house and greet them on the front sidewalk. Walk with them slowly to the front door, while you ask rapport-building questions. You will meet with them in the house, usually at the kitchen counter or table.

STEP 3: BUYER INTERVIEW

You are now seated in a conference room with John and Mary and will offer them a small gift—perhaps something to drink or a pen. Most people are equity sensitive, and when you do something for them, they feel the need to reciprocate. You start your relationship by doing things for each other. You're offering a small gift, and they are offering you their time and answering your questions. You are each jumping through hoops for the other. Psychologists say this mutual hoop jumping builds strong and healthy relationships.

Have a manila file folder prepared with your buyers' names on it. This shows the buyers you are a pro like their doctor, accountant, dentist, or attorney. Open their file and ask, "I would like to ask you a few questions that will help me help you find the right home. Is that OK with you? Is it OK if I take some notes?"

In the case of John and Mary Smith, where you have already visited with them by phone and email, you would modify this question to say, "Let's review what we have so far, and then I would like to ask you a few questions that will help me help you find the right home. Is that OK with you? Is it OK if I take some notes?"

Taking notes is critical. If you don't take notes, John and Mary don't think you're listening. And guess what? You aren't! You must take notes, or you won't remember their details a week from now. Ninjas call this the *power of the pad*.

Three Common Mistakes

This is a critical point in the process where most Realtors make one of three mistakes. Some manage to make all three!

1. **Launching into a Presentation.** Realtors who jump into their presentation are still stuck in the old three-step sales process. They've done a great job of connecting but now they can't wait to show their stuff. "Let me start by telling you about the market.

I've researched the following neighborhoods and houses. Let's talk financing . . ." Blah! Blah! Blah! They take over time of possession.

2. **Not Taking Notes.** Obviously, Realtors who are making a presentation are so busy with their time of possession that they are not taking notes. If you have learned the Ninja Sales Process, you know the next step after the connection is to ask questions, identify pain and pleasure, and *take notes.*

3. **Asking the Wrong Questions.** The next series of questions need to be *foundational questions.* These are questions that build a foundation of trust and confidence in your buyers. As we learned earlier, these are questions that access your buyers' prior learning. You want to start by asking easy questions that your buyers know the answers to. This way, they get into a rhythm and their confidence builds, as does their trust in you.

Here are some typical foundational questions. If you have asked John and Mary these questions over the phone before they arrived, you would simply start out by reviewing their answers to help them get in a rhythm and build their confidence. The questions can be modified, depending on if they rent or own their home. The key is to only ask questions about the past (access prior to learning).

1. "Where are you living now?" (This might be an apartment or rental home.) "How long have you lived there?" "Tell me a little bit about it."

2. (*If they own their home*) "About how many homes have you owned?" (*If they are renting*) "Have you owned a home in the past?"

3. (*If they own their home*) "When you purchased your current home, what was the process you used to find it?" "How did you start

looking?" "What did you do next?" "Did you work with a Realtor?" "How long did it take for you to find your home?" (If they are renting and have never owned a home, go to question 5.)

NOTE: Do you notice how I modified these simple questions for a commercial buyer, such as Mr. CEO? Instead of asking him where he lived, I asked him to tell me the story of his company. Rather than asking him how many homes he owned, I asked him how many stores he had. I then asked him about his process in deciding where and when to open a store. People are very process driven and tend to repeat a process that works for them.

4. "How did that process work for you?" "Is there anything you would like to change on this purchase?" "If you could wave a magic wand and have this purchase go just the way you want it, what would that look like for you?" At this point we are starting to move into diagnostic questions.

5. "Are you familiar with how real estate works here in (location)?" If they are from the local area, modify your question and ask, "Are you familiar with the current market conditions?"

Whether they answer either of these questions yes or no, your response is always the same: "I prepared a packet of information for you that has everything you need to buy real estate in (location)."

STEP 4: BUYER PACKET

By preparing a buyer packet, you once again show that you are a pro. Plus, it is one more hoop you are jumping through for the buyers, which further enhances your relationship. Here are the basic items you need in your packet:

- **Maps of the Area.** They need to know their way around.
- **Websites for the Area.** This includes the school district, chamber of commerce, city, and so on.

- **Mortgage Application.** This will inform them on what they will need for a lender.
- **Closing Costs Brochure.** Most title companies will provide this.
- **Contracts and Addendums.** It helps for them to look at the contract and get comfortable with it *before* they find their home. If your state uses standard contracts, mention that this is the state-approved contract that all Realtors are required to use. This comment will reduce their fear of the contract, as they know the state has approved it.
- **Agency Disclosure.** This represents your working relationship with them. Confirm that they are not working with another Realtor.
- **Your Personal Brochure.** They want to know more about you.

Open the packet, and you will notice them lean in toward you. You have their attention and their connection. Briefly review the packet and show them what you have prepared.

When you are meeting buyers at a house, you probably have never met each other. The buyers may have several appointments set up with a different Realtor at each place. Your buyer packet will help you slow the buyers down, build rapport, and build a working relationship. When buyers come through the front door, they typically want to see the house and quickly go away. If that happens, you've temporarily lost control of them. Once they've satisfied their curiosity about the home and you see them again—usually in the kitchen—it is an appropriate time to ask them, "By the way, do you folks have a buyer packet?"

They will usually say, "No. What's a buyer packet?"

You reply, "Well, it has everything in it that you need to buy real estate in Colorado. I prepared a buyer packet for you." They will immediately come to you like fish to food. They will lean in over the kitchen counter to look through the packet. You have just taken control of the process!

One of the great Ninja real estate companies is 8z Real Estate. Its founder, Lane Hornung, is a genius, and 8z has the best Internet strategy of any company I've seen. With its business model of capturing Internet leads and turning them into appointments, the 8z Realtors are meeting most of their buyers for the first time at the property. Lane tracks everything, and he told me their buyer-conversion ratio jumped 43 percent once his Realtors started using the Ninja Ten-Step Buyer Process. He now requires all his 8z Realtors to go through our four-day Ninja Installation class.

STEP 5: THE FUNNEL PROCESS

Step 5 is the critical step that starts eliminating the buyers' fears about missing something or paying too much. Our goal in Step 5 is to help them have the green light. Here's the dialogue:

"John and Mary, our goal is to help you find a great home and, at the same time, make sure you don't miss out on anything or pay too much. We have a process called the Funnel Process that will help us accomplish those goals. Would you like to see how it works for you?"

I've never had a buyer say no to this question. In fact, they usually offer an enthusiastic yes! Their internal dialogue is, *Hallelujah, a Realtor with a process!* Also, see how we have addressed their two greatest fears of missing out on something and paying too much? We will continue to restate these two phrases throughout the Funnel Process.

The Funnel Process was developed by Keith Huntsman, a partner at The Group, Inc. He is a pro who really understands the power of a process and knows his numbers. After he had been in the business about thirteen years, I asked him one day, "Keith, what percentage of the buyers you work with end up buying with you?" His response? "Larry, so far, it's 100 percent. I've never had a buyer buy from somebody else. I guess I'm really fortunate." Or you have an amazing process!

Here's what you say next:

"The basic idea of the funnel is for us to put everything in the funnel that might work for you. This way, *you don't miss anything*. Then, we'll filter out all of the properties that don't fit your criteria."

You say this while drawing a picture of a funnel on a sheet of paper.

This process is the exact opposite of what most Realtors do. Rather than starting with everything and using a *process of elimination* to find the properties that fit, most Realtors use a *process of selection*—usually properties selected by the buyer. Their buyer goes on the Internet, selects some properties, and then calls the Realtor to set up appointments. They all run out and look at those properties, but because they are using a process of selection, the buyer's nonconscious fear of missing something causes them to think about it. A few days or weeks later, the buyer selects another batch of houses to look at, calls the Realtor again, and the process repeats.

Who is in control of this process? The buyer. Is it a process that works? It can, but it takes a long time. The process of elimination and the Ten-Step Buyer Process are far more effective.

Here's what you say next: "Let's start with what you have so far. Do you have a list of homes you have found that you are interested in?"

Most buyers do. They have found homes on the Internet, in advertising, or that they have driven by. Review what they have. This is an opportunity for them to show and tell. As they bring up each home, ask two questions:

1. "What was it about that property that attracted your attention?" The first thing out of their mouth is their dominant motivation. Write it down! As they show you several houses, and you ask this question about each one, you will start to see a pattern developing as to what is driving their motivation.

2. "Have you gone inside this home?" If so, find out their reaction to it. Also, if there was another Realtor with them, find out what their relationship is with that Realtor.

Next you say: If it's alright with you, let's start by putting these homes into our funnel. To make sure *you don't miss anything*, let's also put into the funnel any home you might consider. Will that be okay with you?"

At this point in the conversation, you should discuss the following:

- **Multiple Listing Service (MLS).** "Let's put all of them (thousands of properties) in the funnel right now, so we make sure *you don't miss anything*. We will also load in the home search function, so if a new listing comes on the market later, we will get a notice, and it will automatically go into the funnel."

- **New Construction.** Encourage the buyer to at least consider new construction at this stage. At this point we should consider everything *so we don't miss anything*. Sometimes buyers will say they are not interested in new construction, but later, when they see the resale inventory is low and they can't find what they want, they may reconsider new construction. Encourage them to put it in the funnel—at least at this stage.

- **For Sale by Owner (FSBO).** Have this discussion. "When we are driving around, if you see a For Sale by Owner that you feel might work for you, I want you to be comfortable discussing it with me. I haven't found a For Sale by Owner yet who wouldn't work with me. So I can help you if you want my help. If you would prefer to work with them on your own by yourself, that is fine, too. I just want you to find the right home and not miss anything." This dialogue might be different if you have a buyer brokerage agreement, but if you don't, the transparency and customer concern of this dialogue is powerful. The phrase "on your own by yourself" speaks to their internal dialogue. Based on the rapport you have built, the idea of being "on your own by yourself" is terrifying to them.

- **Foreclosures and Short Sales.** Depending on market conditions, if there are foreclosures and short sales, have this discussion and put the properties in the funnel.

Next you say: "Once we have everything in the funnel, we'll start a simple process of elimination to remove those properties that don't work for you. We'll use the comfortable process of elimination versus the often-frustrating process of selection. This way, we'll make sure *you don't miss anything*."

Have you ever had buyers who say they want to look at everything? They really don't want to look at everything. The reason they say that is that they don't want to miss out on anything. Now you have a process to help them accomplish that goal.

Your next move is to say the following: We'll go from potentially hundreds of properties in the funnel and then to dozens, as we begin to eliminate those that don't work. Some of them, you will simply look at online. The ones you like the best, we will drive by or make an appointment to go inside. You will be in control of the decisions.

"As we go through this process of elimination, our goal will be to find your top three favorite homes that could work for you. This can be a rolling top three, so if you find a home you like better than one in your current top three, you can substitute. Once you have identified your three favorites, I'll do a comparative market analysis (CMA) showing you sold properties to help you get a feel for value. Our goal is to make sure you don't pay too much."

Funnel Process

ALL HOMES (MLS, NEW, FSBO)

Don't Miss Anything!

Don't Pay Too Much!

PROCESS OF ELIMINATION—ROLLING TOP THREE (CMA)

During the funnel step, it is very important that you repeatedly reiterate that this process is designed to *"make sure you don't miss anything or pay too much."* This settles the fears stored in their nonconscious. You also want to draw the funnel and illustrate the process. When you do that, two things happen. First, your buyers lean in, as they want to see the drawing, and you are even more connected. Second, it's more effective, since most people are visual. Showing is better than telling.

Conclude Step 5 with this question: "Does this look like a process that will work for you?" Their internal dialogue is, *I'm relieved that we have a process that protects me from my two greatest fears.*

This process gives them the green light when they find a home they like.

STEP 6: SCALE OF 1 TO 10

This next question is done in pretend state:

"Just for fun, to give me an idea of where you are in the process, on a scale of 1 to 10 (with a 1 being you are just starting the process and a 10 being you would like to find a home today) where would you rate yourself?"

The use of the 1 to 10 scale is very helpful in getting clarity. I remember taking Pat's mother to the emergency room when she was having chest pains. The nurse came over and said, "Evonne, I'm here to help you manage your pain. To give me an idea, on a scale of 1 to 10, with a 1 being you're totally comfortable and a 10 being the worst pain you've ever had, how would you rate yourself?" Evonne said she was probably an 8. This was much more meaningful to the nurse than a patient who simply says, "I'm in pain."

In my experience, most buyers rate themselves as a 5 or a 6. Then, you ask: "What would have to happen for you to be a 10?"

The buyers will now start to list what needs to happen. Usually, the first words out of their mouth are, "We would need to find the right home." Take a moment here to have them describe the right home. You can probe a bit, but don't get stuck here, because we will revisit the specific things they are looking for in a home a little bit later. Whatever they say, *write it down!* Ask, "What else would have to happen?"

At this point, John says his corporate transfer papers would need to come through. He doesn't have the final paperwork yet. *Write it down!* "What else would have to happen?"

"We'd need to finalize our loan," says Mary.

"Have you talked to a lender?" you ask. Mary says they talked to a lender before they left California but have not made a formal application. *Write it down!* "What else would have to happen?"

Sometimes, you will need to help them along with the list of what needs to happen. For example, you ask, "How about your house in California? Will you need to sell it to buy here?" They say they will, and you discuss whether it is on the market yet and whether John's company will guarantee the sale. *Write it down!* "Is there anything else that would have to happen?"

John and Mary say, "No, I think that's it."

Now, you all have very clear marching orders. You look at your pad of paper, and here's what you have written down. We need to do the following (not necessarily in this order):

- Find the right home.

- Get John's transfer papers.
- Get a loan on the new home.
- Get the California home sold or guaranteed by John's company.

This process clarifies what needs to happen not only for you but also for John and Mary. They are now clear that when these four things have happened, they have bought a home.

I recommend you say, "What would have to happen for you to be a 10?" Say it in a calm, nonchalant way and use these exact words. I once had a student in class complain that this question was backfiring on him. He said that it seemed the buyers raised a shield when he asked it, and he lost their trust.

In an effort to troubleshoot what he was saying, I had him role-play with me. When we got to this step, he asked, with edginess in his voice, "What do I have to do to get you to a 10?" The entire class erupted with similar sentiments. "Wow! That feels like pressure." You are not trying to get anyone to do anything. That approach is old school and non-Ninja. Just use your nonanxious presence and casually ask, "What would have to happen for you to be a 10?" Don't be attached to the outcome.

STEP 7: DREAM HOME EXERCISE

Have you ever had two buyers disagree on what they wanted in a house? Do you feel you are a negotiator, trying to find common ground between them? Are they sometimes not really clear on what they want in the first place? This exercise will help them clarify and prioritize.

Give each buyer a blank sheet of paper. It is important that they each have their own sheet of paper, not a joint sheet. Have them each make a list of what they want in a home. It is a bit of a dream sheet. Once they each have their list complete, have them put a star beside the three things they can't live without. Also, if there is something they simply can't possibly stand in a home, have them jot that down as well. In the case of John and Mary, you could have asked them to do this before they arrived in town. You simply ask them if they brought their homework.

STEP 8: WHATS (FEATURES) AND WHYS (BENEFITS)

Now take out a blank sheet of your own and draw a T on the paper similar to the one in the following illustration. You are going to summarize their top three *have to haves* or top three priorities in the left column. You sense John is the Power personality, so you start with him. Then you go to Mary. Then back to John. Here's what they say:

John: "I want to live on a golf course."

Mary: "We need four bedrooms."

John: "I want a three-car garage."

Mary: "I want a large kitchen."

John: "I had the four bedrooms on my list as well." (They have a duplicate.)

Mary: "I would like to live on a large lot."

Features (Whats)	Benefits (Whys)
Golf course	
Four bedrooms	
Three-car garage	
Large kitchen	
Large lot	

John and Mary have five home features on their list. These are the five things they have to have. Here is where many Realtors step into a trap. They now think they know what John and Mary want in a home, so they load these five features into their MLS search criteria and start looking for homes that fit this description. Unfortunately, John and Mary are not going to buy a home with these five features. Buyers don't buy their *whats*. They buy their *whys*.

As a Ninja, you need to take this process to the second step: Why do they want these features? Now that you have the list on the left side, you start with John again and clarify why these features are important.

You: "John, tell me about why you want to live on a golf course."

John: "I want to live where I have a view and a sense of open space. Right now, we live on a really small lot, and I look out my back window at another house. It would be great to look across an expanse of green that someone else takes care of."

Can John get views and open space someplace besides a golf course? John doesn't play golf, and neither do 80 percent of the people who live on golf courses in the United States. There are other reasons to live there—views, prestige, perception of value, networking if it is a private country club, among others. For John, it is views, and he can get that in other places as well.

You: "Mary, tell me about the four bedrooms."

Mary: "Well, John and I need a master bedroom. Then, we need a guest bedroom with its own bathroom. We have adult children, and when they visit, it would really be nice for them to have their own suite. Also, John has business associates visit, and it would be nice if we had a nice suite for them. I guess the ideal house would have the equivalent of two master suites. Then John needs an office, and I need an office."

What Mary described is not the typical four-bedroom house. It is two master suites and two offices. You could probe a bit about the location of those two offices—lower level? Shared?

You: "John, back to you. How about the three-car garage?"

John: "Well, I have a Harley. Plus, if I decide to learn to play golf, I may want room for a golf cart."

You: "Would an oversize two-car work?"

John: "If all I have is the motorcycle, an oversize two-car could work for sure."

You: "Mary, how about that large kitchen?"

Mary: "John and I like to entertain. In fact, we entertain a lot."

So this kitchen is not just about cooking. It is more about entertaining, and that drives the whole main floor plan. Mary and you start discussing her ideal floor plan for entertaining—the size of groups they entertain, whether it is formal or informal entertaining, and so on. This is clearly a lot bigger item than just the kitchen.

You: "Mary, John had a duplicate with the four bedrooms, so it is back to you again with the large lot."

Mary: "Well, John mentioned how right now, when we look out of our house, we see our neighbors. When I look out my kitchen window, I see my neighbor looking out their kitchen window. I would really like some privacy."

As we are going through the whys with John and Mary, you start filling out the right side of the ledger. Here's what it looks like now:

Features (Whats)	Benefits (Whys)
1. Golf course	1. Views and open space
2. Four bedrooms	2. Two master suites and two offices
3. Three-car garage	3. Three-car or oversized two-car garage
4. Large kitchen	4. Entertaining floor plan
5. Large lot	5. Privacy

John and Mary will buy their *whys* (the right column), not their *whats* (the left column). Ninjas will load the whys into their MLS search and start showing John and Mary homes that fit.

In the end, John and Mary bought a house on a lake with a fabulous view. It was basically a two-bedroom home, but both bedrooms were master suites. There was a large room upstairs, looking out over the lake, that John and Mary made into their office. Although the house had a relatively small kitchen, the open floor plan was perfect for entertaining. The lot was really small, but with the orientation to the lake, John and Mary felt they had a lot of privacy.

I have an amazing number of cards and emails from Ninjas who describe how their work with buyers improved dramatically once they started focusing on the buyers' *whys* instead of their *whats*.

STEP 9: CASH OR LOAN? MLS SEARCH

When you ask, "Will you be paying cash for this home or will you be getting a loan?" most people will say they are getting a loan. Between 20 percent and 30 percent of home buyers pay cash.

If they are getting a loan, the next thing you should ask is this: "Have you met with a lender? Do you have a loan arranged?"

If they are using a lender you're not familiar with (their sister's boyfriend in Florida), ask this question: "Would you like a second opinion? I can recommend several good lenders to you. There is no obligation to use them, but at least you would have a second opinion." Most people will agree to this. They like the idea of a second opinion. Also, you want the buyers checked out by a lender that you know and trust and can deliver the goods.

I'm often asked why we wait until Step 9 to discuss financing. We touch on it a bit in Step 6 but not in detail. Financing is a complicated subject and should not be discussed first, because you will start your buyer off in a confused state of mind. By Step 9, they are in a rhythm; they are feeling clear and confident. They are now in the right mindset to handle financing. Second, you now know the specifics of the kind of house they are looking for and its price range.

At this point, you have a couple of options: You can start doing the first cut on the MLS search, while John and Mary meet with the lender, or you can have them meet with the lender first and then sit with you at the computer to do the elimination process on the funnel. In my experience, Perfection buyers will want to be part of sitting at the computer and doing the elimination process.

A Mismatch on Price

What if there is a mismatch between what John and Mary want and what they are qualified to borrow? After meeting with the lender, they say they are qualified for a loan up to $500,000. They have $100,000 to $150,000 for a down payment, so their total package is about $600,000 to $650,000. The problem is the houses that have their whys start at about $750,000. What do you do now? Discuss the options:

- Are they willing to give up any of their whys?
- Do they have other resources they can bring to the game (other assets, family)?
- Are they willing to "drive 'til you qualify?" What they want in Fort Collins starts at $750,000, but if they are willing to drive fifteen minutes to Windsor, they can get it for less than $600,000.

Ask the buyer, "Are you familiar with the 1 percent = 10 percent rule of thumb?" Most buyers (and Realtors) are unaware that every 1 percent change in interest rate affects a buyer's borrowing power by 10 percent. A 1 percent increase in interest rate lowers the loan amount that can be supported by that same payment by 10 percent. Here's what it looks like:

- 4.5 percent, 30-year loan, $1,013/month payment = $200,000 mortgage amount
- 5.5 percent, 30-year loan, $1,013/month payment = $178,476 mortgage amount
- 6.5 percent, 30-year loan, $1,013/month payment = $160,326 mortgage amount

In a rising rate environment, a buyer's greatest risk is probably their loss of buying power if interest rates go up. They may not realize this. As their trusted advisor, you are there to show it to them.

Avoid the Confusion Trap!

As you are doing the computer search, eliminating houses that don't fit the whys and printing off the ones that do, make sure you have this conversation with your buyer:

"John and Mary, once we decide on the homes you want to look at, we'll set up appointments to see them. I'll print you a copy of the MLS sheet for each home. I'm also going to print the information on all the homes that are for sale or have sold in that neighborhood during the past year. That way you will have all of the information.

"We may drive past a home with a For Sale sign in the front yard, and you may wonder why we are not stopping to see it. There is a reason. Perhaps it's under contract, or maybe it is not in our price range. If you see any properties that you have a question about, will you let me know? We'll have all the information with us, and I want to make sure all of your questions are answered so we *don't miss anything*."

Today, we also have the option of providing this information electronically, with an application that syncs the MLS with a GPS. You can set it up on an iPad for your buyer, rather than taking the printed sheets. Ask your buyer which they would prefer.

I can't emphasize enough the importance of this conversation with your buyers. Unfortunately, most Realtors skip this step, and they pay the price later. They head out to show property and are driving through a neighborhood when the buyers notice a beautiful home, great curb appeal, and wonderful landscaping. The Realtor drives right on by without saying a word. What goes through the buyer's mind? *Hey, what about that one? I like the looks of that one.*

The buyer now starts to look for street signs to figure out the address of that house, so they can look it up later online. The Realtor has just lost them. The buyer is confused and will not be buying a house today. The red light is on until the buyer gets online to check out that house.

I have seen reports that say 60 percent to 70 percent of all buyers check the Internet within two hours after leaving their Realtor. Why? They are trying to find the answers to the confusion created by the Realtor when they were looking at homes. Keep your buyers clear, and give them the green light. Take the active and sold listing data with you for the neighborhoods you are showing property in, and make sure you share this information with your buyers.

Why take the sold data? When your buyer finds a home he or she likes and wants to buy it, what is the first thing to pop in their mind? Exactly! *How much should I offer? I don't want to pay too much.*

You can now say, "Let's take a look at what has sold in this neighborhood to get an idea of fair market value."

STEP 10: WHAT HAPPENS NEXT?

You have four objectives in this step. They all relate to clarity and creating the proper buyer expectations *before* they get into the heat of battle. When buyers are prepared for what is about to happen, it is easier for them to be clear and confident. I've asked Ninjas who are very successful with buyers, "What is your success secret?" They universally say, "Invest more time with your buyers up-front. Prepare their expectations so they don't get surprised."

Here are four areas you want to cover before looking at homes:

1. **Is There Anything We've Missed?** John may say, "Oh, I would need to have my brother look at the house." His brother is a contractor, and John wants him to inspect it. Very often, young, first-time buyers will say, "Oh, we would need to call our parents for the down payment." Earlier in Step 6, we thought we had all of this out on the table and had our marching orders,

but it's a good idea to find out if there is anything we've missed *before* we get in the middle of negotiating a contract.

2. **Review the Market.** Prepare your buyers for the kind of market they are about to enter. Do this before they are in the middle of it. Having them learn about the market solely from personal experience can often cause confusion and fear. Prepare their expectations. Stories and metaphors can be helpful. Here are some sample dialogues.

   - **Market Conditions.** "The market is active right now. In your price range, about 58 percent of the homes for sale are under contract right now. So far this year, 70 percent of the homes have sold for full price or more."

   - **Cream Puff Story.** Review what your buyers are looking for. Then, summarize by saying, "So you are looking for a great home, in a great neighborhood, in great condition, at a great price. Right?" The buyers nod. "You know, we have a name for a house like that. It's called a *cream puff*. And guess what the other buyers are looking for? They are looking for cream puffs, too. As a result, cream puffs don't last on the market very long. When we see a cream puff—and believe me you'll recognize it when you see it—if it's a home you can see yourself living in, my recommendation is that you take action on it right away. It won't last."

   - **85 Percent Perfect House.** The 85 percent house metaphor was mentioned in the section on external and internal dialogues. This is a great place to have that conversation.

   - **Lost House Story.** If you want to tell a lost house story, now is the time. There is less pressure if you tell it while you are in a conference room. If you tell it in a house, it comes off as a pressure tactic. When your buyer is in a house they clearly love and they say they want to think about it, how does it feel when the Realtor says, "Well, let me tell you a story about one of my buyers who wanted to think about it. . . ." This comes off as high pressure. Don't do it! Instead, simply ask, "If this home sells tonight, are you OK with that?" It's their decision.

3. **Prepare Their Expectations.** "When we find a home you like, I will notice that you start doing what we call *the dance*. You will start giving signals that you like the home. When I see you do the dance, I'm going to ask you this question, 'Can you see yourself living in this home?' If you say yes, I'm going to ask you, 'Is this a home you would like to own?' If you say yes, I'll ask you if you want to write a contract on this home."

Dr. Flow, Wynn Washle, says part of his success is setting the proper expectations with buyers. Wynn tracks his numbers and knows what percentage of his buyers find their home the first time they are out looking. After the buyers tell Wynn what they are looking for in a home, and before they start looking at homes, Wynn initiates the following dialogue:

"So, would you like to know your odds?" Wynn asks.

"The odds of what?" asks the buyer.

Wynn says, "Well, 60 percent of the buyers I work with are able to find their home on their first time out. You might be one of the 40 percent who doesn't find it on the first time out, in which case, the odds are 50/50 we'll find it on the second time out."

What just happened? First, Wynn has given the buyer permission to buy on the first time out. Second, he sets the expectation that there is an 80 percent chance they will find their home on the first or second time out. Wynn's odds are high, because he follows the Ten-Step Buyer Process, helps his buyers make a balanced brain decision, and gives them permission to make a decision (find a solution).

We find that Wynn's odds are not unusual with Ninjas who follow our Ten-Step Buyer Process precisely. In fact, if you follow the buyer process precisely, and you find your buyer is looking at more than about ten or twelve homes, it may be because the buyer has issues that are beyond your scope to handle. These issues could be family, financial, or marital. If they have issues, just showing more houses will not be a solution.

4. **Prepare for Negotiations.** Especially in multiple-offer markets, prepare your buyers for the negotiation process up front. Discuss negotiation strategies and ways to reduce or eliminate contingencies—especially inspection, loan, and appraisal contingencies.

   Most states have multipage real estate contracts. (Colorado's contract is seventeen pages.) However, all those pages of legalese are designed to help buyers and sellers come to agreement on just five negotiating points. Those points are the following:

   - Price
   - Terms (earnest money, down payment, and financing or cash)
   - Dates (closing and possession)
   - Inclusions and exclusions
   - Contingencies (loan, inspections, attorney approval, etc.)

Go over these five negotiating points with your buyer *before* they are in a negotiation.

Appendix B

THE ART AND SCIENCE OF SHOWING PROPERTY

Here are some rules of thumb for showing property:

- **MLS Map.** Print off a map and give it to your buyers so they can see where you are as you are looking at properties. This is especially important for out-of-town buyers who are not familiar with the area. Most people are visual learners and will appreciate the map.
- **Active and Sold Properties.** As mentioned in Step 9 of the Ten-Step Buyer Process (Appendix A), make sure you have active and sold properties for those neighborhoods you are showing.
- **Plan Your Route and Show Big Values.** Big values are schools, parks, shopping and employment centers, and so on. Small values are homes. In appraisal, the big values support the small values. Make sure you point out the big values on the way to the homes you are showing.
- **Park Across the Street.** Your buyers will have a better view of the home than if you pull in the driveway, where their only view of the home might be the garage door.

- **Go in First.** I recommend you enter the home first for two reasons:

  1. One reason is security and safety. Ring the doorbell or knock. If there is no answer, open the door slightly, being careful that there is not a dog or other animal waiting inside. Announce yourself. "Hello! Anybody home?" If the coast is clear, open the door all the way, step into the home, and step to the side, so your buyers can see the home. With a gesture of your hand, invite them across the threshold.

  2. When they step across the threshold, watch their eyes. If your buyers go in first, you are looking at the backs of their heads. If your buyers like the home, their eyes will dilate. This is an involuntary reaction that occurs when people see something they like. If they don't like what they see, their eyes will contract, and they will become beady eyed. Watching their eyes gives you an early clue if they like or dislike the home.

  Safety Note: If your buyer is a stranger, and especially if you are female, the National Association of Realtors recommends you never turn your back when showing a house. In that case, you would invite them to enter the house first.

- **Watch Body Language.** Be careful about talking too much when showing property. Instead, listen and observe your buyers' behavior and conversation for clues as to what they think of the house. If they like the house, you will see buying signals, such as sitting down in the home, going through the home more than once, and mentally moving in (placing furniture, picking kids' rooms, etc.). We call this *doing the dance*.

- **See Again?** Point out features and rooms of the house that they may not have noticed. If you are not sure whether they like the home (some buyers are more difficult to read), ask this question: "Is there any portion of the home you would like to see again before we leave?" If they say, "No, I think we've seen it," this is a clue they don't like the house. Most buyers will go through a home at least twice before they buy it.

- **Best Part of the House.** Make sure you discuss the buyer's feelings about the home when you are standing in the best part of the house—usually the kitchen, family room, or deck. Ideally, stand in the part of the house you noticed the buyer most liked. A common mistake some Realtors make in showing houses, especially houses with basements, is that they show the upper floors first, then they end up in the furnace room in the basement, where they start asking the buyer, "How do you feel about this house?"

- **What Stage?** By watching your buyers' behavior, you can determine what stage of the buying process they are in. Buyers typically go through these four stages:

  Stage 1: Curiosity

  Stage 2: Interest

  Stage 3: Desire

  Stage 4: Commitment

  If they are in the desire stage, you will notice the buying signals, and it is appropriate to start asking soft closing questions such as "Is this one of our top three?" Never ask soft closing questions unless you are sure your buyers are in the desire stage.

- **Avoiding Buyer's Remorse.** Buyers sometimes get hot to buy a property and then later have second thoughts and want to cancel the contract. When your buyers are hot, and quickly say, "We'll take it," there are six things you can do when showing property that will help your buyers avoid buyer's remorse later on.

  1. Encourage them to walk through the home more than once.

2. Encourage them to walk through every room. If they don't, they will start to ask themselves about it later. "We didn't see the bedroom in the basement."

3. If the listing Realtor has a floor plan of the home in their brochure, make sure your buyers take it. Later, they can refer to it, and it will help answer their questions.

4. Make sure they tour the home privately. If they are looking at the home at the same time as other buyers (e.g., at an open house) make sure you set up another showing for them to see it privately.

5. Encourage them to review the photos of the home after the showing.

6. Have them read the seller's disclosure statement before writing the contract.

Appendix C

SOFT CLOSING QUESTIONS

There's an old saying in sales, "Only close when the *gate of the mind is open*." What is the gate of the mind? It's the desire stage. Only ask your customer a closing question when they are in the desire stage as described in Appendix B. If they are in the curiosity or interest stages, you will come off as an annoying, pushy salesperson. You must learn to read your customer and know what stage they are in.

What is a soft closing question? It is an easy, low-risk question that requires a small, low-drama decision. Hard closing questions are high-risk questions that create drama because they require a big decision.

Here's a list of favorite Ninja soft closing questions:

- Of the homes we've seen so far, is this home one of your top three?
- Would you rate this an 85 percent or better home?
- Can you see yourself living in this home?
- Is this a home you'd like to own?
- When would you like to move in?
- Shall we see if you can buy this home (Power and Party personalities)?
- Shall we make sure you don't lose this home (Peace and Perfection personalities)?

- Is there any portion of the home you would like to see again before we leave?
- Which home do you like better (comparison of two homes)?
- If I call you later tonight and tell you one of these homes has sold, which one would you be most disappointed to lose? (Do this if they are noncommittal on which home they liked the best.)
- If this home sells tonight, will you be OK with that? What is your plan B?

Ninjas seldom close in the traditional sense. Instead, we ask questions with the goal of helping customers become clear and confident, so they feel comfortable committing to purchase. The scratch-pad solution is an example.

THE SCRATCH-PAD SOLUTION

When you can tell your buyers love a home, but for some reason they want to think about it, they are either confused, afraid, or both. Two strategies that can help them become clear and confident are first, to prepare a scratch-pad or practice contract for them to look at, and second, if the scratch-pad contract is not helpful, ask them if they would like for you to set up another appointment to see the property again later.

Buyers are often either afraid to make the big decision to purchase or they are afraid of the lengthy real estate contract. The scratch-pad solution helps them with both these fears. There are just five basic decisions a buyer has to make—price, terms, dates, inclusions/exclusions, and contingencies. (These are also the five negotiating points of a real estate contract.)

The scratch-pad solution chunks the big decision to buy into these five smaller decisions. This also simplifies the contract in the buyer's mind and helps them become clear. Here's how the scratch-pad solution sounds. It is done in a pretend state.

You: "Of the properties we've seen so far, would you rate this home in your top three?"

Buyer: "I would rate it as my first choice. I love it!"

You: "Can you see yourself living in this home?"

Buyer: "Oh, yes!"

You: "Is this a property you would like to own?"

Buyer: "I really like it a lot, but I'm not ready to buy just yet. I would like some time to think about it."

You: "Absolutely. You need to feel comfortable with your decision. Let me offer you this. If it's all right with you, why don't I scratch out the basics of a contract on a blank sheet of paper that you can take home with you? It will give you something to look at tonight."

Buyer: "Sure. That would be helpful."

You (price): "Let's see. This property is priced at $425,000. If you were to buy this property (pretend state), would you be comfortable with this price?

Buyer: "I think the property is worth it, but I would feel better if I could get it for maybe $410,000."

You write $410,000 on the blank sheet of paper. No matter what the buyer says for price, write it down, even if it is low. You can come back and discuss raising the price later.

You (terms): "I know when you met with Jason (lender) you talked about going with either a thirty-year or a fifteen-year fixed rate loan. If you were to buy this home, which way do you think you would go"

Buyer: "I would probably go with the thirty-year loan."

You write down the down payment, loan amount, and monthly payment on the blank sheet of paper. Some Ninjas will already have calculated the payment and written it on the property MLS sheet prior to showing. That way, the buyer easily knows what the payment is, and it is readily available for the scratch-pad close. You could also do this scratch-pad close on the back of the property's MLS sheet.

You (dates): "If you could wave your magic wand and close and move into this property when you want, when would that be?"

Buyer: "Ideally, it would be before school starts. Say August 15."

You write down August 15 closing and possession date.

You (inclusions and exclusions): "Here's a list of personal property that is either included or excluded in the sale, are you okay with this list?"

Buyer: "Those items look good to me."

You (contingencies): "Let's see. We would want to make the contract contingent on getting your loan. If you don't get the loan, you don't have to buy the property. The same is true if the property doesn't inspect, so we have the contingency on the inspection. Is there anything else you would want to have as contingencies?"

Notice how this dialogue reassures the buyer that they are protected and helps them feel safe.

Buyer: "No. I think that about covers it. You know, why don't we just go ahead with it? I guess the more I think about it, I'm comfortable going ahead."

You: "OK. Let me take this worksheet and prepare a contract for you."

In our experience, the buyer will choose to go ahead about 50 percent of the time. Why? Because they've chunked a big, scary decision into five smaller decisions. You've helped them think through the decision by simplifying, clarifying, and reassuring them. They feel safe, clear, and confident.

About 50 percent of the time, your buyer will decide not to buy right then. They truly want to think about it. That's okay. Don't push them. It's their decision. You control the process. They control the decisions.

Buyer: "Gee, thanks. This really helps. I'll take this paper home tonight and look it over again and get back with you."

You: "Great, if you have any questions tonight, feel free to call me.

In the meantime, would you like for me to set up an appointment for you to take another look at the home?"

Buyer: "That's a good idea. I would like to see it tomorrow right after work."

You: "OK, I'll get that appointment set up for tomorrow. When I talk with the listing Realtor, if they say they have an offer coming in on the property, shall I call you?"

Buyer: "Please do. If I need to move quicker, I can."

When the buyer really likes a home, give them every opportunity to buy it. Finish your appointment with either a contract or an appointment to see the home again.

THE AUCTION SOLUTION

Sometimes, when the buyer says they will take the scratch-pad contract home and look it over, it could mean they are headed to another city or even another country and will not be back for six months. This especially happens in resort markets. The auction solution is another tool in your tool kit.

Buyer: "I really like this property!" (They are doing the dance.)

You: "Of the properties we've looked at, is this one your favorite?"

Buyer: "Oh, yes! By far! I love it!"

You: "Is this a property you would like to own."

Buyer: "Definitely, but I want to think about it first."

You: "Absolutely. You need to feel comfortable with your decision. Let me offer you this. If it's all right with you, why don't I scratch out the basics of a contract on a blank sheet of paper that you can take home with you? It will give you something to look at tonight."

You and the buyer do the scratch-pad solution.

Buyer: "Thank you very much. This really helps clarify everything. We'll talk it over and get back with you."

You: "Let me ask you this. (You know the buyer is leaving that night for Chicago.) This home is priced at $3.2 million. Just for fun (pretend state), if you could wave a magic wand and buy it for $2.7, what would you do?"

Buyer: "I'd buy it in a heartbeat. It would be a steal at $2.7."

You: (smiling) "Just for fun, if you could buy it for $2.8, what would you do?"

Buyer: "At $2.8, it's still a great buy."

You: "I agree. How about $2.9?"

Buyer: "I'm still in at $2.9. That's still a good deal."

You: "How about $3.0?"

Buyer: "At $3.0, I would have to think about it."

You: "I can tell you are comfortable at $2.9 but not at $3.0. Would you like to go ahead at $2.9?"

About half the time, the buyer will say yes. You have clarified with the scratch-pad solution and found a price at which they are comfortable with the auction solution.

However, you will be writing an offer for substantially less than full price, and this may upset the seller. You will need to explain to the seller (or their Realtor) that this is the best you could do and it is better than no offer at all. Once the game starts, our experience is that both buyer and seller get into the negotiation and the odds of a signed agreement are high.

Appendix D

SELLER DECISIONS

What is the single most important factor in getting a home sold? In a Ninja workshop, our students will shout out "price" or "location." In fact, the single most important factor in getting a home sold is "seller decisions." What are the key decisions? The seller decides the following:

- List price
- Condition
- Showing availability
- Contract acceptance
- Realtor (which affects marketing and negotiating)

You can have a great house in a great location, but if you have a dysfunctional seller, you will have your hands full trying to sell that house. As a result, Ninjas don't list houses. We list sellers.

Evaluate the house, the market for the house, and the seller's decision-making ability. We recommend you look at four factors when evaluating your seller:

1. **Expectation.** Is your seller realistic or unrealistic? Can you coach them to have realistic expectations?
2. **Motivation.** Is your seller motivated to sell? Do they have a *gap*—a difference between where they are and where they want to be and a timetable for making that happen?

3. **Cooperation.** Are they cooperative and coachable? Does it feel like you are on the same team and working together? Or are they adversarial and uncooperative?

4. **Communication.** Is your seller open and honest in his or her communication? Are they readily available to respond to offers? Or are they unavailable and closed in their communication, perhaps with hidden agendas?

If you don't feel you have a motivated and functioning seller, you may choose to pass on this assignment. We will give you the dialogue for gracefully walking away in Step 9 of the Seller Process.

GET TO PRICE RIGHT AWAY

When you meet with a seller, what do you think is the number one question on their mind? *What's the price?* They want to get to price quickly. A mistake many Realtors make is starting with a presentation on their company, themselves, and their marketing plan. They do this thinking they need to demonstrate their value to the seller first. Their presentation turns into a seminar with the Realtor having time of possession, and the seller becomes restless. Their internal dialogue is saying, *When will we get to price?* Often, the seller checks out, and the Realtor's presentation sounds like Blah! Blah! Blah!

The Ninja Selling process gets to the market and price early in the consultation for two reasons:

1. That's what the seller wants.

2. If you run into rough weather on the price or your fee, you can say, "Let's set the price (or fee) aside for just a minute, and let me show you how we plan to market your home." You have a

plan B. If you've already gone over your marketing plan earlier, your tool kit is empty.

CRUCIAL CONVERSATIONS

Keep in mind that when you sit down with a seller, you are often entering a *crucial conversation*. The book *Crucial Conversations, Tools for Talking When the Stakes Are High*, by Kerry Patterson, Joseph Grenny, Ron McMillan, Al Switzler, and Laura Roppe, lists three elements that make up a crucial conversation:

1. The stakes are high.
2. There is a difference of opinion.
3. Emotions are high.

When these three elements are present, Power and Party People will often respond with violence (anger, tears, emotional outburst) whereas Peace and Perfection People will often respond with silence. (They clam up and become uncommunicative.) The following are good ways to avoid violence or silence:

1. **Make It Safe.** Be calm, cool, soften your voice, display your nonanxious presence, and communicate that you are here to help them and that you are on the same team. It's you and them against the market. The market is the bad guy, not you.

2. **Make It Clear.** Confusion causes fear and poor decisions. Sellers may be confused by many factors: neighbors' home prices, an appraisal, their personal situation, other Realtors bidding for their listing, and so on. Your mission is to turn this confusion into clarity.

In addition to confusion, sellers may fear they're selling their house too cheap, paying the Realtor too much, or not getting sufficient value for the fee paid. And, if the house does not sell, it will mess up their life plans.

Keep in mind that selling a home is a big change for most people. You are their *change master*. Your mission is to help them through the five stages of change, which are the following:

1. **Denial.** They may be in denial about the market and the real value of their home. Or perhaps one spouse may be in denial about the move.

2. **Anger.** Typically, sellers move from denial to anger. It is important here that they yell at the market, not you. You are there to help them. You are on the same team.

3. **Sadness.** They are distraught that their sales proceeds are less than their original expectations.

4. **Acceptance.** They start to work things out in their mind and accept reality.

5. **Renewal.** They become excited about moving on to their new future.

Some sellers will go through the five stages of change in a matter of minutes. For others, it may be weeks or months. Your mission is to help them through it—remaining calm and cool, or what we call a *step-down transformer*.

What is a step-down transformer? Electrical power comes out of a power plant at thousands of megawatts. If it ran directly into your home, your home would explode because of too much power. There are a series of transformers that step down the power, so it is safe to enter your home. You are the step-down transformer in the transaction. You take the negative energy and drama and lower the wattage.

Have you ever been in a transaction with another Realtor (or a customer) who is a step-up transformer? They take the smallest issue and magnify it into high drama. Not Ninjas! Ninjas are like ducks, calm and cool on the surface and paddling like crazy underneath.

Appendix E

THE SIXTEEN-STEP SELLER PROCESS

The Ninja Sixteen-Step Seller Process is a series of questions to ask the seller. These questions give the seller time of possession. As a result, it is a listing consultation not a listing presentation.

Here's a summary of the Ninja Sixteen-Step Seller Process:

- Step 1: Prelisting Interview
- Step 2: Prelisting Package
- Step 3: Property Walkthrough
- Step 4: What Are We Selling?
- Step 5: Other Properties to Sell?
- Step 6: The Calendar
- Step 7: Prelisting Package Review
- Step 8: Questions Regarding Package
- Step 9: Qualified to Market Your Home?
- Step 10: My Mission and Your Odds
- Step 11: Fair Market Value
- Step 12: Selling "On the Line"
- Step 13: Where Will It Sell?
- Step 14: Pricing "On The Line"
- Step 15: On Time and Plan B
- Step 16: The Next Seventy-Two Hours

Let's walk through each step in detail.

STEP 1: PRELISTING INTERVIEW

The phone rings, and a voice says, "Hi, my name is John Smith. You don't know me, but we have mutual friends, Jason and Heather Brown, and they suggested I call you. We are interested in visiting with you about selling our home."

What do you do next? You connect (build rapport), and then take control of the process. It sounds like this:

"John, thanks for the call. How do you know Jason and Heather?" (Build rapport and common ground.) "If it's all right with you, I would like to ask you a few questions and then set up a time for us to get together. These questions are to help me prepare for our meeting and should take about ten minutes. Is this an OK time with you?"

You then pull out your prelisting interview questionnaire and start asking the questions. The questions are organized with prior learning questions first, to build a foundation of trust and confidence. The goal of the prelisting interview is to gather basic information, so you are prepared when you meet with the seller. You will also pick up subtle nuances in the conversation, such as the seller's personality type, priorities, and so on.

It is important that you simply ask the questions and take notes. Be conversational, but do not allow yourself to become engaged in a discussion on any particular question such as price. Avoid selling over the phone. You are simply examining the patient not performing surgery. Just read the questions, take notes, and move on to the next question. (You can download this prelisting interview questionnaire at www.NinjaSelling.com.)

Prelisting Interview

1. Name _____
2. Property Address _____
   Mailing Address _____
3. Owners/Decision Makers _____
   Phones: (H) _____ (B) _____
   Fax _____ E-mail _____
4. Why are you selling? _____
   If a corporate move: Is your company helping you with the move? _____
5. When do you need to move? _____
6. Could you describe your house for me? _____
   _____

Beds _____ Baths _____ Sq. Ft. _____ Style _____
Lot Size _____ Bsmt? _____
7. How long have you owned your home? _____
   _____

8. What sold you on your home when you bought it? What features did you like? _____
   _____

9. Have you done any updating to the home since you bought it? _____
   _____

10. If you were to stay in your home another 5 years, is there anything you would do to it? _____
    _____

11. For a moment pretend to be a buyer and look at your home through what we call "Buyer Eyes." On a scale of 1 to 10, how would you rate its condition? (Poor Condition = 1; Model home = 10) _____
    What would it take for your house to be a 10?
    _____

12. What are you going to be asking for the property?
_____

Have you had a recent appraisal? _____ Have you recently refinanced? _____

13. Do you own your property free and clear, or do you have a loan? (If they have a loan) Do you happen to know the approximate balance? _____

14. What are three things you are looking for in a Realtor?
_____
_____

15. Are you interviewing any other brokers for this job? Do you have any appointments set up?

Name _____ Company _____ Time _____
Name _____ Company _____ Time _____

16. Have you sold a property before?
_____

17. Have you considered going for sale by owner?
_____

18. Have you considered selling to an institutional investor (iBuyer)? (Optional question)
_____

19. Is there anything else I should know about your home?
_____

How do I get access to your property (if out-of-town owner)?
_____

20. To help me prepare for our meeting, do you have any questions for me?
_____

21. Explain what happens next: One Call _____
Two Call _____ Prelisting Packet _____

22. Set appointment: Day _____ Time _____
Place _____

Explanation and Comments on the Prelisting Interview Questionnaire

- **Questions 1 through 8.** These are foundational questions that access prior learning. I'm often asked why we ask some of these questions when we could simply look up the answers in county records. The reason is to have the sellers get comfortable answering questions to which they know the answers. If the seller mentions they are relocating to another city, should you ask them if they would like for you to connect them with a broker in that city? Yes, but not on the phone. Wait until you have met each other face-to-face at their home and have had a chance to build rapport.

- **Questions 9 through 12.** These questions will give you a pretty good idea of the home's condition. In fact, how the seller answers questions 10 through 12 is a list of what most buyers will expect to have done in the home and will provide a list of items that need to be done to get the home ready for market. These questions are especially valuable if you are doing a one-call listing.

- **Questions 13 and 14.** These questions can be touchy and are optional, depending on the situation and how much rapport you feel you have with the seller. When we were in the Great Recession market with a very high percentage of the properties being underwater financially, these questions were very important.

- **Question 15.** Listen very carefully to how sellers answer this question. They will give you their top priorities, your marching orders. Make sure you cover these concerns when you meet with them. Also, this is a qualifying question for them. If they don't say they are looking for a Realtor who can get the job done, it may mean they are not very motivated.

- **Question 16.** You do not need to ask for the names of the brokers they are interviewing, but if they volunteer them, you need to have somewhere to write them down. What you're really curious about is if they have any other appointments set. You would prefer to be the *first* appointment for several reasons:

  - Eighty-two percent of all sellers only meet with one broker (NAR Profile of Buyers and Sellers). Of the 18 percent who meet with more than one Realtor, half of them don't want to meet with a second Realtor, but the first one didn't meet their expectations and they feel they need a second opinion. If you're first and do a great job, there is a very good chance you will list their home. Most sellers prefer to only have to talk to one Realtor.

  - By being first, you will set the bar so high it will be difficult for the other Realtors to match it. Your goal is to be the standard by which the others will be compared.

  - By being first, you open yourself up to the risk the seller will say, "I really like what you have shown me and would like to list with you, but I have appointments with two more Realtors. I'm the kind of person who keeps my commitments, so I need to talk to them first."

    Respect their commitments and say this.

    You: "If you didn't have those appointments, would you be comfortable hiring me as your Realtor?" (This is a pretend state question.)

    Seller: "Absolutely, but we do have those appointments and feel we should honor them."

    You: "I agree. It's important that you keep your commitments. When is your last appointment?"

    Seller: "Monday at 4:00 p.m."

    You: "If it's all right with you, let's do this. Let's get

together Monday at 6:00 p.m. You'll have had all your appointments by then, and we can sit down and see if you are still comfortable moving forward."

They will keep this appointment with you because they keep their commitments.

- **Question 17.** Why ask this question? Aren't we just putting ideas in the sellers' head about selling it themselves? First of all, sellers are smart. If they are thinking about going for sale by owner, it is in their mind before they call us. I like this question for one reason: the brutal honesty and transparency of it. Most sellers are surprised that we have the courage to ask this question. It sets the stage for the kind of relationship the seller can expect from us—open, honest, transparent, everything on the table.

- **Questions 18 through 20.** These are general "have we missed anything?" questions. Again, be careful on question 20 not to get engaged in a discussion or selling over the phone. You are simply getting a list of their questions and concerns so you can be prepared to address them when you meet. Sometimes the seller will ask, "What's your fee?" or "What do you think our house will sell for?" Respond by saying, "I'll show you what your options are when we get together." Or "Our goal at this point is for me to get a list of your questions so I can be prepared to answer them when we get together. I'll make sure I bring information on _____."

- **Question 21.** Here you have an important decision to make. Are you going to use a one-call or a two-call listing process? You have to make a decision and communicate what happens next to the seller. Some of our top-listing Ninjas use only a one-call process, while others exclusively use a two-call process. Still others use both, depending on the situation. There is no right or wrong way. The important point is to make sure you communicate the process to your seller. Here are the benefits of each process:

One-Call:

- House is easy to price based upon the phone interview
- Seller indicates urgency to "get this done" (Power or Party personalities)
- You are in competition with other brokers

Two-Call:

- Home is unique and difficult to price without seeing it
- Seller is Peace or Perfection personality and will want to take more time
- You are not in competition with other brokers

Several years ago, a young man named Anthony showed up in one of our Ninja Selling classes. Anthony was twenty-two years old, a fresh college graduate, and a brand-new real estate licensee. When it came time to practice the prelisting interview, it just happened to be at the same time Anthony was scheduled to call his first seller. Rather than practicing with another Ninja, Anthony decided to go live on his first interview.

Afterward, he came back to the room all excited. At the end of the interview, the seller had asked him, "Anthony, how long have you been doing this?" Anthony had replied, "Only a few weeks." The seller said, "Really? You sound like you've been doing this for years. You are a pro." This simple questionnaire process will make you sound like a pro, too.

STEP 2: PRELISTING PACKAGE

If you plan to use a one-call process, explain this process to the seller, make sure all decision-makers will be present, and explain that you will be having a packet of information delivered to them in advance that will help them understand the market and the sales process. Ask for their commitment to read the packet before you meet. If they only have time to read one thing, ask them to read your marketing plan.

If you plan to use a two-call process, explain this process to the seller. You will come to their house to take a tour of the property. At that time, you will leave them with a packet of information on the market and the sales process. You will ask for their commitment to read the packet before their next appointment with you. If they only have time to read one thing, ask them to read your marketing plan. Set a second appointment to meet at your office with all decision-makers. Meeting at your office accomplishes several objectives: They see you have an office and are a professional, you can introduce them to your staff, and you are in a controlled environment, where you will not have the interruptions that might occur when you are at their home.

As a minimum, your Prelisting Packet should contain the following:

- Information on you and your company (including testimonials)
- Information on the market
- Your marketing plan
- Examples of your marketing materials
- All documents they will need to sign

STEP 3: PROPERTY WALKTHROUGH

When the seller comes to the door of their home, use your three-step greeting: "Hi. How are you today? Thanks for your time. My name is_____. It's great to meet you." If you already know each other, you would simply say, "Hi. How are you doing today? Thanks for your time. It's great to see you again."

When they invite you into their home, remove your shoes, if appropriate. This small gesture shows respect to them and their home. They will appreciate it.

You have four goals during the property walkthrough:

1. **Build Rapport.** Smile and ask questions (FORD). Look for common ground with them, such as hobbies, photos of trips,

pets, and so on. Make sure you take a lot of notes (power of the pad). The more notes you take, the more they feel you care about them and their home. They also feel you are a pro.

2. **Review.** "Let's see, according to my notes, you purchased this home eight years ago." (Look at them and nod.) "You remodeled the kitchen two years ago." (Look at them and nod.) Review the major points of your prelisting interview to make sure both sellers are on the same page. After reviewing several points about the home, review their reason for selling and their timing. "Let's see, according to my notes, you are headed to San Diego and John starts work on October 1. Is that right?" (Watch for Mary's reaction. Does she nod approval, or does she give an icy stare indicating she's not happy about this move?)

3. **Qualify the Seller.** Are both sellers in alignment on selling their home? Do they have experience selling a home in the past? What are their expectations and motivations? Are they cooperative? Open and honest in their communication? Are they functional decision-makers? Here are some questions to ask:

    - "Have you sold a home before?" If they answer yes, then ask, "About how many homes?"
    - "When did you sell your last one?"
    - "What were your experiences with that sale? How did it go for you?"
    - "What did you like the best? What did you like the least?"
    - "What would you like to do the same or different on this sale?"
    - "If you could wave a magic wand and have this sale go just the way you want it, what would that look like?"
    - "Is your company assisting you with this move?"
    - "Do you have a Realtor helping you in your new city? Would you like me to help you find a good Realtor?"

4. **Qualify the House.** Look at the condition, location, size, floor plan, features, and amenities. Ask about inclusions and exclusions. Take notes!

STEP 4: WHAT ARE WE SELLING?

You have toured the home and have a feel for its condition. If you notice items that a buyer will object to, now is the time to find out what the seller is willing to do (if anything) to improve the condition of the property. It sounds like this: "One of our goals is to help you enhance the value of your property, so you can get top dollar for it. A good way to think about it is this: Do you want to sell your house at wholesale with items a buyer would need to fix, or at retail where your home is in move-in condition? For example, do you want to price your property with this carpet or with new carpet?" Another example would be to say, "Do you want to price your home in its current condition or with the home freshly painted?"

Sometimes, the seller will ask, "What would you do?" or "What do you recommend?" Be careful about jumping on their side of the ledger. Remember, you control the process, and they control the decisions. If you recommend new carpet and paint and then the house doesn't sell, they will blame you.

Instead, use the common metaphor of selling a car. "Let me ask you this, have you ever sold a car or traded a car in?"

Most people have had this experience, and they answer yes.

"When you got ready to sell your car, did you clean it up? Touch up the paint? Wax it?" (They nod.) "Why did you do that?"

They say, "Because we thought it would sell faster, and we would get more money for it."

"Well, the same is true in houses. If you are willing to do a few things, your home will sell faster and for more money. It is totally your call. What would you like to do to the _____ (carpet, paint, etc.)?"

STEP 5: OTHER PROPERTIES TO SELL?
"Do you have any other properties that you need to sell? Would you like me to help you with those properties?"

We had a young rookie salesman named Matt. On his very first listing appointment, he was reading the questions straight from the Sixteen-Step Process. When he read the questions "Do you have any other properties that you need to sell? Would you like me to help you with those properties?" the seller said, "Well, Matt, as a matter of fact we do. We have eighteen properties. We are transitioning to Arizona and ultimately want to sell these properties here or trade them for property in Arizona. If you do a good job on our home, you can handle the others as well." Matt came running back to the office to tell me, "Boy, I'm sure glad I asked those questions!"

STEP 6: THE CALENDAR
You are now at the kitchen counter or table. The dialogue goes like this:

"So John, you mentioned that you need to be in San Diego to start work on October 1." (John nods.)

Pull out a yearly calendar that shows a month on each page. "Let's see what we need to do to keep you on schedule." When you pull out the calendar, John and Mary will lean in to see it. All three of you are now very connected.

Go to the October page. "Let's see, October 1 is a Monday, so that is probably your first workday, right John?" (John nods.) "Would you like to be there a little early to get settled?" Mary says, "I think we should be there at least a week before." John agrees.

"OK, so let's work backward and see what we need to do. To get there a week early would be September 24, so let's say we closed on your home here around September 20. That would give you four days to move." (John and Mary nod approval.)

"Now, most buyers will be getting a loan, and we should plan on at least four weeks for the loan process. Six weeks are better. Working backward, that means we want to have a contract by August 23, at the latest, to keep you on schedule. Today is July 12, so (counting weeks on the calendar) our mission is to get your home on the market and under contract in the next six weeks." John and Mary express surprise at the fast timetable. October seemed too far away.

What has just happened using the calendar? You and the sellers have become very connected as you problem solve together, using the calendar; you have clarified for them the timing and schedule; and you have shifted their focus from *price* to *schedule*.

Now you explore consequences.

Consequence 1

"John and Mary, if for some reason your home is not sold and closed by October 1, what will you do?" Discuss their options: John gets an extension on starting work; John moves to San Diego alone, while Mary and the kids stay here to sell the house; the whole family moves to San Diego, and they leave the house here—having two house payments. Any of these options are less desirable than plan A, which is to get the home sold on time. This discussion builds motivation.

Consequence 2

"What if your home sells right away and the buyer needs to move in? Can you move before September 24?" John and Mary think this is a better option than not having the house sold on time.

What if you have a seller who says, "We're really in no hurry." They don't have a time line. See if you can help them create one. The best way is use a pretend state. Here's how it sounds:

Seller: "Well, we really don't have a schedule. We're in no hurry."

You: "Remind me again why you want to sell."

Seller: "We would like to move to Denver to be closer to our kids and grandkids."

You: "If you could wave a magic wand and move whenever you want, when might that be?"

Seller: "Oh, ideally before the snow flies. Probably sometime before Thanksgiving."

You now have a date to work with.

One-Call or Two-Call Process

If you are using a two-call process, at this point you will say, "I will work up a detailed market analysis and pricing strategy for your home and see what we need to do to get you to San Diego on time. Let's meet at my office to go over it, and I'll also introduce you to the people who will help us make it happen."

Set an appointment for the second call. Then provide the sellers with your prelisting package and say, "I prepared a package of information for you. It will help you understand the market and the process of selling your home. There's also background information on me and my company, as well as all the documentation you will need to sell your home. If you don't have time to read everything, probably the most important thing to read is the marketing plan. Would you take a few minutes and review the packet before we get together at my office?"

If you are using a two-call process, after giving them a tour of your office and staff, you are now in a conference room or private office and ready to proceed with Step 7.

If you are using a one-call process, you have already had the package delivered. You are now at their kitchen counter or table and ready to proceed with Step 7.

STEP 7: PRELISTING PACKAGE REVIEW

"I prepared a package of information for you. Have you had a chance to review it?"

If they say "yes," go on to Step 8. If they say, "No, we got busy and didn't have a chance to look at it," then briefly review what's in the prelisting package, focusing mostly on your qualifications and your marketing plan.

STEP 8: QUESTIONS REGARDING PACKAGE
"Do you have any questions regarding the package?"

Most of the time they will say no and be very complimentary of the package, thanking you for putting it together. Occasionally, they will have a question or two. In that case, take the time to answer their questions. If they have a big question, such as "What do you think the price of our home should be?" or "What is your fee?" you will use the process described in Step 9—writing down their question and asking if there is anything else.

You summarize Step 8 with your value proposition and job description: "Our goal is to get you to (location) on time. My job is to do the following:

- Help you enhance the value of your property so you get top dollar for it
- Help you with a pricing strategy that nets you the most dollars
- Give your property maximum exposure in the marketplace
- Help you negotiate the best contract
- Manage your transaction so it is as smooth as possible and gets you where you want to go on time"

STEP 9: QUALIFIED TO SELL YOUR HOME?
"Based on the information in the package, do you feel we are qualified to sell your property?"

The Step 9 question is a soft trial close. You are not asking the sellers for a decision to hire you. You are simply asking them if they feel you are qualified. In more than forty years in real estate sales, I've never found a seller to say no to this question. Why? A prelisting package is one of the most important things a seller wants—and something that less than 20 percent of Realtors provide. Immediately, you are differentiated in a way that is valuable to the sellers.

Sellers will always say either "Yes" or "Yes, but . . ." to this question. They are most likely to say "Yes, but . . . ," so let's start with that option.

Option 1: The Seller Says, "Yes, but . . ."

Their hesitation may be about price, fee, or appointments with other Realtors, among other things. As the sellers begin to list their questions or concerns, it is very important that you do three things:

1. Repeat back to them their question or concern. This acknowledges them and lets them know you are listening and heard them.

2. Take out a sheet of paper and write down their question or concern. This lets them know you are going to address their question, and it will not be forgotten about or swept under the rug. The paper will lay everything out for all to see.

3. Ask, "Is there anything else?" Get all of their concerns out on the table at once. As they have a question, repeat it back, write it down, and ask if there is anything else? Make a list of their concerns.

Do not answer each one at this point. Simply make a list. Here's what it sounds like:

You: "Based on the information in the package, do you feel we are qualified to sell your property?"

Seller: "Absolutely! I'm very impressed with your package and your company, but it will depend on the price."

You: "So you feel we're qualified, assuming we can agree on price?" (Write *price* on a sheet of paper.) "Is there anything else?"

Seller: "Yeah, we want to discuss your fee."

You: "So, two things that are important to you are price and fee." (Write *fee* down on the paper.) "Is there anything else?"

Seller: "Well, we are talking to two other brokers."

You: "OK, you need to get comfortable with the price, the fee, and compare the three brokers. (Write *two other brokers* on the paper.) Is there anything else?"

Seller: "No. I think that's it."

Notice how, when the seller mentioned price as a question, you did not take that bait like a bigmouth bass and start going into a pricing analysis. That would have gotten you out of your process. You will cover price but not yet. You want to get all the questions out first. You maintain control of the process.

You: "So, after we answer your questions about price, fees, and you have had the opportunity to interview the other brokers (you hold up the sheet of paper), one of three things will happen. First, you may decide to hire me. Second, you may decide not to hire me. Third, if I feel I can't help you achieve your objectives, I have a responsibility to tell you that. It would not be right for me to list your home knowing down deep inside that it is mission impossible. If I feel that way, is it OK if I tell you the truth? I won't list your home unless I feel I can help you."

Seller (a bit surprised by the honesty and transparency): "We really appreciate your honesty with us. That's the kind of relationship we want."

You: "Shall we proceed and see where we are?" (You are now ready for Step 10.)

This "one of three things can happen" dialogue accomplishes three things:

1. It is a bit of a takeaway close. Our top-listing Ninjas report that about a third of the time, the sellers say, "Wait a minute, we want to work with you."

2. It shifts the need-power dynamic. The person with the highest need has the lowest power, and the person with the lowest need has the highest power. Most Realtors, when they go on a listing appointment, have a goal to get the listing and, without realizing it, end up psychologically groveling for it. This dialogue changes all of that. You would like to work with the seller, if possible, but you do not need the listing.

3. If it truly is mission impossible, you have set up a graceful exit strategy. Have you ever had a good friend or client refer you to

somebody who was totally unrealistic, but you took the listing anyway, simply because it was a referral and you figured you better take it out of respect for your friend or client? Then, you discover you're trapped in an impossible situation. This dialogue provides a graceful exit for you, the seller, and the friend or client who referred them.

Option 2: The Seller Says, "Yes."
You: "What questions do you have?"

If they have questions, you will handle their questions as described above.

If they don't have questions, you say, "OK, let's look at the market and what we need to do to get you to (location) on time. Before we do that, I want you to know that if I feel I can't help you achieve your objectives, I have a responsibility to tell you that. It would not be right for me to list your home knowing down deep inside that it is mission impossible. If I feel that way, is it OK if I tell you the truth? I won't list your home unless I feel I can help you."

STEP 10: MY MISSION AND YOUR ODDS
"My mission is to help you get to (location) on time. Would you like to see your odds?"

This is a great question that immediately gets us into the pricing process. It also grabs the attention of all four personality types. Here are their internal dialogues:

- Power People: "Yes! Now we are going to get right down to it."
- Party People: "Odds? Game on!"
- Peace People: "Oh, my, I hope we have good odds."
- Perfection People: "Great! Some numbers to look at!"

Regardless of the sellers' personality, you have their attention with this question.

At this point, you will start to share your market analysis. Brokers have their own format they like to use. Generally, their market analysis includes information on supply and demand, a comparison of similar properties that have sold, are for sale, and have not sold. We recommend your market analysis and pricing discussion follow four rules:

1. **Work from General to Specific.** Organize your information starting with the general and working to the specific. It's clearer for most people when information is presented this way. Start with the big picture (the overall market), then go to the market in their price range, then go to the market in their neighborhood, and finally to their home. If you start with the specific (their home), sellers have no context of what is going on in the neighborhood or their price range. They get confused. Confused sellers tend to make poor decisions.

2. **Be Visual.** Most people process information visually. Showing is better than telling. Use a visual format rather than talking about the market.

3. **Be Socratic.** Be careful about being too professorial and conducting a seminar when you are going over your market analysis. Ask questions and have the seller participate. You want to avoid having time of possession for more than two minutes at a time.

4. **Be Clear.** The goal is to help the sellers become clear. The number-one way Realtors confuse their sellers is by putting a stack of twenty or so multiple listing sheets in front of them. First of all, most sellers struggle to read these sheets. Second, their analytical brain likes to deal with just three to five key pieces of data. The Ninja process summarizes all those complicated MLS sheets into just the five vital few determinants

of value: price, location, size, condition, and amenities. These determinants are then displayed visually on a chart that is very easy to understand. Sellers become clear, confident, and make a good balanced-brain decision. In fact, the seller becomes so clear and confident they end up making the pricing presentation to you!

Visual-Pricing Tools

Visual-Pricing Tools will help you both price and communicate the price to your seller. There are now a number of companies and MLS's that offer visual pricing tools. We highly recommend these tools for three reasons.

1. **Visual.** The tools take complex data (MLS sheets) and turn them into simple, usable information that's easy to see and understand.
2. **Clear.** The assorted MLS data is summarized on just a few visual charts. Sellers are clear and less confused than when they look at a stack of MLS sheets.
3. **Value and Differentiation.** Before the Internet, providing your seller a stack of MLS sheets used to be a valuable differentiator. Today, your seller can get that same information online. If that is all you're doing, you aren't bringing much value. With the Visual-Pricing Tools, you provide valuable decision-making tools that differentiate you from other Realtors.

One Visual-Pricing Tool used by many Ninjas, Focus 1st, was founded by Tim DeLeon, a partner at The Group, Inc. It runs on every MLS in the United States and is available at www.Focus1st.com. An example follows. This is the chart you show after asking the question, "Would you like to see your odds?"

Odds of Selling Your Home

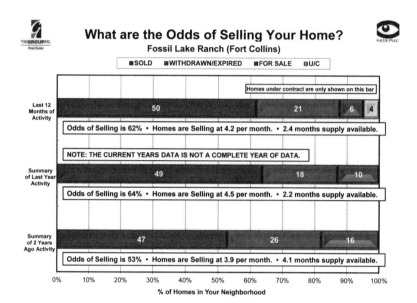

As a point of differentiation, you can also show them your personal sales statistics and their odds of selling with you versus the marketplace.

One of the great Ninjas in our company is Chris Doyle. He has listed and sold nearly two hundred homes in his career and only had ten homes not sell. A seller's odds of selling with Chris are over 95 percent! That's a difference!

Two Prices

Whenever you go into a listing consultation, you should have two prices in your head. One price is your *ideal list price*. You don't say this price to your seller. (It's their decision.) Instead, you help them understand the market, and they end up making the pricing presentation to you. You either accept or reject their price. You control this process through your questions.

Your second price in your head is your *walk-away price*. At a certain price this listing assignment becomes mission impossible, and you will exercise Option 3 of the "one of three things will happen." Your walk-away price is a function of the market, your assessment of the seller's motivation, and your ability to coach them into reality. If you can't coach them to reality, you are better off walking away. Overpriced listings that don't sell drain your energy and your marketing dollars and reduce your income per hour. They also hurt your reputation as a Ninja who gets results.

If you are not using the Visual-Pricing Tools, you can still calculate the seller's odds of selling by price range and neighborhood from the multiple listing service data. Then show their odds with you from your personal sales statistics.

STEP 11: FAIR MARKET VALUE

"Are you willing to list your home at fair market value?"

Sellers will usually ask, "What is fair market value?"

Your response is, "Fair market value is determined by what buyers are willing to pay for a property, given their choices and what sellers are willing to sell for, given their choices and the market competition. Would you like to see how buyers and sellers determine fair market value?"

Sellers will respond, "Yes."

You: "Let's start by looking at the market through what we call *buyer eyes*. Buyers start selecting homes based on three criteria: size/style, location, and price. Later, they also consider condition and features/amenities. These are the five determinants of value in housing.

"By looking at this information, the market will speak to us and tell us what fair market value is. It's important that we are listening."

Show your seller your Visual-Pricing Tools—odds of selling for their neighborhood, days on the market, and so on. Then, show them the scattergram. (Note: *If you are not using scattergrams or Focus 1st Visual-Pricing Tools, show your market analysis, including sold, active, and expired data. Then, go to Alternative Questions 12 through 16 at the end of Appendix E.)*

A scattergram shows the relationship of price and size in a particular location (neighborhood). Of the five determinants of value, the scattergram shows three of the five (price, size, location) on a single sheet. You will need to refer to the MLS sheets for condition and amenities, so these sheets are typically underneath the scattergram for easy reference.

Here's a sample scattergram:

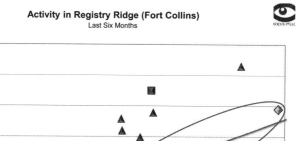

Price is on the vertical axis. Square footage is on the horizontal axis. The homes on this scattergram are shown by total square feet (TSF). The dots represent the homes that are sold. The trend line is calculated as the average distance between the dots. (For the engineers and those who remember your college statistics class, this line is calculated using a linear regression equation.) The easier way to explain this to most sellers is to tell them the trend line is the average distance between the dots. We could also call this trend line the *fair market value line*.

By looking at the trend line, we can see there is a definite relationship between price and size—the larger the home, the higher the price; the smaller the home, the lower the price.

Cream puffs will generally sell above the line, and properties in poor condition will generally sell below the line.

The scattergram shows homes for sale as well as homes that have not sold or expired. The homes in the ellipse are under contract.

Once you have explained the scattergram to your sellers, and they are clear on how it works, you are now going to use the simplest, most powerful pricing dialogue I have seen. Here it is:

Have your sellers find their square footage on the horizontal axis with their pen. In this case, total square footage is approximately 3,800 square feet. Have the sellers place their pen on the 3,800-square-foot mark and draw a vertical line straight up and off the page. Once they have done that, ask the question in Step 12.

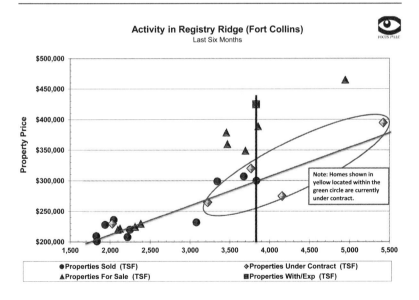

STEP 12: SELLING "ON THE LINE"

"Would you agree, your home will sell somewhere on this line?"

The sellers will usually laugh at how simple and obvious this question is. Of course their house has to sell somewhere on that line. It's the square footage of their house!

STEP 13: WHERE WILL IT SELL?

"Based on current market conditions represented on this chart, where do you feel your home will sell on this line?"

The sellers will usually say that their house will probably sell somewhere close to where the vertical (square feet) line and the trend line (fair market value line) intersect.

STEP 14: PRICING "ON THE LINE"

"Based on current market conditions, where do you feel we should price your house on this line to get you to (location) on time?"

If they name a price you are comfortable with, agree with them. If they name a price you are uncomfortable with (you feel it is mission impossible), ask the question in Step 15. Notice how the Ninja process has the seller making the pricing presentation to you!

STEP 15: ON TIME AND PLAN B

"Do you feel that price will get you there on time? If not, what is your plan B?"

"If we get to (date) and your house isn't sold, what will you do?"

Have a discussion about timing and being able to stay on schedule.

If the seller is still hung up on a price that is too high in your opinion, put them in a pretend state and discuss consequences and carrying costs. Using a pretend state, you can ask several what-if questions here.

For example, if the market is showing the price to be about $375,000 and the seller wants $425,000, you could ask, "If we had a contract lying on the table right now for $400,000 cash, what would you do?"

If they say they wouldn't take it—even though it is $25,000 above market—you probably have mission impossible on your hands and may want to exercise Option 3 of "one of three things will happen."

You can also use this question to call their bluff. I recall an instance where it was clear the husband wanted to move and his wife did not. He had received a big promotion, so this was great for his career, and he was excited. It was obvious, however, that while she wanted to support her husband's career, she clearly did not want to leave her friends and move the kids. I picked up the vibe that her strategy would be to insist on a price that was so high it would not sell. She could say she supported her husband by putting the house on the market, and when it didn't sell, she could say, "I guess it just wasn't meant to be."

I decided to call her bluff. The market showed $375,000, and she insisted they would not take a penny under $450,000. I pointed out the market data and then I asked her, "If we had a contract on the table right now for $450,000, what would you do?"

She sat there in stunned silence for a moment, and then with tears in her eyes, she said, "I wouldn't be able to take it."

I said, "I think you and Paul should talk over what you want to do." The next day, Paul called to say he was turning down the promotion, and they were staying.

STEP 16: THE NEXT SEVENTY-TWO HOURS

"If we find a buyer for your house in the next seventy-two hours, are you going to be OK with that? What if it is the first person who looks at your house?"

This is a very important discussion to have with your seller. Point out to them that there are buyers on the sidelines who have seen everything that is currently on the market. When something new hits the market, these sideline buyers jump on it, and there is an initial flurry of activity. They are excited about anything that is new and fresh. This is often when we get our best offers.

Properly prepare your sellers' expectations. If you don't have this conversation, what happens when you bring a full-price contract (or multiple contracts), and the ink isn't even dry on the listing agreement? The sellers don't feel good about it. They feel they underpriced their home, and you didn't earn your fee. Step 16 helps avoid this issue.

ALTERNATIVE QUESTIONS FOR STEPS 12–16

If you are not using visual pricing tools or scattergrams, here are some alternative questions for Steps 12 through 16:

- **Step 12: Price.** "Based on current market conditions, where do you feel you should price your home to get to (new place) on time?"
- **Step 13: On Time and Plan B.** "Do you feel that price will get you there on time?" "If not, what's your Plan B?"
- **Step 14: Consequences and Plan B (If you feel their price is too high).** "If we get to (date) and your house isn't sold, what will you do? What is your Plan B?"
- **Step 15: What if? (Pretend State).** "If we get a contract on your house for $_____ today, what would you do?"
- **Step 16: The Next Seventy-Two Hours.** "If we find a buyer for your house in the next seventy-two hours, are you going to be OK with that? What if it is the first person to look at your house?"

The next appendices highlight three additional ideas for working with sellers.

Appendix F

PRICING ON THE BRIDGE

In today's digital world, buyers and brokers generally search the Internet and the MLS in price blocks. For example, they look for homes priced from $450,000 to $500,000 or from $500,000 to $550,000. In those cases, there is a pricing bridge at $500,000. If you are listing a home and the market shows a value close to $500,000, you would be wise to price it on the bridge—that is, at $500,000. By doing this, the home will show up in both searches. If it is priced at $499,900, it won't show up in the $500,000 to $550,000 search. Big mistake! Don't price houses the way you price sweaters! A national study showed that homes priced on the bridge receive 28 percent more showings.

Every market's pricing bridges are different, and the range tends to increase as you go higher in price. For example, buyers may search in $50,000 ranges when looking between $500,000 and $550,000 but increase to $100,000 ranges when looking at homes in the $800,000 to $900,000 range. Know the pricing bridges for your market.

If you are in a market with a shortage of inventory, look under the bridge. When Realtors say to me that they have a great buyer but can't find them anything, I ask, "What is their price range?"

The Realtor responds, "$500,000 to $550,000."

I say, "Go do a search from $490,000 to $550,000. Realtors are notorious for pricing right under the bridge." A study in our market showed that, depending on price range, 12 to 22 percent of the homes were priced right under the bridge.

Want to find additional inventory for your buyers? Look under the bridge.

Appendix G

DYNAMIC PRICING

"I don't go to where the puck is. I go to where the puck is going to be."
—**Wayne Gretzky, professional hockey player**

Are you in a seasonal market? Is there a time of the year when the market is hotter and there are more sales than other times of the year? Are you aware of it? Most markets have patterns of hot and slow times of the year. Knowing these times and anticipating them gives you the ability to price not just where the market is but also where it is going to be. Here's an example:

Joanne DeLeon, a master of dynamic pricing, received a call from a seller whose listing had just expired. They were on the market for six months at $289,900 and were frustrated. They had heard good things about Joanne from a friend and called her.

The first thing Joanne did was to pull up a scattergram of their neighborhood. In the following illustration, the seller's home is the square, and it is obvious why it didn't sell. It was overpriced at the time. Notice the other houses that are similar in size that sold for less.

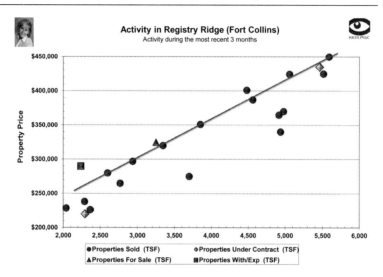

Notice also that all the homes in this neighborhood had either sold or were under contract except for the subject property and one other home priced at $320,000.

Joanne decided to check this neighborhood for seasonality. Look at the following.

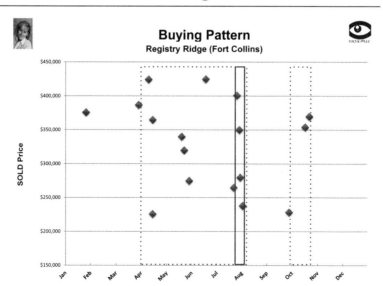

You can see that all of the homes, except for four, sold between April and August. That is the hot season in this neighborhood. Joanne also noticed that the seller's home had been on the market for six months from September through February. That is the slow season. The home didn't sell, and now the sellers were calling her. It was the first of March, the start of the hot season.

When Joanne looked at the home, she saw it was a cream puff—a beautiful home in showcase condition. In addition, the one other home that was for sale went under contract. Joanne's listing would be the only home for sale in the neighborhood heading into the busy spring market.

Where would you price this home for the spring market? It had been on the market for six months at $289,900. But now, it would be the only one available entering a hot market. After going through her pricing tools with the sellers, they decide to raise their price and place it on the bridge at $300,000. They had three offers the first week, and the home sold and closed for $306,000—more than $16,000 above its previous list price. The sellers were ecstatic! Dynamic pricing was the key. Did Joanne create value? She is a master.

You may be wondering how could this home possibly appraise? Joanne prepared an appraisal package showing her Focus 1st Pricing Tools, including the market-timing chart. She also attached copies of the three offers to the appraisal package. The home appraised for $306,000.

Appendix H

YOUR NEXT TRANSACTION IS EMBEDDED IN THIS ONE

Remember the 15 to 20 percent transaction rate? Statistically, there are three to four real estate transactions that will be done this year by the twenty neighbors close to your new listing. In fact, the number is probably higher, because something happens in a neighborhood when someone puts their house up for sale. The neighbors start thinking, *Maybe we should do something.*

Here's your system:

CONTACT THE NEIGHBORS.

Within a day after your sign goes up, make a point to call on twenty neighbors face-to-face. Here's your dialogue, with key phrases noted in italics:

"Hi. How are you today? Thank you for coming to your door. My name is Joanne DeLeon with The Group Real Estate Company. I just listed your neighbor's home three doors down. *As part of my service to my sellers*, I make a point to visit the neighbors to let them know about the property." (Hands the neighbor a property brochure.) "*We want you to be the first to know about it. Also, we want you to be able to associate a face with the name on the sign, so you know who is working in your neighborhood.* Do you have any questions about the property or real estate in general?" (If you are having a private open house just for the neighbors, this is also an excellent time to personally invite them.)

The first phrase "as part of my service to my sellers" causes the neighbor to think, "*Gee, that is really a nice service. I don't believe my last Realtor did that.*" The second phrase, "We want you to be the first to know," makes them feel special. The third phrase, "We want you to be able to associate a face with the name on the sign, so you know who is working in your neighborhood," is an embedded command. The next morning, when they leave home for work and drive by the sign, whose face pops into their mind? How about when they come home that night? How about every day? You are becoming top of mind for them and potentially their *Realtor of Choice*.

BRING YOUR A GAME.

Make sure your listing is beautifully staged and pre-inspected; have a professionally photographed brochure; and prepare a kitchen counter display with additional information on the utilities, homeowners' association, and a contract-writing packet. In a hot sellers' market, I often see Realtors "cheap out" on their service—no brochures, no staging, no counter display. They figure why do it? The house will sell with multiple offers in just a few days. Big Mistake! They are being short sighted. Who will go into this home? Neighbors and buyers who will also be sellers. What will they see? Do they see your A game and notice how differentiated you are and the value you bring? If so, they will want to work with you. Your next transaction is embedded in this transaction.

AFTERWORD

When I first heard Sylvia Castillo speak, her words touched my heart. She has an amazing gift of using language to express feelings of inspiration. Sylvia wrote the Ninja Prayer as a gift to the Ninja Nation.[1] As our commencement speaker, she often delivers it on the last day of our classes. As you commence your life on the Ninja Path, it's only appropriate that we close this book and send you off with the Ninja Prayer.

The Ninja Prayer

I give thanks for this day, and I awaken grateful. Giving thanks for this life and for my place in it. As I begin brand new this day, I give thanks for the breath that breathes and sustains me. I begin with an attitude of gratitude, and I give thanks for the infinite opportunities that are available to me. For I know that as I rise, I Am.

I Am enough, and today I release all fear, all doubt, and all separation. I move into this day grounded in the absolute truth. I am guided by the infinite intelligence that lives within me, and I powerfully co-create this day. Today I begin with a profound sense of understanding and clarity.

---

1 More words by Sylvia Castillo can be found at SerenitysWay.com.

I know that my consciousness is a gift, and I transform situations by way of my beingness. I move through this day fully embracing the strength and the power that lie within me. I give thanks for the opportunities disguised as challenges, for I absolutely know that they allow me to use my wisdom, my kindness, and my intelligence. There is no situation or obstacle that moves me from this path of least resistance.

I meet each meeting, each transaction, and each closing as an opportunity to bring my authentic self—to be fully engaged and inspired. I negotiate with purpose, inviting the highest and best outcome for all of those involved. Knowing that creative solutions, positive communication, and masterful ideas are my art and my craft, and it is good and very good.

I give thanks for these experiences that continue to nurture and grow me, for each day I become more and more of who I have come here to be. How wonderful it is to know that there is no one and no thing that stands between me and my highest truth and vision.

Today I stand grounded in this awareness, and I recognize that life is always conspiring for my greater good. I find balance in all that I do; there is enough time, enough energy, and enough resources for all of my dreams and desires. As I create this day, I choose well in all my endeavors.

I release this word, and I give thanks for all that I have, for all that I Am and for all that I Am becoming.

I Am Successful. I Am Powerful. I Am Ninja.

—Sylvia Castillo

INDEX

A

A game, 299
A relationship status, 159
absorption rate, 85
abundance mind-set, 94–95
acceptance, as stage of change, 264
Acknowledge step, in greeting, 197
actions, as key to mastery, 11–12
active properties, 247, 251
activity goals, 144
advisors. *See* Proactive Trusted Advisors
affirmations, 12, 24, 43–49
Alexander, F.M., 42, 124
Allen, James, 43
analytical brain, 219, 220, 221
anchors, 46
anger, as stage of change, 264
Aristotle, 122
art, in flow program, 109–110
asking, versus telling, 218. *See also* questions
Aspromonte, Don, 226
attention, paying, 90
auction solution, 259–260
auditory thinkers, 213
auto-flow, 106–107

B

B relationship status, 159
balanced brain decisions, 219–221
basic services, 80
Beckwith, Michael, Dr., 25
beliefs, 34, 37
Bell, Alexander Graham, 50
benefits, in Buyer Process, 241–244
big picture, going to small picture from, 215–216, 284
big values, showing, 251
body language, customer, 215, 252
books, role in programming, 42
brain
    analytical, 219, 220, 221
    balanced brain decisions, 219–221
    conscious, 33
    creative nonconscious, 34, 47–48
    emotional, 219, 220–221
    learning to run, 32–33
    nonconscious, 33–36, 44–46
    RAS in, 27
brand, building, 79, 83–87, 118
Brewer, John, 177
bridges, pricing, 294
Brinton, Howard, 4
brokers, 73–74, 78, 271–272
Buie, Nate, xvi–xvii, 54, 60, 71–72

business
    doing, 120
    generating, 120–123
    working on versus working in, 121
business strategy, xvii, 93–101
Business Tracker, 130–131
buyer eyes, looking at market through, 287–288
Buyer Interview, 230–232
buyer packets, 86, 232–234
buyers
    flow, power of, 103
    next seventy-two hours question about, 292
    overtaxing analytical brain, 220
    top six services most relevant to, 86
    types of, 73–75
    See also Ten-Step Buyer Process
buyer's remorse, avoiding, 253–254
buying process, 103–104, 253

C

C relationship status, 160
calendar, 157, 277–279
calls, flow through, 107–108, 113.
    See also customer service calls
capacity, as key to trust, 100
Capano, Clara, 96
Cash or Loan? step, Buyer Process, 244–247
Castillo, Sylvia, 300–301
categorizing database, 159–161
change, 68–69, 127–128, 222, 264
character, as key to trust, 100
clarity, customer, 201, 204, 247–250, 263, 284–285

closing questions, 204–205
closing techniques, 2
closings, follow-up after, 117–118, 161–163
clothing, role in establishing trust, 100
commission breath, 91, 216
commitment to excellence, 10
commitments, keeping, 90
common ground, 134
communication, 82, 86, 211–212, 218, 262
competence, as key to trust, 100
condition, of house, 276
confidence, customer, 201, 203–204
confusion, avoiding, 246–247, 263
Connect and Communicate (Principle 4), xvii, 171
connection
    in Ninja Consultation, 188, 189, 196–200
    in Ten-Step Buyer Process, 229
connection questions, 202
conscious brain, 33
consequences, discussing with seller, 278–279
consistency, 100, 101
construction, new, 236–237
consultation. See Ninja Consultation
contact information, in database, 158
contracts, 165–166, 233, 250, 256–259
convenience services, 81
conversion ratios, 97
Cook, Bobbie, 183
cooperation, seller, 262

core values, 70
core/basic services, 80
correction, in mastery, 11
cream puff story, 248
creative nonconscious brain, 34, 47–48
crucial conversations, 263–265
Crum, Thomas, 3
curiosity stage, buying process, 104
custom services, 81
customer service calls, 132–136, 155–156
customers
    attracting, 55–56, 57–58
    being Proactive Trusted Advisors for, 88–91
    building relationships, 98–101
    communicating difference to, 82
    decision strategies of, 179–180
    "Differentiate or Die" mantra, 86–87
    flow, power of, 102–105
    focusing on, 147
    follow-up, after closing, 117–118, 161–163
    generating continuous flow of, 120–123
    giving permission, 185–186
    helping make good decisions, 219–221
    matching and mirroring, 214–215
    in Ninja Selling, xvii
    P time, 165–166
    personalities, 172–178
    Platinum Rule, 172, 178
    pretend states, 181–184
    pursuer-distancer dance, 57–58
    services most relevant to, 85–86
    showing property to, 251–254
    talking by, 62
    two-minute warning, 63
    types of, 73–75
    See also buyers; Ninja Consultation; sellers; Sixteen-Step Seller Process; Ten-Step Buyer Process
customized flow items, 109

D

D relationship status, 160
daily affirmations, 46, 47–49
daily habits, Ninja Nine, 124–131
Daily Routine, Ninja, 120–123
database
    building, 150–152, 153–156
    categorizing, 159–161
    choosing correct product, 157–158
    discussing with customers, 164
    formatting, 158–159
    importance of, 148
    post-closing contact, 161–163
    rejuvenating with 8 in 8 system, 118–119
    scalability, 149–150
    three laws of real estate, 149
    three-step process for, 151–152, 153–156
    updating, as Ninja Nine habit, 142–143
    warm list, building from, 127–128
    See also customers
decision strategies, 179–180, 197

decisions
  control of, 194, 200, 201–202, 204–210
  helping customers make good, 219–221
  seller, 261–262
DeLeon, Joanne, 295–297
denial, as stage of change, 264
Depression-Era Selling, 1–2, 57
desire stage, buying process, 253, 255
diagnostic questions, 203, 204
differentiation, 80–81, 84, 86–87, 285, 286
direct mail, in flow program, 106–107, 110–111
discount brokers, 73–74, 78
distractions, handling, 43
doing the dance, 249, 252
Dornan, Dave, 218
Doyle, Chris, 286–287
Dream Home Exercise, 240–244
dreams, 67, 159
dress, role in establishing trust, 100
Dunlap, Jim, 4, 5–7, 12, 53, 223, 224
dynamic pricing, 295–297

E

E time, 166–170
8 in 8 system, 99, 114–119, 133
8Z Real Estate, 234
80/20 rule (Pareto's principle), xix–xx
85 percent house metaphor, 185–186, 248
elimination, process of, 235, 237–238

email, 106–107, 110, 124, 135–136, 211–212
Emery, Stewart, 9–11, 54
Emmons, Robert, Dr., 26
emotional brain, 219, 220–221
emotional energy, 18–23
energy
  emotional, 18–23
  sending and receiving, 15–17
Enroll step, Three-Step Greeting, 196–197
entering home, when showing property, 252
events, finding database contacts at, 153–154
excellence, commitment to, 10
expectations
  buyer, 247–250
  seller, 261, 292
external dialogues, 180
eyes, watching customer, 252

F

fabled service, 87, 132
Facebook, finding database contacts on, 155–156
face-to-face communication, 211–212
face-to-face flow, 107–108, 113
fair market value, 287–290
family information, in database, 158
family questions. *See* FORD questions
Fanning, Jack, 222
Fanning, Michael, 222

farming, geographical, 119
fears
    buyer, 226–227, 234, 238
    overcoming, 145–147
    seller, 263–264
features, in Buyer Process, 241–244
feelings, 25, 47
Fifteen Post-Closing Contacts, 161–163
files, customer, 164
financial crisis, 88–89
financing, 244–247
first person, 12, 44–45
first two minutes, importance of, 199–200
Five Rules of Ninja Selling, 90–91
five-step customer service call process, 133–134, 155–156
flow, 58
    auto-flow, 106–107
    budgeting, 111–112
    Business Tracker and, 131
    customer service calls and, 132
    8 in 8 system and, 114–119
    example of, 112
    importance of, 96
    live flow, 107–108, 113
    post-closing contact and, 162–163
    power of, 102–105
    quality of, 108–110
    relationship status and, 160
    role in building relationships, 101
    system override with, 113
    tips for success, 110–111
    working on business with, 121
flow time, 166–170
focus, 28–31, 50, 51–54
Focus 1st Visual-Pricing Tools, 85, 137, 285–287, 288
follow-up, after closing, 117–118, 161–163
For Sale by Owner (FSBO), 237
FORD (family, occupation, recreation, and dreams) questions, 65–72
foreclosures, 237
formatting database, 158–159
foundational questions, 203–204, 231–232, 270
Four Pillars of Brand Building, 83–87
four-step sales process. *See* Ninja Consultation
frequency of interaction. *See* flow
Frey, Garrett, 87
Frey, Walt, 4, 47, 165
friends, 41–42, 66
from decision strategy, 179
Fun Facts form, 163
Funnel Process, 234–238

G

generating business, 120–123
geographical farming, 119
George, Bud, 87
gestures, matching and mirroring, 215
goals
    activity, 144
    for Information step, 201–202
    key steps to programming, 44–46
    Net Forward Energy Ratio, 51–54
    nonconscious brain and, 34–35
    property walkthrough, 274–276
    relation to RAS, 30–31
Goddard, John, Dr., 30–31
go-givers, xiii–xiv

Golden Rule, 172
good vibrations, 15–17, 25
gratitude, 24–26, 122, 124
Gray, Helen, 112
Green Light Selling, 226
greeting, three-step, 196–198, 228, 274
Greeting step, Buyer Process, 228–229
Grenny, Joseph, 263
Gretzky, Wayne, 295
grinders, 74

H

habits, role in programming, 42–43. *See also* Ninja Nine
Hansen, Debbie, 129
hard closing questions, 255
harmony, increasing, 167–168
Helder, Chris, 173
high negative emotional energy, 18, 22–23
high positive emotional energy, 19, 20, 21
highest price, buying based on, 74–75
Hobbs/Herder marketing firm, 114
Holsten, Jon, 112
Hornung, Lane, 234
hot list, 126, 130–131, 160–161
humility, 25
Huntsman, Keith, 234

I

I (indirectly productive) time, 166–170

ideal list price, 287
income, increasing, xix–xx, 78
incremental change, 222
Information step, Ninja Consultation, 188, 189, 201–205
interaction, frequency of. *See* flow
interest rate, 245–246
interest stage, buying process, 104
internal dialogues, 180, 181–186, 203
Internet, changes in selling caused by, 56
interviews
  Buyer, 230–232
  live, 139–142
  prelisting, 267–273, 275
investing
  in flow, 111–112
  time, 165, 168–169

J

Jacks, Lawrence Pearsall, 167–168
job description, in Seller Process, 280
Johnson, Terri, 87
Jones, Charles, 41

K

Kane, James, 100
Kendall, Larry, xiii–xiv, 5–6
Kendall, Pat, 181–184, 206–210
kinesthetic thinkers, 213–214
Kiyosaki, Robert, 3
knowing, role in building relationships, 98–99
Koch, Richard, xx

L

Law of Value, 59–60
laws of real estate, 149
learning modalities, matching, 212–214
level of service, improving, 76–78
life, quality of, 30–31, 38
life changes, 127–128
life lists, 30–31
liking, role in building relationships, 99
listening skills, 61, 62, 68–69, 108
live communication, 211–212
live flow, 107–108, 113, 142
live interviews, 139–142
live real estate reviews, 137–139
loans, 244–247
location, as law of real estate, 149
Loehr, James, Dr., 3, 19
lost house story, 248–249
love, overcoming fear with, 146–147
low negative emotional energy, 19, 22–23
low positive emotional energy, 19, 21
lowest price, buying based on, 73–74
Lozanov, Georgi, 185

M

magic wand exercise, 181–184
mail, in flow program, 106–107, 110–111
Malvey, Mike, 64–65, 167
maps, MLS, 251
market
    answering questions about, 152–153
    fair market value, 287–290
    reviewing with buyers, 248–249
    timing patterns, 295–297
market analysis, 283–290
market statistics, 109
marketing systems, 85
mastery, xvii, 9–12
matching
    customer, 214–215
    learning modalities, 212–214
Matthias, Nolan, 125
McCarty, Andrea, 78
McIlroy, Rory, 216–217
McMillan, Ron, 263
McWhinney, Chad, 54, 190
measurable goals, 44
media, role in programming, 42
Meeting step, Ten-Step Buyer Process, 229
meetings, finding contacts at, 153–154
mental energy, in NFER, 51
mental push-ups, 48–49
mental rehearsal, 44–46
mentors, 41–42
menu pricing, 78
Merrill, Rick, 223
mind-set, 11, 12, 13–14
miracles, 10, 53–54
mirroring customer, 214–215
mission, presenting to seller, 283–287
morning routine, 13, 24–26
Mother Teresa, 30
motivation, seller, 261
Multiple Listing Service (MLS), 236, 244–247, 251, 285–286

N

name, mentioning in Three-Step Greeting, 197–198
name tag table, finding contacts at, 154
nasties, on customer service calls, 136
National Association of Realtors (NAR), 4
need-power dynamic, 217, 282
negative energy, 16–17, 18–19, 22–23, 51
negative pathway of RAS, 28–30
negotiating, 71–72, 250
neighbors, contacting, 298–299
Net Forward Energy Ratio (NFER), 51–54
networking, 153–154
neural reconditioning, 44–46
new construction, 236–237
next seventy-two hours question, 292
Ninja Business Strategy (Principle 3), xvii, 93–96
Ninja Consultation
    Connection step, 196–200
    example of, 190–193
    Information step, 201–205
    overview, 187–189
    process and decisions in, 194
    Proposal step, 211–218
    Solution step, 206–210
    summary of, 194–195
Ninja Daily Routine, 120–123
Ninja mind-set, 13–14
Ninja Morning Routine, 13, 24–26
Ninja Nine
    daily habits, 124–131
    fear, overcoming, 145–147
    focusing on productive activities, 143–144
    as generating P time, 166, 167
    overview, 122–123
    weekly habits, 132–143
Ninja Path, 222–224
Ninja Prayer, 300–301
Ninja Selling® System
    birth of, 4–5
    ninjas versus samurais, xviii
    overview, xiii–xiv, xv–xvi
    principles of, xvii, 9–12
    role of Larry Kendall in developing, 6–7
    success case, xx–xxi
    summary of, 69, 194–195
nonanxious presence, 216–217
nonconscious brain, 33–36, 44–46
nonproductive mental energy, 51
notes
    personal, 24, 124–125
    taking, 230, 231, 239–240, 275

O

occupation, 66, 158
odds of selling, 283–287
"on the line" pricing, 290–291
on-accident salespeople, xvi
"one of three things can happen" dialogue, 282–283
1 percent = 10 percent rule, 245
1 to 10 scale, 238–240
one-call listing process, 272–273, 279
100 percent full-on state of consciousness, 53–54

onion process, 79–81
on-purpose selling, xvi–xvii
open houses, finding contacts at, 154–155
outcome, attachment to, 90–91, 216

P

P (productive) time, 165–170
pain, 60–61, 69, 73
Pareto's principle (80/20 rule), xix–xx
Parnegg, Peter, 67
parties, finding contacts at, 153–154
Party People, 174–175, 177–178, 179, 283
Patterson, Kerry, 263
paying, buyer attitude toward, 73–75
paying attention, 90
Peace People, 175–176, 177–178, 179, 283
peak performance state, 20
people, role in programming, 41–42
Perfection People, 176–178, 179, 283
Performance Quadrant, 19
permission, giving, 185–186
personal mastery (Principle 1), xvii, 9–12
personal notes, 24, 124–125
personal sales statistics, 286–287
personalities, xv, 99, 172–178
personalized flow items, 109
Peters, Tom, 3
phone calls, flow through, 107–108, 113. *See also* customer service calls
PIE log, 166–167, 170

Pillars of Brand Building, 83–87
Pink, Daniel, 5
plan B, working out with seller, 291–292
Platinum Rule, 172, 178, 212, 214
player mind-set, 13–14, 19–20, 38–40, 41–42
pleasure, 60–61, 69, 73
positive energy, 16–17, 19–20, 21, 51
positive goals, 44
positive humility, 25
positive pathway of RAS, 28–30
positive reading, 24
post-closing contact, 117–118, 161–163
Power People, xv, 173–174, 177–178, 179, 283
power-need dynamic, 217, 282
pregame rituals, 21–23
prelisting interview, 267–273, 275
prelisting packets, 80, 85, 273–274, 279–280
present, being, 68–69
present tense, stating goals in, 45
pretend states, 181–184, 238–240, 256–259, 291
price
    buying based on, 73–75
    discussing with seller, 262–263
    dynamic pricing, 295–297
    fair market value, 287–290
    Focus 1st Visual-Pricing Tools, 285–287
    ideal list, 287
    menu pricing, 78
    odds of selling and, 283–287
    "on the line", 290–291

and quality of real estate services, 76
in value proposition, 75
walk-away, 287
working out with seller, 290–292
price mismatches, 245
pricing bridges, 294
pricing systems, 85
printing database, 143
prior learning questions, 203–204, 231–232, 270
Proactive Trusted Advisors, 85, 86, 88–91
process
    control of, 194, 199–200, 229
    of elimination, 235, 237–238
    focusing on, 216–217
    of selection, 235
    See also specific processes
productive (P) time, 165–170
productive activities, focusing on, 143–144
programming
    daily affirmations, 47–49
    key steps to, 44–46
    Ninja Morning Routine, 25
    nonconscious brain, 34–36
    overview, 12
    RAS, 28–31
    results formula, 37–40
    things that control, 41–43
properties
    asking seller about other, 277
    showing, 251–254
    walkthroughs, 274–276
Proposal step, Ninja Consultation, 189, 211–218
prospecting, with FORD questions, 70–71
pursuer-distancer dance, 57–58, 198
pursuing, being proactive versus, 90–91

Q

qualifications, seller opinion regarding, 280–283
qualifying house during walkthrough, 275–276
questions
    Buyer Interview, sequence of, 231–232
    and flow, 108
    FORD, 65–72
    Funnel Process, 236
    hard closing, 255
    for Information step, sequence of, 202–205
    for live real estate reviews, 139
    next, as embedded in last answer, 67–68
    overview, 62
    seller, handling, 281–282, 283
    Socratic method, 63–64
    soft closing, 253, 255–260
    types to ask, 64–65
    See also Sixteen-Step Seller Process

R

rapport, 70, 202, 274–275
RAS (Reticular Activating System), 27–31, 126, 168
reading, 24, 42

real estate information, in database, 159
real estate licensees, xix
real estate reviews, 137–139
real estate services
    asking about in prelisting interview, 271–272
    creating value, 59–60
    embedded transactions, 299
    improving level of, 76–78
    most relevant to buyers and sellers, 85–86
    quality of, 75–77
    in value proposition, 79–82
    value proposition for, 79–82
real estate, three laws of, 149
Realtors, defined, xix
rebranding, 118. *See also* brand, building
recognition, brand, 83
recreation, 66–67, 158
Redd, Estelle, 78
referrals, 98–99, 101, 132, 135
relational databases, 158
relationships
    building, 98–101
    categorizing database by, 159–160
    with 8 in 8 system, 118
    flow, 101, 106, 112
    follow-up, after closing, 161–163
    as law of real estate, 149
relevance, brand, 84, 86–87
renewal, as stage of change, 264
reputation, brand, 83–84
residential sales, 94
response-ability, 19, 22, 38–40

responsibility, 38
results formula, 37–40
retail market, 60
Reticular Activating System (RAS), 27–31, 126, 168
rituals, 21–23
Robbins, Tony, 2
Rohn, Jim, 9
Roppe, Laura, 263

S

sadness, as stage of change, 264
safety, when showing property, 252
sales. *See* Ninja Selling® System; selling
sales laboratory, The Group, Inc., 4
sales presentation, three-step, 187. *See also* Ninja Consultation
sales slumps, getting out of, 95–96
samurais, versus ninjas, xviii
scalability, 149–150
Scale of 1 to 10, 238–240
scarcity mind-set, 95–96
scattergrams, 288–290
schedule, working out with seller, 277–279, 291–292
science, in flow program, 110
scratch-pad solution, 256–259
seasonality, pricing and, 295–297
selection, process of, 235
self-esteem, 34
self-image, 34, 43
self-talk, 34, 43
sellers

crucial conversations with, 263–265
discussing price with, 262–263
dynamic pricing, 295–297
flow, power of, 102
key decisions for, 261–262
overtaxing analytical brain, 220
pricing bridges, 294
qualifying during walkthrough, 275
top services most relevant to, 85–86
See also Sixteen-Step Seller Process

selling
defined, 55
Depression-Era, 1–2, 57
history of, 5
Internet, changes caused by, 56
Ninja principle regarding, xvii, 55–56
"on the line", 290
on-purpose, xvi–xvii
residential, 94
See also Ninja Selling® System

sensory specific goals, 45–46
service, fabled, 87, 132.
  See also real estate services
Sharma, Robin, 43
Shiffrin, Mikaela, 216
Shoptaugh, Jake, 35
short sales, 237
showing property, 251–254
showing up, 90
Sixteen-Step Seller Process
    alternative questions for, 292–293
    asking about other properties, 277
    calendar, focusing on, 277–279
    discussing house condition, 276
    fair market value, 287–290
    mission and odds, 283–287
    next seventy-two hours question, 292
    overview, 266–267
    prelisting interview, 267–273
    prelisting packets, 273–274, 279–280
    pricing "on the line", 290–291
    property walkthrough, 274–276
    questions regarding qualifications, 280–283
    selling "on the line", 290
    on time and plan B, 291–292
    where house will sell questions, 290

skill set, as key to mastery, 11
small values, showing, 251
Socratic method, 63–64, 284
soft closing questions, 253, 255–260
sold data, 85, 247, 251
solution questions, 204–205
Solution step, Ninja Consultation, 188–189, 206–210
solving problems, creating value by, 60–61
Spaulding, Tami, 21, 87, 125, 143–144
step-down transformers, 264–265
Stop Selling! Start Solving! (Principle 2), xvii, 55–56
subconscious, 35
success, three keys to, 11–12
suggestions, giving permission through, 185–186
Sun Tzu, 68
Switzler, Al, 263

T

Tate, Jessica, 155
Taylor, Jack, 38–40
Ten-Step Buyer Process
  buyer fears, 226–227
  Buyer Interview, 230–232
  buyer packet, 232–234
  Cash or Loan? step, 244–247
  Dream Home Exercise, 240–244
  Funnel Process, 234–238
  Greeting step, 228–229
  Meeting step, 229
  1 to 10 scale, 238–240
  overview, 226
  summary of, 227–228
  What Happens Next? step, 247–250
  Whats and Whys, 241–244
The Group, Inc. Real Estate Associates, 2
  attitude of gratitude at, 26
  birth of Ninja Selling, 4–5
  communicating difference, 82
  flow example, 112
  Jim Dunlap's career at, 5–6
  Maximum Exposure marketing, 77
  sold data, customer access to, 85
  success of, 3
  trust, establishing, 88–89
Theriault, Gina, xx–xxi
third person, stating goals in, 45
thoughts
  in results formula, 37, 38
  role in programming, 43
three laws of real estate, 149
three-per-month flow program, 106–107, 111, 113
three-step database dialogue, 151–152, 153–156
Three-Step Greeting, 196–198, 228, 274
three-step sales presentation, 187
Thurber, Marshall, 2, 3
Tice, Lou, 2, 33
time
  categories of, 165–168
  investing wisely, 165, 168–169
  PIE log, 170
time of possession, 62–63, 108
timing, as law of real estate, 149
toward decision strategy, 179
transaction rate, 93–94
transactions, embedded, 298–299
travel, role in programming, 42
Trujillo, Dave, 140, 143
trust, 85–86, 88–91, 100–101, 136, 203–204
truthfulness, 90
two-call listing process, 272–274, 279
two-minute warning, 63

U

updating database, 142–143
urgency, categorizing database by, 160–161

V

value
  buyer types, 73–75
  buying decisions based on, 75
  creating, xvii, 59, 90
  customer service calls and, 133
  differentiation and, 86–87

fair market, 287–290
and flow, 101, 108–109
FORD questions, 70
increasing income by providing, 78
Law of, 59–60
pain and pleasure as drivers, 60–61
proactive versus pursuer, 90–91
providing in market analysis, 285
pursuer-distancer dance, 57–58
and quality of real estate services, 75–77
wholesale and retail, 60
value proposition, 75, 79–82, 280
vibrations, controlling, 15–17, 25
victim mind-set, 13–14, 19–20, 38, 41–42
videos, role in programming, 42
visual format, in market analysis, 284, 285
visual thinkers, 212–213, 218
visualizations, 24, 25–26, 43, 44–46
Visual-Pricing Tools, 85, 137, 285–287, 288
vital few, xix–xx, 165–169
Vitale, Maria, 13–14, 24–25, 54
voice, matching and mirroring, 214
voice mail, customer service calls through, 135
voice-to-voice flow, 107–108, 113

W

walk-away price, 287
walkthrough, property, 274–276
warm list, 126–131, 160–161

Washle, Wynn, 98–99, 140, 161–163, 249
weekly habits, Ninja Nine, 132–143
What Happens Next? step, Buyer Process, 247–250
Whats, in Buyer Process, 241–244
Who You Are step, in greeting, 197–198
wholesale market, 60
Whys, in Buyer Process, 241–244
word-of-mouth advocacy, 87
work habits, Ninja Nine, 122–123

Y

York, Mary Lou, 47–48
Young and Rubicam, 83

Z

zone, being in, 53–54

ABOUT THE AUTHOR

Larry Kendall holds a master's degree in Business Administration from Kansas State University and is one of the founding partners of The Group, Inc., a Colorado real estate company.

The Group, Inc. has been recognized by both Real Trends and *REALTOR Magazine* as the most productive real estate company in the United States in terms of transactions and dollar volume per associate.

Larry is the author of *Ninja Selling*, a sales training system with over 100,000 graduates. He has taught for 10 years in the real estate program at the Colorado State University College of Business and was inducted into their Real Estate Hall of Fame twice. Larry is 2006 Colorado Realtor of the Year.

His book, *Ninja Selling*, was released in 2017 and became both an Amazon Best Seller and the #1 New Release in its first week. It received the Axiom Business Book Awards Gold Medal as the best new sales book for 2018.

In 2020, Larry was inducted into the Colorado Business Hall of Fame.

Larry's mission is to help people and their organizations go from the life they have to the life they dream about.

For more information about Ninja Selling,
please go to:
www.NinjaSelling.com